Stop and Search

Police powers to stop, question and search people in public places, and the way these powers are exercised, is a contentious aspect of police-community relations, and a key issue for criminological and policing scholarship, and for public debate about liberty and security more generally. Whilst monitoring and controlling minority populations has always been a feature of police work, new fears, new 'suspect populations' and new powers intended to control them have arisen in the face of instability associated with rapid global change. This book synthesises and extends knowledge about stop and search practices across a range of jurisdictions and contexts. It explores the use of stop and search powers in relation to street crime, terrorism and unauthorised migration in Britain, North America, Europe, Australia, Africa, and Asia. The book covers little researched practices such as road-blocks and ID checking, and discusses issues such as fairness, effectiveness, equity and racial profiling. It provides a substantive and theoretical foundation for transnational and comparative research on police powers in a global context.

This book was originally published as a special issue of *Policing and Society*.

Leanne Weber is Larkins Senior Research Fellow at Monash University, Melbourne, Australia. Her research interests include the detention of asylum seekers in the UK and migration policing networks in Australia. Previous publications include *Borders, Mobility and Technologies of Control* (2006) and *Globalization and Borders: Death at the Global Frontier* (2011).

Ben Bowling is Professor of Criminology and Criminal Justice in the School of Law at King's College London, UK. He has studied policing since the 1980s and is recognised as a leading authority on police stop and search powers. Previous publications include *Policing the Caribbean: Transnational Security Cooperation in Practice* (2010) and *Global Policing* (2012).

Stop and Search
Police Power in Global Context

Edited by
Leanne Weber and Ben Bowling

Routledge
Taylor & Francis Group
LONDON AND NEW YORK

First published 2013
by Routledge
4 Park Square, Milton Park, Abingdon, Oxon OX14 4RN
605 Third Avenue, New York, NY 10017

Routledge is an imprint of the Taylor & Francis Group, an informa business

This book is a reproduction of the journal *Policing and Society*, volume 21, issue 4. The Publisher requests to those authors who may be citing this book to state, also, the bibliographical details of the special issue on which the book was based.

British Library Cataloguing in Publication Data
A catalogue record for this book is available from the British Library

ISBN 13: 978-0-415-63100-6 (hbk)

Typeset in Times New Roman
by Taylor & Francis Books

Publisher's Note
The publisher would like to make readers aware that the chapters in this book may be referred to as articles as they are identical to the articles published in the special issue. The publisher accepts responsibility for any inconsistencies that may have arisen in the course of preparing this volume for print.

Contents

Citation Information

The chapters in this book were originally published in the journal *Policing and Society*, volume 21, issue 4 (December 2011). When citing this material, please use the original page numbering for each article, as follows:

Chapter 1
Introduction: Stop and search in global context
Leanne Weber and Ben Bowling
Policing and Society, volume 21, issue 4 (December 2011) pp. 353-356

Chapter 2
The formation of suspicions: police stop and search practices in England and Wales
Paul Quinton
Policing and Society, volume 21, issue 4 (December 2011) pp. 357-368

Chapter 3
Stop and search in London: counter-terrorist or counter-productive?
Alpa Parmar
Policing and Society, volume 21, issue 4 (December 2011) pp. 369-382

Chapter 4
Ethnic profiling in ID checks by the Hungarian police
Balázs M. Tóth and András Kádár
Policing and Society, volume 21, issue 4 (December 2011) pp. 383-394

Chapter 5
The usual suspects: police stop and search practices in Canada
Scot Wortley and Akwasi Owusu-Bempah
Policing and Society, volume 21, issue 4 (December 2011) pp. 395-407

Chapter 6
The fantastical world of South Africa's roadblocks: dilemmas of a ubiquitous police strategy
Monique Marks
Policing and Society, volume 21, issue 4 (December 2011) pp. 408-419

Chapter 7
Police stop and search in India: Mumbai nakabandi
Jyoti Belur
Policing and Society, volume 21, issue 4 (December 2011) pp. 420-431

Chapter 8
'War on Illegal Immigrants', national narratives, and globalisation: Japanese policy and practice of police stop and question in global perspective
Mitsuru Namba
Policing and Society, volume 21, issue 4 (December 2011) pp. 432-443

Chapter 9
Ethnic profiling in the Netherlands? A reflection on expanding preventive powers, ethnic profiling and a changing social and political context
Joanne P. van der Leun and Maartje A.H. van der Woude
Policing and Society, volume 21, issue 4 (December 2011) pp. 444-455

Chapter 10
'It sounds like they shouldn't be here': immigration checks on the streets of Sydney
Leanne Weber
Policing and Society, volume 21, issue 4 (December 2011) pp. 456-467

Chapter 11
Suspecting immigrants: exploring links between racialised anxieties and expanded police powers in Arizona
Doris Marie Provine and Gabriella Sanchez
Policing and Society, volume 21, issue 4 (December 2011) pp. 468-479

Chapter 12
Stop and search in global context: an overview
Ben Bowling and Leanne Weber
Policing and Society, volume 21, issue 4 (December 2011) pp. 480-488

Introduction

Stop and search in global context

Police, Stop! Halte! Igazoltatás! Thamba! Tomare! Pare! Alto! Halt! Arrêtez-vous immédiatement! The command – issued verbally or in the form of a road sign, a roadblock, or a flashing light on the top of a police car – is universal. Police officers around the world have the power to stop, question and search people, their clothing, bags and vehicles in public places. This ranges from street stops of people suspected of possessing prohibited items; 'suspect passengers' passing through ports, airports and railway stations; and proactive stop and search carried out in an attempt to prevent serious crime and terrorism. The power to stop, check, interrogate and search, and the way it is exercised, is a contentious aspect of police–community relations and a key issue for criminological and policing scholarship. It offers a fascinating case study in the state use of legal powers. It is a visceral manifestation of coercive and intrusive power and the most publicly visible interaction between state agent and citizen or, increasingly, between state agent and non-citizen. This collection examines the power to stop and search in the context of police studies from various parts of the world. The diversity of geographic examples in this collection of essays is echoed in diverse *forms* of stop and search and in *where*, *how* and *why* it is used. The similarities and differences in the everyday use of stop and search in different countries enable us to look at some key issues.

While the pressure to monitor and control minority populations has always been a feature of police work, new and renewed fears about emerging and existing 'suspect populations' – often accompanied by new powers and technologies intended to control them – have arisen in the face of instability associated with rapid global change. This special issue synthesises and extends knowledge about stop and search practices across a range of social, political and cultural contexts. Starting from specific socially, geographically and historically situated locations, the contributions engage with globally relevant themes such as the resurgence of nationalism in the face of globalising pressures; patterns of ethnic and racial targeting; increasing reliance on surveillance and identification technologies; and the convergence of criminal, migration and security paradigms. It is now evident that things happening in one part of the world are shaped by events occurring many miles away and vice versa (Held and McGrew 2002). The world economy has integrated. Transport and telecommunications networks have thickened and widened. Global flows of all kinds have become more extensive, intensive and faster-flowing. Global interconnectedness has created new possibilities for police and criminal justice cooperation and the sharing of technologies, policies and practice (Bowling 2008, Bowling and Sheptycki 2011). Through sharing of information, nodes and networks of power are emerging that involve a range of different organisations – locally, nationally and globally.

Ironically, because of their dispersed nature, these globalising processes may be best understood through situated studies of the local. As Sassen (2007, p. 6) has observed, globalisation does not always manifest at a self-evidently global scale but may involve 'transboundary networks and entities connecting multiple local or "national" processes and actors, or the recurrence of particular issues or dynamics in a growing number of countries or localities'.

Although they may manifest in different forms, and be directed against different suspect populations, police stop and search powers are undoubtedly a recurring dynamic across the globe. Powers to stop and search often provide the starting point for exclusionary projects aimed at people occupying the social, legal and economic margins. In many parts of the world these powers developed from laws against vagrancy. In others they emerged as strategies to control colonised or subjugated populations. Historically, they have been directed towards those perceived to be outsiders. Globally, it seems, the task of policing is increasingly to select, immobilise and eject suspect populations, not just from public spaces or localities, but increasingly from national territory (Weber and Bowling 2008). An important focus for the study of police practice is therefore to examine the policing of border crossing, and the policing of peoples, in ways that connect local, national and transnational mechanisms (Weber and Bowling 2004). Street policing intersects with migration controls through informal questioning at the border and within the domestic sphere. Assisted by new information technologies, once a person has a criminal record, or an irregular migration status, the capacity for police to exercise control and surveillance multiplies rapidly. Globalised counter-terrorism measures also criminalise diverse transnational connections between migrant communities and contribute to social exclusion.

The articles in this collection explore the use of stop and search powers against a range of suspect populations, and in a variety of contexts. Collectively, they develop recurring themes about the search for security and the fluid boundaries of belonging in a rapidly changing world. Contributions are drawn from Japan, India, Australia, South Africa, Hungary, the Netherlands and from Britain, Canada and the United States. By juxtaposing perspectives from the 'periphery' and the 'metropole', the special issue responds to calls by Australian sociologist Raewyn Connell to reconceive social science as a 'mutual learning process on a planetary scale' (Connell 2007, p. 222). According to Connell, long-lasting patterns of inequality in power, wealth and cultural influence resulting from European and North American imperialism have produced a North Atlantic stranglehold on mainstream social science and blinded its practitioners to the potential benefits of intellectual engagement with knowledge from the periphery. Despite the global scope of its ambitions, Connell's vision is predicated on an intellectual workforce engaged in intimate and essentially human forms of dialogue: 'Once an overlapping problem area is defined, a common interest in truth and depth of understanding can be discovered ... voluntary association, goodwill and mutual liking are not trivial bases for intellectual cooperation. They provide a basis for shared labour that points forward to emerging shared interests, rather than backward to interests founded in structures of inequality' (Connell 2007, p. 229).

The production of this special issue has followed this prescription in many respects. The first step was defining the exercise of stop and search powers by police as an overlapping problem area of mutual concern. The second was to come together at a workshop held in London – an iconic metropolis – to mobilise the knowledge and experience of academics, lawyers and activists from 10 countries in an act of shared intellectual labour. The resulting collection reflects our collective concerns about police stop and search practices across a range of differing contexts and our mutual interest in harnessing the 'deep understandings' produced by this dialogue to move beyond existing structures of inequality. At the same time the contributions highlight diversity in the scope of police powers; public acceptance of police stop and search practices; and expectations for accountability arising from deep cultural, political and historical differences. Attention to context ensures that these global themes are given a distinctively local inflection. The view from the periphery – exemplified by contributions from post-Soviet societies such as Hungary (Tóth and Kádár); post-colonial societies such as India (Belur) and South Africa (Marks); and Australia with its continuing colonial dynamic (Weber) – complements the more extensively researched and debated views from the metropole. Adding to the diversity, contributions come from human rights activists and legal practitioners, as well as academics.

The papers also represent a range of criminological traditions, from the sophisticated quantitative analysis reported by Wortley and Owusu-Bempah to the fine-tuned qualitative approach exemplified by Quinton. Authors have looked beyond reviews of the established stop and search literature to find appropriate theoretical frameworks. Van der Leun and van der Woude draw on Garland's culture of control thesis to contextualise their discussion of the policing of immigrants in the Netherlands; Mitsuru Namba frames his account of the war against illegal immigrants in Japan in terms of globalisation, risk and nationalism; Monique Marks embeds her discussion of police roadblocks in South Africa in the literatures of community policing and police effectiveness; and Weber looks to research on police legitimacy and ideas about governance through surveillance to provide a critical perspective on everyday migration policing in Australia.

The papers uncover a range of targets for stop and search practices, defined by race, religion, ethnicity and legal status, each able to be linked to specific local histories and perceptions of threat and belonging. In Arizona (Provine and Sanchez) the nineteenth century redrawing of national borders shapes the contemporary targeting of Mexican immigrants. In Toronto, the evidence shows that Black populations remain the 'usual suspects' (Wortley and Owusu-Bempah), while counter-terrorism in London has shifted some of the police focus towards young Muslims (Parmar). Long-standing antipathy towards the Roma minority in Hungary (Tóth and Kádár) and towards Chinese and Korean neighbours in Japan (Namba) earmarks those groups for disproportionate police attention under contemporary social conditions. While a history of exclusionary, colonial policing against Aboriginal people appears to normalise the surveillance of non-citizens in Australia (Weber), active political and social rhetoric against foreign criminals in the Netherlands is challenging the long-standing presumption of cultural tolerance in that country (van der Leun and van der Woude). In both Mumbai (Belur) and Durban (Marks), roadblocks appear as a common form of stop and search, and seem to be rather loosely targeted and overshadowed by deeper concerns about serious violence committed by criminals, terrorists and police, as well as other forms of potentially harmful behaviour such as drunk driving. More generally, reliance on categorical signals, as described by Quinton, seems likely to increase as police around the world adopt supposedly 'intelligence-driven' approaches.

Taken as a whole, we believe that this collection, and the process which produced it, has made a small but genuine contribution towards reconceiving criminology as a globally connected mutual learning process. More specifically, this approach has yielded new insights into stop and search practices around the world, which are informed by a global perspective. We would like to express our gratitude to the contributors to this volume; to all the participants at the Stop and Search in Global Context workshop held at King's College London on 7–8 July 2011, especially Rebekah Delsol, Loraine Gelsthorpe, Paddy Rawlinson, Mike Shiner and Layla Skinns who acted as expert discussants to Lea Schönfeld for research assistance to our respective universities – Monash University, Melbourne, at the geographic (although not economic) extreme of the periphery, and King's College London situated at the heart of the metropolis – for financially supporting this venture in global dialogue; and to *Policing and Society* editor Martin Innes for promoting this model of globally engaged scholarship.

Leanne Weber
Monash University, Melbourne
Ben Bowling
King's College London

References

Bowling, B., 2008. Transnational policing: the globalisation thesis, a typology and a research Agenda. *Policing: a Journal of Policy & Practice*, 3, 149–160.
Bowling, B. and Sheptycki, J., 2011. *Global policing*. London: Sage.
Connell, R., 2007. *Southern theory: the global dynamics of knowledge in social science*. Sydney: Allen & Unwin.
Held, D. and McGrew, A., eds., 2002. *The global transformation reader; an introduction to the globalization debate*. Cambridge: Polity.
Sassen, S., 2007. *A sociology of globalization*. New York: W.W. Norton & Company.
Weber, L. and Bowling, B., 2004. Policing migration: a framework for investigating the regulation of global mobility. *Policing & Society*, 14 (3), 195–212.
Weber, L. and Bowling, B., 2008. Valiant beggars and global vagabonds: select, eject, immobilize. *Theoretical Criminology*, 12 (3), 355–375.

The formation of suspicions: police stop and search practices in England and Wales

Paul Quinton

Department of Sociology, University of Surrey, Guildford GU2 7XH, UK

This paper explores the interpretative practices of the police when carrying out stops and searches. Drawing on ethnographic research carried out in England and Wales, a conceptual framework is developed to understand how officers become suspicious and decide to initiate encounters. It is argued that officers use tacit knowledge to make sense of new situations and determine what action to take, and base their suspicions on signals they come across on patrol. In examining these social processes, the paper shows that categories and stereotypes are central to decision-making which result in a police focus on the socially marginal. Looking beyond the immediate influences on officer action, the paper also explores the role played by the law in regulating police practice.

Introduction

When police officers conduct stops and searches, they make legal decisions. These everyday decisions can have a profoundly negative effect on the public particularly when the encounters are carried out with little reason, perceived to be unfair, or are poorly handled (Stone and Pettigrew 2000). Ironically, if these decisions undermine the legitimacy of the police, they are likely to weaken the public's willingness to comply with the law (Tyler 1990). It is, therefore, crucial to understand the processes by which officers become uncertain about people or anticipate wrong-doing, and decide to initiate encounters.

Suspicion was a feature of many of the first policing studies, and it has since become regarded as a pervasive aspect of cop culture (Reiner 2010). The early literature drew a distinction between idealised notions of suspicion as it appeared in books, and how it was used in practice. Skolnick (1966) argued that the police characterised people as symbolic assailants through the use of perceptual shorthand, which resulted from the dangers faced by officers and their ability to use force. Others regarded suspicion more as a way for police to exert control over their workload and territory, and thought it intrinsically bound to officer knowledge and uncertainty (Rubenstein 1973). Matza (1969) placed greater emphasis on social control. He described how the ordinary mode of suspicion involved 'rounding up the usual suspects' and focusing on categories of people who 'looked like criminals' (see also Marx 1988). Subsequently, commentators have viewed suspicion as a means of re-establishing social order (Ericson 1982), constructing criminality (McConville *et al.* 1991), or disciplining social groups (Choongh 1997). Furthermore, it has been argued that suspicious are grounded in a series of working rules (Smith and Gray 1985, McConville *et al.* 1991) which draw on public information about criminals (Young 1994).

These accounts of police suspicion are not unproblematic. The early ethnographic studies did not recognise the law as providing context and setting for police action, and portrayed culture as deterministic of behaviour (Dixon 1997). Similarly, more recent structuralist accounts have tended to neglect the active role played by officers in the decision-making process. This paper, therefore, seeks to examine the interpretative practices of the police when carrying out stops and searches, and looks at how discretion is situated in a particular legal and social context. The work of Goffman is used as the conceptual lens to examine these social processes because he was largely concerned with understanding how suspicions were communicated in mundane social encounters and were central to the production of order. The paper sits in the Anglo-American tradition, and is based exclusively on empirical research conducted in England and Wales. Its scope is necessarily limited and concentrates largely on ordinary police powers that require officers to have reasonable grounds before conducting a search, and on less intrusive encounters requiring no formal power.

Research methods and analysis

This paper draws on ethnographic fieldwork carried for two related studies (Bland *et al.* 2000, Quinton and Olagundoye 2004). These studies sought to evaluate changes to police stops and searches introduced following the Stephen Lawrence Inquiry, but were also designed to enable a qualitative exploration of police decision-making (Quinton *et al.* 2000, Quinton 2010). Research was conducted in 10 research sites across England and Wales, over two separate time periods:

- In 1999/2000 – Central Leicester, Chapeltown, Greenwich, Hounslow and Ipswich.
- In 2003 – Bournville, Hackney, Sefton, South Notts and Wrexham.

In total, 198 officers were interviewed across the sites. The interviews focused on what prompted their suspicions, how they initiated and handled encounters, and the impact of policy changes. Observations of patrols were also conducted to gain first-hand experience of decision-making in a more naturalistic setting. Most of the time was spent with officers on vehicle patrol, although some foot patrols were also studied. Officers were accompanied for over 565 hours across 70 shifts. During that time, 249 people were: stopped and searched; or stopped and asked questions about who they were, what they were doing, or similar.

An initial coding framework was developed from the interviews and the existing policing literature. These codes were used to examine individual encounters in the fieldnotes to identify the prompts for police action. Comparisons were made between similar encounters to highlight the contingencies in police practice. This analysis enabled the codes to be refined or rejected, and for new codes to emerge. The revised framework was then applied across the fieldnotes to understand the overall patterns in the data. After the main prompts for action were identified, the conceptual apparatus was used to help make sense of the decision-making process both within and across the encounters. While it was not possible to 'get inside the heads' of the officers, their tacit knowledge was not entirely beyond empirical reach. As well as the shared meanings developed through immersion into their social world, inferences were grounded in comments and gestures made during encounters, as well as conversations with officers afterwards. Of course, it was not always possible to interpret what they were thinking because of a lack of empirical clues. Moreover, the presence of a researcher will have influenced their behaviour. While some encounters were seemingly done for show or by the book, there were many examples that were unrecorded, poorly handled, or probably unlawful.

Signalling and framing

Erving Goffman (1972) argued that the strategies used by formal agents of social control to identify whether something was amiss were the same as those used by ordinary people in their everyday lives. People were said to engage in constant monitoring to ensure their surroundings took on a 'normal appearance'. They were able to participate in their usual routines until such monitoring revealed the presence of a *sign* which, if it had meaning and prompted alarm, would function as a warning *signal*. As Innes (2004) noted, it is the reaction caused by a signal that crucially marks it out from the mass of information in the social environment. For Goffman (1971), these fleeting communicative processes were central to social interaction. He argued that people continually gave off information about themselves, but sought to control the flow of information as part of an impression management strategy. People simultaneously projected and concealed different aspects of their 'real' identity which others inevitably responded to. If the audience became suspicious, they attempted to see around the presented self in order to reveal 'true' character and intent. This signalling process was seen to be particularly risky for people with 'undesired differentness' because, if the source of their stigma was revealed, they could be reduced 'from a whole and usual person to a tainted, discounted one' (Goffman 1968: 12). Thus, people were thought to deliberately cover 'discreditable attributes' in an attempt to pass unnoticed.

While signalling describes the communicative processes within encounters, the concept does not explain *why* certain cues stand out from the background noise beyond stating they cause a reaction. Without a complementary understanding of how cues are interpreted, signalling could be seen as an unmediated process based on stimulus/response. Officers render familiar the unfamiliar by drawing on their stock of experiential and cultural knowledge – the so-called common-sense of policing (Holdaway 1983, Ericson 2007). In so doing, they will use tacit sense-making schema to organise their experience and answer the question: What is going on here? As Goffman noted, a frame will allow 'its user to locate, perceive, identify and label a seemingly infinite number of concrete occurrences defined in its terms' (1974: 21). This process has been seen to play a crucial role in decision-making because, in addition to enabling people to tune in and attribute meaning to particular signals, frames allow them to determine what the matter is at hand, how to proceed, and how to account for their actions (Chan 1996, Manning 1992). Moreover, because cognitive schema are relatively stable and reflect wider relationships of power, they are likely to affect patterns in decision-making over time and reproduce existing social boundaries.

Legal and organisational influences

A conceptual focus on the here-and-now of police decision-making is not to suggest that wider influences on action are unimportant. Interaction is not only highly situated but also requires those involved to attend to structural issues – such as authority, economics, and power – before they can proceed (Maines 2001). Furthermore, in the context of both legal discretion and policing, it has been argued that experiential knowledge is embedded in, and stands in relation to, the prevailing organisational, legal and structural conditions (Hawkins 1992, Manning 1992, Chan 1996). For Chan, it is the *primacy* of these relationships that is important. Thus, the interpretative practices that shape officer decision-making only function in relation to their legal powers and the socio-political status of different communities.

Although mainly focused on interaction, the fieldwork also looked at the influence of law on police behaviour. The interviews revealed that officers were not able to describe exactly what reasonable suspicion meant in practice, and nobody attempted to provide a concrete definition. Instead, officers talked about when they might carry out a search or the types of factor they would consider. There were clear differences between officers in the level of suspicion they required before initiating contact. A few said they would not search a person under reasonable suspicion unless they had enough evidence to arrest, while others worked to a much lower standard: '[Y]ou didn't need much... you only need about two things' (Chapeltown/L3). Overall, the observations showed that legal considerations were not foremost in officers' minds when they conducted searches.

The law was not, however, completely irrelevant to decision-making. Many sought to work within their own understanding of the rules (in as far as they could be articulated). Some officers were found to be more careful than others, and sometimes took greater care over their grounds in particular situations. There was also a widespread belief that the legal rules around searches had been tightened. The fact that reasonable suspicion was unaltered suggested its constraining effect had to be consciously activated by officers and was mediated by other factors. Greater awareness of the rules seemed to stem, for example, from concerns about complaints, being labelled a racist, and media reporting of the Stephen Lawrence Inquiry.

The fieldwork also indicated that weaker forms of legal regulation fostered a more permissive discretionary environment (see also Parmar, this issue). Under s60 *Criminal Justice and Public Order Act* 1994, officers could be authorised to search anyone in a particular location for a defined period without reasonable grounds in order to prevent violence. Its introduction can be seen as part of a broader expansion of enabling powers which emphasised collective security over suspects' rights. Observations of an authorisation in one site found officers conducting searches in large numbers and with very low levels of suspicion (compared to their usual working practice). While the s60 had been granted to tackle knife crime, few searches were expressly carried out to find weapons. Decisions tended to be based on general signals of disorder and demeanour. Threatening and abusive behaviour, challenges to police authority, and acts of criminal damage were all key prompts. The absence of reasonable suspicion, therefore, seemed to considerably widen officer discretion and allowed them to discipline people for minor acts of disorder.

The more immediate organisational setting was also found to situate officer practice. For example, Chapeltown and Hackney were found to use stop and search in wholly different ways despite both having inner-city crime problems, diverse populations, and long-standing community tensions. Police data revealed that four times as many searches per 1000 residents were recorded in Hackney than in Chapeltown. Moreover, while Chapeltown officers tended to recognise how their actions could adversely affect local people and were cautious about initiating contact, a more overtly confrontational approach was taken in Hackney. Officers portrayed themselves as the 'thin blue line' and were primarily concerned with asserting their authority. Although it was difficult to be conclusive, these differences could be partly attributed to the policing models that had been implemented. In contrast to Chapeltown's community- and problem-oriented approach, Hackney had a more reactive model based around rapid response and enforcement. Likewise, whereas supervision in Chapeltown reportedly emphasised quality, Hackney seemed to have a much stronger performance culture based around numerical measures and targets.

Forming suspicions

Officers often struggled to put into words what made them suspicious, either describing recent encounters or talking vaguely about hunches (see Smith and Gray 1985). Their accounts suggested that suspicions were skilful taken-for-granted accomplishment that could not be taught. This highlights the importance of socialisation in policing and how cultural knowledge is developed, shared and reinforced via the training school and the work-setting (Fielding 1988). The examples given by officers during the interviews highlighted the often contradictory and elastic nature of suspicions (see McConville *et al.* 1991, Reiner 2010). Staring, not making eye contact, driving too fast and driving too slow were all said to generate suspicions. Given that many of the signals in police talk rarely featured in practice, they might primarily be regarded as a way of communicating practical insights about policing (see Waddington 1999).

The observations provided more tangible insights about the processes by which officers constructed their suspicions. The following extract describes the build-up to an archetypical suspicion-based stop. The encounter was notable because it contained a number of signals that often attracted attention and which were framed around a series of taken-for-granted categories. In this example, the signals were identified in a problem neighbourhood during a particularly quiet shift in which the officers were actively looking for action. The encounter also immediately followed an aborted 999 call, which may also have provided some additional encouragement. As Dixon *et al.* (1989) previously noted, a person who fits a stereotype only becomes suspicious in the right context.

> [The officer] sees three kids hanging around by a takeaway and then go up side street. We turn back to see where they have gone. They are not in the side street… Went down street to look – see smashed glass on floor next to car. As we drive pass, can see that glass is old and not from car that is parked there. Circle back up next street and kid is

> standing in road swinging arms. He is young – mid teens and is wearing a furry cap and a white Adidas top. (Chapeltown/L4/3)

Given that the boys were not visibly engaged in criminal activity, their presence carried symbolic value to the officers beyond the immediate situation. Teenagers, particularly those in groups, were often assumed to be 'up-to-no-good'. Also, the police typically held strong ideas about what normal behaviour looked like, so it was relatively common for officers to presume that someone loitering or hanging around had criminal intentions. Sports clothes were often taken as a symbol of a person's status, marking them out as someone who was not respectable. These particular signals – in combination – were likely to have had special meaning for the officers. It is highly questionable whether a different combination would have generated quite the same response (e.g. older people, working, wearing school uniform). After these initial signals attracted interest, the officers were seen to focus on additional signals that supported their emerging frame. The apparent disappearance of the teenagers was likely to have confirmed their preliminary suspicions; particularly as they quickly drove around the corner to find them. The view that criminals would act furtively around the police was widespread on the basis that innocent people had nothing to hide. No consideration was given to the possibility the boys had entered the takeaway (which they had). The presence of smashed glass next to a car also seemed to sensitise the officers towards vehicle crime. Even though the glass was soon found to be old (which could have signalled the all-clear), it later provided justification for the encounter: '[I]f they were thinking of stealing a car they might be put off it now'. However, none of these considerations were articulated in the written stop records. The encounters were described vaguely as 'routine stop checks', which presented them as 'typical cases' and meant it would have been difficult to assess whether contact was justifiable (see Dixon 1997).

The strategy of seeking out additional signals to confirm suspicions and reject alternative explanations was widespread. The level of confirmation officers needed before they initiated contact seemed to be context-dependent. Prior knowledge about places or people was an important influence on action, and determined whether the cues they identified carried significance (Rubenstein 1973, Holdaway 1983). Signals in locations known for drug-dealing or linked to known offenders had particular resonance, and were almost taken as immediate proof of wrong-doing. An officer was observed searching two well-known drug addicts simply because they had been described as 'acting suspiciously' over the radio (Sefton/L2/1). The searches were likely to have been unlawful as there was no evidence to indicate they had done anything illegal. In another encounter, a black man was searched because officers saw him put his hands down his trousers (Hackney/N2/3). Out of context, his behaviour would have been ambiguous but, near a crack house in the early hours, became a strong signal of furtiveness and drug possession. The frame used to make sense of this situation, and which excluded alternatives, resulted in the police mistakenly jumping to conclusions about a piece of foil they found: 'The officer makes an "ah" sound, but it turns out to be a KitKat wrapper'. The foil contained chocolate rather than drugs.

Forming suspicions was not always a closed process based on a fixed interpretation of events. Framing was contingent, and if new signals were identified that did not fit the officer's initial interpretation, reframing could occur (Goffman 1974).

Although rare during the fieldwork, officers often talked about initiating a stop for a one reason only later to pick up on different signals after the interaction was under way. This process was perhaps most relevant for encounters involving drugs because many of the relevant signals could only be identified at close quarters. For example, the police pulled over a car because it was untaxed, dishevelled and contained four young white men (Sefton/N2/1). However, the driver was subsequently searched because an officer smelt cannabis in the car. The observer could not smell anything, which raised questions about the subjectiveness of the officer's grounds and the lawfulness of his actions.

Reframing was also seen to result in officer suspicions being allayed. Two officers were seen searching a neighbourhood for a man reportedly chasing his girlfriend with a knife. They paid close attention to a man running down the pavement, but quickly concluded he was just a jogger as he was not running with urgency (Hackney/N2). A signal was identified that gave the officers the all-clear and reassured them that normal appearances had been restored. These types of signals had to be identified and accorded relevance before they discouraged officers, and views about what was incongruent were inevitably infused with moral and normative judgements: 'Young lad, on wall, 2am – should be at home' (Leicester/1/14).

On very rare occasions, the police were seen to interpret the same events from different perspectives which highlighted how frames could be selectively deployed to justify different practices. In the following example, two officers were seen to engage in 'staging talk' (Goffman 1971) about which signals they would regard as suspicious. These planning activities revealed the negotiated character of their suspicions, and allowed them to rehearse how they could account for their actions.

> [We] park up so we can see the cars driving up and down [the road]. They say that they can see which cars keep going backwards and forwards – this would mean that they are kerb-crawlers... [Officer 1] says that he has just seen a white Rover go past twice – the second time with a woman in it... We speed up and follow white car. [Officer 2] says that it might be people coming back from the mosque. The car turns and we follow, and look through the window. Asian man and white woman – she might be a known prostitute, but [they] see she is not as they drive pass. (Chapeltown/L4)

Two competing interpretations were put forward that relied on the same signals but which contextualised them in different ways. Specifically, in order to make sense of the situation, differential use was made of territorial knowledge about the open vice market and the location of the mosque. It was not clear why the first officer persisted with the kerb-crawling frame until the last minute, given that appearances could have been normal. The presence of a researcher raises the possibility that he was playing to the audience, although his readiness to take action could just have reflected traditional cop culture. More importantly, this near-encounter prompts questions about how suspicion is legally defined and accounted for. There is a requirement for reasonable suspicion to be individual, specific, and based on fact. Even though no search was conducted, the example illustrated how 'facts' could be subjectively defined and present almost any course of action as being reasonable to an objective third party depending on how the context was portrayed.

The main prompts for suspicions

The observations revealed that suspicions were prompted by an array of categorical, physical, and behavioural signals, but that a smaller cluster of signals had more of a major influence on decision-making.

Signals that marked people out into broad social categories were found to have the strongest influence on suspicions, and were often symbolically associated with notions of respectability and order (see Reiner 2010). Seeing someone 'known to the police' held most currency with officers. 'Regulars' were instantly recognised on patrol and symbolised habitual criminality. Encounters were frequently initiated and often with low levels of suspicion. In one example, officers searched a teenager they recognised as a car thief over an hour after a call about joy-riding. The teenager matched the suspect description, but there was no evidence any vehicle had been stolen or that he had anything illegal on him: 'We know what you get up – or used to – we know what your history's like' (Hounslow/L4/1). As regulars were kept under close scrutiny and repeatedly 'turned over', they developed long-standing and sometimes antagonistic relationships with particular officers. Contact sometimes bordered on harassment as the lawfulness of the grounds was often questionable.

Other categorical signals had less of a direct effect on police actions, but were seen to attract interest nonetheless. The targeting of young people in their teens or early 20s was pervasive, particularly groups of lads around cars. The stopping of young people was relatively frequent and a widely accepted practice. Suspicions about young people were fairly generalised, and it was difficult to discern what youth symbolised beyond vague notions of criminality and disorderliness. Clothing or general demeanour were often taken as a clearer indication that someone was involved in crime. The connotation of teenagers wearing track suits, baseball caps and hooded tops were that they were not respectable: 'You build the stereotypes up through experience, the people you see are involved in crime. In this area, it's people in sports gear' (Leicester/N2). Inevitably, this focus would have resulted in young people from deprived backgrounds and ethnic minorities being targeted.

Race was also an important feature in police decision-making. Its implicit nature and the guardedness of the officers, however, meant it was difficult to find definitive evidence of encounters being initiated principally because someone was from an ethnic minority. On the whole, being black was found to have a shared meaning among officers and generally heightened their suspicions (Holdaway 1983, Smith and Gray 1985). Race was seen to act as a pivotal signal in a small number of cases. In the strongest example, a car was stopped because the driver and passengers were black: 'Rasta man, worth a look' (Leicester/L4/7). The fact that racist language was used and no other signals appeared to be present suggested race was the most likely reason for the stop. The overt use of racist language was found to be rare, except in relation to gypsies in some sites. Nevertheless, during the interviews officers pointed to racial differences in offending. One officer, in particular, held extremely racist views.

> Afro-Caribbeans commit street robbery... Somalians come from the most violent country in the world. [We] shouldn't be surprised when [they're] violent over here... (Greenwich/2/23)

Most officers took much greater care to contextualise their answers, often explaining differences in terms of locality and social causes. Nevertheless, black people were typically associated with robbery and occasionally drugs, and white people with a wider range of crimes (e.g. disorder, burglary and vehicle crime). At the time of the study, stereotypes about Asians were much less common. These views often led to some officers making exaggerated claims: 'Whenever a robbery comes in, 90% you'll be thinking it's a black male because of the description and because you know who does robbery in the past' (Leicester/1/21).

Hall *et al.* (1998) have argued that, while there is no straightforward link between attitudes and behaviour, stereotypes are structural and widely diffused throughout British society. They added that these rigid mental images persist unconsciously, and can be directive of action because they operate at the level of perception and expectation. Their effect, therefore, is to mark out the boundaries between 'them' and 'us', and sustain relationships of power. Stereotypes were seen to be remarkably stable over time, as they were transmitted and maintained through informal work routines. Stereotyping, however, was seen to be highly contingent, rather than an inevitable or universal process. They also highlighted that efforts to interrupt any automatic link between attitudes and behaviour, and promote a more reflective approach, had largely been ineffective. In respect of stop and search practices, it is clear that reasonable grounds cannot be based on stereotypical images or personal characteristics (including prior offending). However, because the formation of suspicions is regarded as a rational process which involves officers surveying the material facts around them and weighing-up the likelihood of finding a prohibited item, it neglects the extent to which practical rules-of-thumb are central to decision-making (see Dixon *et al.* 1989).

Officers often talked about physical characteristics as important prompts for action, but their influence was variable during the observations. Officers said they stopped vehicles with physical problems (defects, missing tax discs), but enforcement was highly selective despite the availability of these signals on patrol. Cars and people who were thought to be scruffy also attracted attention, but were rarely stopped. Likewise, incongruent items of clothing used by offenders to disguise themselves or hide things (overcoats, gloves, dark clothes) featured more in police talk than in practice.

Overall, physical signals were most relevant when officers thought a person was an addict or were using suspect descriptions to identify people. Officers, for example, had a finely-tuned understanding of the physical cues associated with drug-use: '[G]aunt, sweating, eyes also give it away' (Greenwich/1/4). With suspect descriptions, contact was almost always initiated when a person was thought to physically match the information given out over the radio. However, descriptions were often vague and lacking in detail which meant, in practice, officers had considerable discretion to stop whoever they liked. As time passed following a call, descriptions tended to be used more as a general resource with officers tending to focus on aspects of the description which they thought were most reliable (i.e. reported race or unusual clothing). This process sometimes resulted in stops being made on fairly generalised suspicions, and was very likely to have been racialised. As one officer said following a robbery call involving two black suspects: 'We will look to stop any IC3s [black people]' (Bournville/N1). Responding to a call, however, meant officers could present themselves as having little discretion. The expansion of Automatic Number Plate Reader technology similarly allowed traffic stops to be presented as scientific, routinised and involving low discretion, but masked the decisions taken back-stage about which intelligence databases were linked to the reader. Some of these will be highly-selective, focused on known offenders, and shared transnationally which could exacerbate the self-reinforcing focus on the 'usual suspects'.

It was exceptional for officers to witness criminal behaviour in progress, but when they did it provided strong and direct signals that led to swift action. Officers more readily came across motoring offences (speeding, jumping lights), but contact depended on how interested officers were in traffic matters and whether they were busy responding to calls. It was much more common for officers to respond to behavioural signals that were not directly criminal in nature. Acts of disorder were important signals (street drinking, aggression), especially if they challenged the authority of the police (making pig noises). In addition, the police were seen to make inferences about a person's criminal intentions from a wide range of looser behaviour cues that were more open to interpretation. As mentioned, motivation was often inferred about people hanging around or walking aimlessly. These inferences were often context-specific and sometimes intersected with other rules-of-thumb: '[The officer] says that the young black man nearby was fine too, but if he was standing near some sort of car that would be different' (Bournville/N2). The elasticity of these interpretations meant almost any behaviour could be interpreted as criminal in the right circumstances, and legitimate the use of stereotypes.

Concluding remarks

This paper has shown police practice to be at odds with the law. Rather than suspicions being objective and based on the likelihood of finding something illegal, decisions to initiate encounters tended to draw on broad generalisations and stereotypes that placed people into defined social categories. Many of the observed searches were based on weak grounds and likely to have been unlawful. While the learned rules-of-thumb inevitably made it easier for officers to negotiate their social world, their use will have resulted in innocent members of public coming into unnecessary and intrusive contact with the police, sometimes on a regular basis. Moreover, the categories that dominated police thinking were highly symbolic and would have resulted in suspicions falling disproportionality on the socially marginal – young men, black people, and the 'regulars'. Given that stereotyping and framing reflect wider relationships of power, police action would not only target those worthy, in police eyes, of being 'kept in order', but would also reproduce existing social inequalities. This is not to suggest that decisions were dictated functionally by social structure and based on blanket stereotyping. The use of categorical suspicion was found to be contingent and highly situated, with officers drawing on different interpretative frames to make sense of a range of circumstances.

This paper presents a significant challenge to the view that stop and search is effectively regulated via the law. Legal considerations did not featuring strongly in the decision-making process, and officer practice varied significantly. In some cases, the law was little more than a resource for reasserting authority and disciplining members of the public, particular those already in long-standing relationships with the police. In these instances, the police were seen to 'rule with law' rather than demonstrate the 'rule of law' (Bowling, personal communication). Moreover, the ability of officers to account for their actions after the event, using stock phrases and drawing on their contextual knowledge, also questions the extent to which meaningful oversight of written records is possible. This paper does, however, offer some crumbs of hope. There was some evidence to suggest that discretion was restricted when officers were required to have reasonable suspicion, and that external events could encourage officers to actively constrain their own behaviour. Given stops and searches are to remain police tactics for the foreseeable future, there may be value in trying to understand why the police comply with the rules at all given officers' low visibility, and to identify the conditions in which regulation is most likely to be effective.

Acknowledgements

I would like to thank Nigel Fielding and Martin Innes for their support during my doctoral research. I am also grateful to Ben Bowling, Simon Holdaway, Paul Johnson, Robert Reiner and Layla Skinns for their comments. This paper was written by the author in a personal capacity. His views do not represent those of the National Policing Improvement Agency (his employer) or the Home Office (who part-funded his studies).

References

Bland, N., Miller, J., and Quinton, P., 2000. *Upping the PACE? An evaluation of the Stephen Lawrence Inquiry recommendations on stops and searches.* London: Home Office.

Chan, J., 1996. Changing police culture. *British Journal of Criminology*, 36 (1), 109–134.

Choongh, S., 1997. *Policing as social discipline.* Oxford: Clarendon.

Dixon, D., 1997. *Law in policing: legal regulation and police practices.* Oxford: Clarendon.

Dixon, D., Bottomley, A.K., Coleman, C.A., Gill, M., and Wall, D., 1989. Reality and rules in the construction and regulation of police suspicion. *International Journal of the Sociology of Law*, 17, 185–206.

Ericson, R., 1982. *Reproducing order: a study of patrol work.* London: University of Toronto Press.

Ericson, R., 2007. Rules in policing: five perspectives. *Theoretical Criminology*, 11 (3), 367–401.

Fielding, N., 1988. *Joining forces: police training, socialization and occupational competence.* London: Routledge.

Goffman, E., 1968. *Stigma: notes on the management of spoiled identity.* Harmondsworth: Pelican.

Goffman, E., 1971. *The presentation of self in everyday life.* Harmondsworth: Pelican.

Goffman, E., 1972. *Relations in public: microstudies in public order.* Harmondsworth: Pelican.

Goffman, E., 1974. *Frame analysis: an essay on the organization of experience.* New York: Harper and Row.

Hall, S., McLaughlin, E., and Lewis, G., 1998. *Racial stereotyping in the police: statement on research on racial attitudes and stereotyping.* Report prepared for Deighton Guedalla Solicitors. Milton Keynes: Open University.

Hawkins, K., 1992. The use of legal discretion: perspectives from law and social science. *In*: K. Hawkins, ed. *The uses of discretion.* Oxford: Clarendon, 11–46.

Holdaway, S., 1983. *Inside the British police.* Oxford: Blackwell.

Innes, M., 2004. Signal crimes and signal disorders: notes on deviance as communicative action. *British Journal of Sociology*, 55 (3), 335–355.

Maines, D., 2001. *The faultlines of consciousness: a view of interactionism in sociology.* New York: De Gruyter.

Manning, P.K., 1992. Big-bang decisions: notes on a naturalistic approach. *In*: K. Hawkins, ed. *The uses of discretion.* Oxford: Clarendon, 249–285.

Marx, G., 1988. *Undercover: police surveillance in America.* London: University of California Press.

Matza, D., 1969. *Becoming deviant.* Englewood Cliffs: Prentice-Hall.

McConville, M., Sanders, A., and Leng, R., 1991. *The case for the prosecution: police suspects and the construction of criminality.* London: Routledge.

Quinton, P., 2010. *Becoming suspicious: a study of police-initiated encounters with the public.* Thesis (PhD). University of Surrey.

Quinton, P. and Olagundoye, J., 2004. *An evaluation of the phased implementation of the recording of police stops.* London: Home Office.

Quinton, P., Bland, N., and Miller, J., 2000. *Police stops, decision-making and practice.* London: Home Office.

Reiner, R., 2010. *The politics of the police.* 4th ed. Oxford: Oxford University Press.

Rubenstein, J., 1973. *City police.* New York: Farrar, Straus and Giroux.

Skolnick, J., 1966. *Justice without trial: law enforcement in democratic society.* New York: Wiley.

Smith, D. and Gray, J., 1985. *Police and people in London.* Aldershot: Avebury.

Stone, V. and Pettigrew, N., 2000. *The views of the public on stops and searches.* London: Home Office.

Tyler, T., 1990. *Why people obey the law.* New Haven: Yale University Press.

Waddington, P., 1999. Police (canteen) sub-culture: an appreciation. *British Journal of Criminology*, 39 (2), 287–309.

Young, J., 1994. *Policing the streets: stops and search in north London.* London: Islington Council.

Stop and search in London: counter-terrorist or counter-productive?

Alpa Parmar

School of Law, King's College London, London, UK

The principle of 'reasonable suspicion' aims to prevent the abuse of the police power to stop, search and arrest and to increase accountability. The lack of a 'reasonable suspicion' requirement in stop and search under Section 44 of the Terrorism Act 2000 generated controversy and demands for legislative reform. Questions were raised about whether counter-terrorist policing efforts under s44 were effective of merely compromising civil liberties and sanctioning 'ethnic profiling'. Drawing on observations of stop and search operations, interviews with police and people in London, this paper examines the implementation, experience and perception of s44 from the perspective of police and policed. The paper contends that the spectre of terrorism has legitimated unfair policing – both conceptually and practically – and ethnic minority communities have become suspect and potential intelligence sources. This is inherently problematic, generating a binary framework of expectations which are intangible and contradictory in pursuing human security. Ethnic minority communities have been criminalised, reified in reference to their religious backgrounds, and intra-ethnic tensions and ambiguities have deepened.

Counter-terrorist legislation in the UK: stop and search practice

This paper is based on an empirical study of counter-terrorist policing in London focussing on the experience of people stopped and searched under s44 of Terrorism Act 2000 (TA 2000) between July 2008 and July 2009. Section 44 (1) and (2)[1] enabled the police and the Home Secretary to define any area of the country and a time period wherein they could stop and search any vehicle or person, and seize 'articles of a kind which could be used in connection with terrorism' (Terrorism Act 2000). There is little in-depth empirical research on s44 and how it was experienced by communities. This paper responds to this lacuna by detailing the way in which s44 was conceptualised and deployed by the police and explores citizens' experiences of being subjected to this power.

Legal and socio-political context

Terrorism Act (TA) 2000 widened the definition of terrorism and granted the police extended periods to detain suspects, and most controversially permitted the police to stop and search a person or vehicle without 'reasonable suspicion' that an offence had been committed (s44(1) and (2)). The law was changed after 7 July 2005 London Underground attacks and the UK government's 'Contest' policy[2] was updated in 2009 to respond to the 'evolving threat' of terrorism. Although the Contest policy was presented as a coherent and mutually reinforcing strategy, the contradictions underlying the practical implementation of the policy were apparent early on. The Prevent strand's goal to stop radicalisation through community engagement and building trust with Muslim communities does not sit easily alongside an approach which 'over-polices' Muslims. Indeed, Hazel Blears in 2005 publicly announced that 'Muslims should accept as a reality that they would be stopped and searched more often than others'. The guidelines for stop and search specify that 'you should not be stopped because of your age, race, gender, sexual orientation, disability, religion or faith; the way you look or dress, the language you speak' (Association of Police Authorities 2010). Ironically, however, the intention to reassure the public about their security translated to undermining some of the policing advances engendered the by Macpherson inquiry (Kundnani 2007) and instead legitimated the practice of labelling Muslim communities as suspect.

Charting the controversy

The absence of a requirement for reasonable suspicion with s44 and the increased discretion it accorded to police officers prompted questions about whether effective counter-terrorism policy could exist without undermining citizens' rights. The principle of 'reasonable suspicion' is associated with the power of arrest as an important safeguard and to underline the presumption of innocence until guilt is proven. In Dumbell v. Roberts [1944] 1 All ER 326, Scott stated that:

> The power possessed by constables to arrest without warrant ... provided always that they have reasonable grounds for their suspicion is a valuable protection to the community; but the power may be easily abused and become a danger to the community instead of a protection (329)

Analysis of the use of s44 between 2001 and 2006 had also shown that there was a low rate of terrorist arrests through the use of this power, a high rate of non-terrorist arrests, a disproportionate impact on Asian ethnic minorities and uneven geographical delivery of the power with most stops occurring on the City of London (Walker 2008). After the July 2005 London attacks, the use of s44 stop and searches rose dramatically for all ethnic groups and suggestions that ethnic minorities were targeted more than others were reported in the media (Travis 2009). Recent figures affirm this pattern – the biggest increase on figures from 2008 was for Black people (322%), then Asians (277%), then the 'Other' category (262%), followed by white people (185%) (Ministry of Justice 2009). In 2009, more than 100,000 searches under s44 were conducted, but none resulted in an arrest connected to terrorism.

The targeting of ethnic minorities and the large increase in the number of Asians[3] who were stopped and searched under s44 provided further indications of ethnic profiling (Moeckli 2005, Walker 2008, Parmar 2010). The London underground attacks also represented a shift in the perception of 'threat' as defined within the 'war on terror' framework. The discursive move from the idea of the 'external threat' to the idea of the threat as coming from 'the enemy within' was apparent in media and political accounts (Bigo 2006, Hudson 2007). Self-contradictory political rhetoric emphasised that the majority of Muslim people were law-abiding and peaceful – Jacqui Smith, then Home Secretary, even stated that terrorist activity committed by Muslims was 'anti-Islamic', yet the undertone of official policy was that Muslim communities were disengaged and posed a threat because they lacked the sense of belonging and national pride necessary to engender a cohesive social order. As Pantazis and Pemberton argue, 'the designation of Muslims as the principal suspect community . . .and the fixing of Muslim communities rather than individual suspects within the gaze of counter-terrorist policing is underpinned by the discretionary nature of the powers contained in the Terrorism Act' (2009, pp. 652–653).

Legislative change?

In January 2011, shortly after the fieldwork was completed, s44 stop and search powers were ruled unlawful by the European Court of Human Rights. It was held that the use of s44 violated Article 8 of the European Convention on Human Rights (the right to respect for private and family life). In the landmark ruling it was stated that s44 powers were 'not sufficiently circumscribed' and lacked 'adequate legal safeguards against abuse' (Gillan and Quinton v The United Kingdom, ECtHR).

The Metropolitan Police Service (MPS) use of s44 search powers ended on 8 July 2010 on the authority of the Home Secretary, Theresa May. During the six-month interim between the ECtHR ruling and the withdrawal, police officers were confused about whether it should or could be used. Once a decision was made, senior police officers were critical of the withdrawal s44 as it was thought that few safeguards existed to 'protect the public' against attempted attacks with the planning of events such as the 2012 Olympics in London, state occasions and major summits (Dodd 2010). The criticism towards 'rolling authorisations'[4] was responded to in a review of the Terrorism Act 2000 (Protection of Freedoms Bill, 146, 2011) and in order to promote more accountability, s47A (which replaced s44) allows authorisations to be implemented after being subject to higher thresholds – permitted only where a senior police officer reasonably suspects an act of terrorism will take place and considers that the stop and search powers are necessary to prevent such an act. Notably, however, once an authorisation has been granted, s47A(3) confers powers on a constable in uniform to stop and search a pedestrian or anything carried by the pedestrian for evidence that they are a terrorist and the powers may be exercised *whether or not the constable has reasonable suspicion* that there is such evidence.

The debate about s44 was unfolding when the study was at the design stage. The importance of empirically grounded research in this area was clear, as was the need for a response to the question of whether counter-terrorist policing could be effective whilst maintaining the principles of democratic accountability. Such debates are,of course, not hermetically sealed but are subject to changing public opinion and political priorities. Although the socio-legal context may now have changed, it remains important to understand how s44 was received, not least because the legislation has had a lasting impact on individuals and the groups to which they belong. Moreover, the symbolic aspect of policing generated from the controversy about law in practice was profound.

Table 1. Summary of data collected.

Data description	Participant description	Number/ time
Semi structured interviews	Beat patrol police officers, counter-terrorism trained police officers, counter-terrorist unit senior police officers, British Transport Police officers	28
Semi structured interviews	Citizens stopped and searched under s44 of the Terrorism Act 2000	40
Semi structured interviews	Agency representatives and members of the public who have implemented and participated in PREVENT initiatives	15
Participant observation	Counter-terrorism stop and search operations including foot and vehicle stops, larger counter-terrorist exercises, handling of complaints and station based work	25 × 8 hour shifts
Semi structured interviews	Policy makers and Metropolitan Police Service Advisors including researchers and statistical experts	6
Metropolitan police figures	Statistics on stop and search under s44 of the Terrorism Act for the period January 2008–July 2010	n/a

Research process

Data collection included primary research and secondary analysis of police statistics. The research collection process spanned one year, during which access to two central London police stations was negotiated and I was able to join specified counter-terrorist operations and was based at the police stations at other times. A typical counter-terrorist operation involved beat patrols in a defined geographical area, in which stop and searches of both citizens and vehicles took place. It was unknown to me whether or not the operations were based on specific intelligence, but discussions with the superintendent in charge of the operation suggested that the places for the operations had been suggested centrally and were based simply on the fact that they were crowded central London locations and, therefore, potentially 'high-risk' sites. The counter-terrorist operations also often involved the use of an Automatic Number Plate Recognition (ANPR) device scan the number plate of vehicles. If the database recognised that there was an issue with the vehicle, then the driver would be asked to be stopped further along the road (Table 1).

Policing the threat of terror in London: empirical findings

Section 44 Stop and Search: ethnicity and disproportionality

Figures on the ethnic background of those people stopped and searched across London from January 2008 to July 2010 were provided on a monthly basis and analysed for the rate of disproportionality.[5] Disproportionality figures are revealing, because more than simply providing the number of people who were stopped and searched from each ethnic group, they allow comparisons between each ethnic group. As shown on the graph below, the highest rate of disproportionality was for the 'Other' category which indicates that the rate was consistently close to or above 2.0 and with peaks in May 2008 and July 2008. There were further peaks in disproportionality for people belonging to the 'Other' ethnic group in March,

May, June and July 2010 which is surprising given that this was after the January 2010 ECtHR ruling that s44 was being used unlawfully. This was at a time when the overall rate of s44 stop and searches across London had been dropping and use of the power was being 'phased out'.

A similar pattern can be seen for the rate of stop and search for Asian people in that the figures for disproportionality were consistently around 1.5 times above what would be expected from their numbers in the population. From October 2009 we can see a consistent rise in the rate of disproportionality for Asian people which continued over the period when s44 was being used less overall. For Black people who were stopped under s44, the rate of disproportionality remained later (between 0.9 and 1.4) the figure for Asian and Other groups (Figure 1).

The interpretation of disproportionality figures is complex because of the range of factors which may intersect to cause the visible patterns. The 'available' search population (Waddington *et al.* 2004) in London is more ethnically diverse than other areas of the UK and this is likely to contribute to part of the disproportionate number of ethnic minorities stopped and searched, along with the factor of the younger demographic age profile of Asian, Black and people of Mixed ethnic background. Given the location of previous terrorist attacks, previous terrorist attack locations, large crowds of people and commuter populations, London is where counter-terrorist policing efforts are targeted, in accordance with the government's risk assessment procedures. As discussed later, officers may have been acting on specific intelligence about the profile of potential suspects and also the area in which a s44 operation may have been directed could result in high numbers of Asians being stopped by virtue of the population in that particular locale. This, of course, raises questions as to how the areas where s44 operations were directed to be carried out were identified and whether it was based on 'intelligence' or a security risk assessment.

Aside from the potentially mitigating factors outlined thus far, for the high s44 disproportionality rates amongst the Asian and Other group, there is the more problematic explanation that the police may have been profiling people who had an outward Asian, 'Mixed' or 'Other' background ethnic appearance. This is explored further in the interviews which were conducted for this study with the police and the people who were stopped and searched. The suggestion that Asian and particularly Muslim men were being profiled would represent an important shift in the empirical information we have about police ethnic minority stereotypes thus far. Research from the 1980s until the mid-1990s tended suggest that some Asian groups were under or proportionately represented in terms of their reports of offending and there was also a corresponding low level of policing directed towards this group (Mawby *et al.* 1979, Jefferson 1993). Scholarship over the last ten years, however, has indicated that Asian males are the 'new folk devil' (Alexander 2000, Parmar 2012). Police stereotypes of Asian people and have shifted from an image of a law-abiding and self-policing community to a moral panic about drug using, violent, gang members and potential terrorists (Webster 1997, Alexander 2000, Goodey 2001, Hudson 2007).

Outcome of stop and searches

One factor which underlined questions about the utility of s44 as an effective counter-terrorist policing tool was the fact that the over-whelming majority of

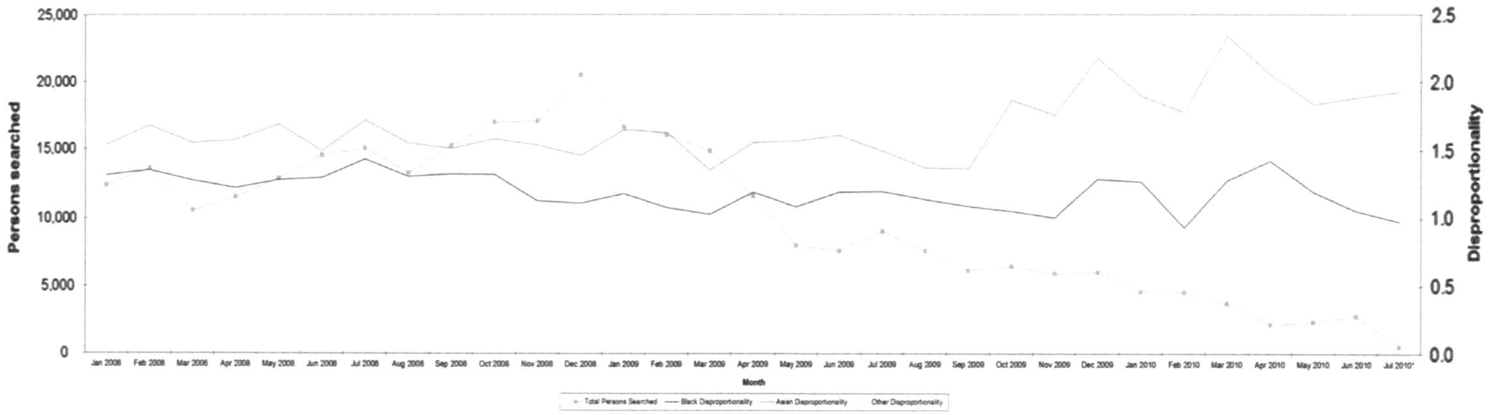

Figure 1. Stop and searches under Section 44 of the Terrorism Act 2000 and disproportionality for the Metropolitan Police Service: January 2008–July 2010.

searches did not result in an arrest for terrorism. The MPS figures show that between January 2008 and April 2009 s44 was being heavily used – for example, the highest number of stops during this period was in December 2008 with a total of 21,594 searches. From these stops, only one arrest was related to terrorism, though it is not known whether this resulted in a successful prosecution. Five hundred and sixty-three people were 'advised' and 20,388 resulted in no further action. Between January 2008 and July 2010, cannabis warnings were given to an average of 14 people per month resulting from a s44 stop and search. Other outcomes included dispersal of groups under the Anti-Social Behaviour Act 2003, verbal warnings and alcohol confiscation. The power was being essentially used in speculative intrusions and the governance of less serious crime.

The police and the policed

The policed

Forty interviews with people who had been stopped and searched under s44 were conducted. All participants were male and the self-defined ethnic profile of this group was 19 Asian, 3 Other Asian 10 Black, 7 White and 1 Mixed. Of the Asian group, 11 described themselves as Muslim, 4 said that they were Sikh and 4 were Hindu. For the Black group, 6 described themselves as Caribbean, 3 as African and 1 as Somalian. Of the White group, 2 said that they were Irish. The person of 'Mixed' background specified that he was White and Asian and that he was a British Muslim. The sample was skewed towards people of Muslim background. Thirty of the males were aged under 25 and the remaining ten participants were aged between 25 and 38 years.

Of the 40 interviews, 27 were conducted immediately and the remaining 13 were conducted within two weeks. The majority of people from a minority ethnic group background (22/34) stated that they felt that had been stopped primarily because of their ethnic background. The resounding claim was that it was they felt that they were searched because they were visibly Asian, Black or 'because they looked Muslim'. Although the interviews cannot necessarily confirm that the police were or were not profiling people on the basis of their ethnic appearance, quotes such as the one below support the understanding that ethnic minorities firmly *believed* that they were unfairly targeted.

> That's the third time I've been stopped and searched. What, do I have terrorist written on my forehead? They think it's OK to brand us as criminals and that we'll just sit back. That's not how it is though is it. The cops can't have it both ways. I was reading that the police have been invited to the mosques. What's the point in that? . . .what's that gonna do? (British-Pakistani Muslim)

The criminalising process

There was a strong feeling amongst Asian youth that they felt labelled, and as though they were not treated fairly by the ways in which the police made their decisions about who to stop and search. Such protests about questioning why they had been stopped were generally absent from the interviews with White citizens who tended to have a positive view about the interventions taken by the police. Nevertheless, two people belonging to the White group said that they felt as though were stopped to 'balance out the numbers' as one person put it, to show that the police were not only stopping Asians.

Previous scholarship on the process of criminalisation has identified police practice as the key to how groups and communities of people come to be associated with types of crime and following this there is an expectation that members from that group will be likely to commit those crimes (Hall *et al.* 1978). The pliability of the criminalising process, which was highlighted by Jefferson (1993) suggested that although South Asians and particularly Pakistani Muslims were seen as the most 'other' of others, the discourse of 'Asianness' was not a criminalising one at that time. Although the literature has analysed processes of criminalisation through media portrayal, the research discussed here suggests that when anecdotal accounts of being treated as 'suspect' by the police are verified through individual experience – the process is validated, particularly amongst young people. The sharing of information (predominantly via social networking media) amongst the Asian men I interviewed also acted to bolster their notions of a criminalising process – many of my interviewees knew of their friends (often from the same ethnic background) who had been stopped and searched which crystallised their perception that they were targeted by the police because of their ethnic background.

Intra-ethnic tensions: 'Don't freak, I'm a Sikh'

One significant finding to emerge was the intra-ethnic hostility that appeared to have been generated amongst non-Muslim Asians who were stopped and searched. The young men I spoke with were frustrated and felt they were stopped and searched because the police thought that they looked as though they were Muslim.

> It's everywhere. I know I've been stopped because that copper thought – he's brown, he follows Islam, maybe he's a terrorist. It's not just the police either – I feel a responsibility to remind people, my friends, that I'm not Muslim and that I think terrorism is really wrong. When I go out, I drink alcohol, even if I don't feel like it, to give people the message that I'm not Muslim. (British Asian Hindu)

These findings are in support of newspaper reports soon after the July 2005 underground attacks which stated that people were wearing T-Shirts with 'Don't freak, I'm a Sikh' written across them. This was thought to be spurred by the report that following the attacks, hate crimes against Asians widely increased and that these were directed to Asians of all faiths (Guardian 2005).

Counter-terrorist, counter-productive?

The research provides empirical evidence for the problematic consequence of the enmeshing of policing and security, imposes a framework for intelligence collection structured around *pre-emption* which is a military based doctrine from which a blended style of counter-terrorism policing has developed (Brodeur 2001, Hocking 2003, Hocking and Lewis 2007). Within this strategy a key security imperative of the state is to anticipate threats and in this constructed state of permanent crisis, in which peacetime is seen only as a time before wartime, exceptional powers become routine and normalised. In Agamben's (2005) analysis, the 'state of exception' is not a special kind of law, but rather the suspension of the juridical order itself and it thus defines law's threshold. The change in policing within the context of counter-terrorist strategies can also be framed within the 'pre-crime logic of security' (Zedner 2007, McCulloch and Pickering 2009). As Zedner explains, the institution of draconian security policies, are interspersed with the assurance and appearance of protection and a concern for human rather than national security. McCulloch and Pickering (2009) explain that counter-terrorism is uniquely suited to the 'pre-crime' shift as the term 'terrorism' is pre-emptive, existing prior to and beyond and formal verdict. Law enforcement, aims to confront threats before they emerge, linking substantial and continuing coercive action to suspicion. Indeed, the 'counter-terrorism legislation demarks a new frontline so that law is always catching up with the "reality" of policing' (McCulloch and Pickering 2009, p. 641).

The research demonstrated that the elision of ordinary policing and counter-terrorist policing practices were generating counter-productive consequences. Indeed, the public were aware of the wide reach of the terrorism powers and commented on their inapplicability, as one young British-Pakistani male explained:

> I mean ... do they really think they will catch terrorists like this? By stopping innocent people on the street? I was going to play football, not set off a bomb. (British-Bangladeshi Muslim)

The resentment generated by s44 stop and search encounters was striking and underlined the problematic consequences of its enforcement. Contrary to the suggestion that British Muslims lacked a sense of civic responsibility and felt as though they did not belong, people expressed that they did feel British and engaged with society. Problematically, some expressed that since the overuse of the powers under the TA 2000 had become widespread, they felt excluded, and 'special cases' for which adherence to the rules of democracy no longer applied. S44 stops were found to be catalytic in generating social and political disenfranchisement:

> I felt alright before I was stopped, I felt like this is my country, I was born here and there are so many parts of me that are all London ... After the second time I was stopped I started to feel like people see what they want to see. The police see me as a terrorist, and then I'm invisible. No-one listens, they just assume and do what they want to do. There's no such thing as democracy, no human rights. How would you feel? (British Pakistani Muslim)

Another interviewee explained that prior to his s44 encounter he felt as though society was fair, and that if something went wrong, he could go to the police, complain and that he would trust the fact that something would be done. After he was stopped and when his complaint came to nothing, the young Bangladeshi man felt as though he did not want to be involved anymore. This is worrying when we consider that some writers have commented on the potential links between radicalisation and the idea that acts of terrorism are the result of a systemic failure in participatory democratic practice and perceptions of alienation and the unfairness of the social order (Hocking 2003, Bramadat and Wortley 2008). Indeed the *Prevent* strategy is premised on the idea that engaging with the Muslim community can yield intelligence about potential terrorist plots and that if the police are attuned and have a strong relationship with ethnic minority groups, that the detection and prevention of acts of terror will be facilitated. The enforcement of s44 was found to, at best, stifle and at worst reverse the development of mutual trust between British Asians and the police.

The police

Views towards Section 44 of the Terrorism Act 2000

Police perception towards s44 and the non-requirement for 'reasonable suspicion' was mainly positive. The officers I spoke with generally felt as though the legislation allowed them to 'get on with the job at hand' rather than worry about 'bureaucracy' as one officer put it.

> It's a really useful piece of legislation, and the fact that we don't need suspicion is because of the seriousness of what the power is actually for. I know it's not popular, but the police need this to be able to keep people safe . . . And actually, after the July attacks, I've had members of the public come and say 'thank–you' for the fact that we are actually implementing our powers under section 44. It's our job now to also make people feel secure. (Police Officer)

Equating the enforcement of s44 with the maintenance of security was common amongst officers. In addition to its assumed reassurance function for the general public, one officer emphasised that it may have a 'deterrent effect' (by making potential terrorists less likely to plan or engage in an attack for fear of being caught) and associated the lack of arrests for terrorist activity as evidence of the fact that s44 operations were having a preventive effect. The ubiquitous threat of terror provided an increased legitimacy to the justification for state intervention despite the fact that the police practices contravened democratic values.

Two officers raised negative concerns about their requirement to enforce s44. A female officer stated that she very much disliked conducting s44 operations because she was worried about the number of public complaints it generated. In one of my observations, the same officer conducted a s44 stop and search on a female at a train station and after the search the officer commented that she 'felt bad' about the search because the person she stopped was Irish and she was worried that the citizen who was stopped may have felt targeted because of her background. The second officer had more practical concerns about s44 as he felt as though the power was not effective enough, as by the time they might stop a suspected terrorist in an underground station or in a crowded place, to him, it was 'too late'. He suggested that counter-terrorist efforts should be more targeted and based on intelligence rather than a 'reassurance exercise'.

Criminal activity and terrorism

I was interested to understand more about the fact that s44 stops seldom resulted in arrests for terrorism and how police officers interpreted this. Some officers stated that they thought the number of stops were justified because s44 had an important 'reassurance function'. Indeed one British Transport Police officer suggested that the main reason for wheeling out an x-ray machine onto the platform of King's Cross station was to give the message out to people that 'something was being done about terrorism.'

Another officer suggested that it did not matter to him that s44 resulted in few arrests for terrorism because it also allowed them to carry out other essential police functions such as drug offence warnings, and thus functioned as a 'gateway' power. Another officer suggested that although s44 allowed them to detect less serious offences, these could often be viewed in terms of 'the bigger picture in fighting terrorism' because drug dealers, illegal DVD sellers and so on were 'often funding terrorism somewhere down the line.' The conflation of regular criminal activity with counter-terrorist policing and the rationalisation of stop and search practice (by way of reference to the terrorist threat) by police officers is problematic. It is indicative of how the institutional mind can overwhelm the rational through the intangible aim to 'protect' people. Firstly there is clear lack of proportionality in the use of a draconian power to stop someone and to then arrest or warn them for an offence which is much less threatening, serious or risky. This is of concern because as we know from Figure 1 above, ethnic minorities are more likely to be initially stopped and searched under s44 and so the collateral impact on ethnic minorities is disproportionate (Bowling and Phillips 2007, Bowling, Parmar, and Phillips 2008). Secondly, the way in which the spectre of terror was used to legitimate unfair police practice is difficult to reconcile in the context of efforts which were said to be being made to engage with ethnic minorities and in particular 'Muslim communities.' It is not surprising that the use of coercive high policing practices whilst aiming to foster legitimate relations based on mutual trust (Innes and Thiel 2008) results in feelings of resentment and concerns about disingenuousness from Muslim citizens towards the police.

Conclusion: security, suspicion and the criminalising process

The pursuit of human security is wrought with complexities which can generate mistakes. We should not expect perfection from the police given the pressures they face to make both precise and swift decisions (Bowling 2007). Arguably, however, mistakes and unfair practice can be assuaged by ensuring that powers to enforce the law are conceptualised correctly and used in line with the rationale and purpose for which they were created. The research described in this paper warns against the individual and community level impacts of expecting the police to achieve 'security' – a state which has been described as unattainable, subjective, impermanent and something for which the public has an insatiable 'ice-cream-like' desire (Mythen and Walklate 2008, Loader 2009, Zedner 2009). This calls into question whether the ends justify the means in the use of s44 given the high cost to public (in particular ethnic minority citizens') perceptions of legitimacy and confidence in the police.

The (mis)use of counter-terror policing powers has an impact which is perhaps intractable in terms of the process of criminalisation to which Asian-Muslim men felt subjected. The combination of local level (individual and community) and macro-level accounts[6] of the use of s44 powers has resulted in Asian men feeling as though the perception of them as inherently suspicious has become normalised. The encouragement of police discretion through the non-requirement for 'reasonable suspicion' resulted in disproportionate numbers of Asian and Black people being stopped and searched and as a consequence 'over-policed' across London. Whether this was a *direct* result of the absence of 'reasonable suspicion' is not clear. Whether the withdrawal of s44 and the apparent safeguards proposed in the new s47 counter-terrorist legislation will mitigate for the negative cost to the perception of police legitimacy amongst ethnic minority communities is even more uncertain. The disenfranchisement of Asian males of Muslim background highlighted in this paper is of paramount social significance. Arguably, the aim to 'prevent' terrorism and radicalisation on a wholesale basis by targeting Muslim citizens through community programmes and policing efforts further entrenches the criminalising process. As Sen suggests, 'in the downplaying of political and social identities as opposed to religious identity, it is civil society that has been the loser, precisely at a time when there is a great need to strengthen it' (2007, p. 83). Recognising the multiplicity of identities would militate against the conception of such groups and people in exclusively religious terms.

Acknowledgements

I thank the participants of the study, the Metropolitan Police and the Metropolitan Police Strategic Research and Evaluation Unit for access to the data and reproduction of the graph on page 6. I am grateful to Ben Bowling for advice throughout the research and to Paddy Rawlinson, Leanne Weber, Layla Skinns and Tariq Mughal for their insightful comments on earlier drafts of the paper.

Notes

1. Section 1 refers to the search of an individual and Section 2 refers to the stop and search of a vehicle and its contents.
2. The UK had a strategy for Countering International Terrorism in place since 2003 called CONTEST which had four principal strands: Prevent, Pursue, Protect and Prepare. This strategy was updated in 2006.
3. The Asian category is not disaggregated in the police figures, so it is not possible to understand whether there was an increase stop and searches of people from Muslim backgrounds.
4. 'Rolling authorisations' enabled a police commander in a particular area (usually covering the whole of London) to implement s44 stop and search powers without redress to the Secretary of State for confirmation.
5. Disproportionality figures are based on the subject's self-defined ethnicity and calculated by the result of minority searches being divided by White searches which is then multiplied by a multiplier based on the ratio of population per the 2001 census. The multipliers are 5.74 for Black, 5.5 for Asian and 20.01 for 'Other' search subjects.
6. For example the fatal shooting of Jean Charles de Menezes in July 2005, wrongly suspected to be a terrorist and the arrest and detainment of six Muslims of North African origin working as street cleaners falsely tipped off to be plotting to kill the Pope earlier in 2010.

References

Agamben, G., 2005. *State of exception.* K. Attell 2005, Trans. Chicago: Chicago University Press.

Alexander, C., 2000. *The Asian gang: ethnicity, identity, masculinity.* Oxford: Berg.

Association of Police Authorities, 2010. *Police stops: know your rights leaflet.* Association of Police Authorities. Available from: http://www.apa.police.uk/Admin/uploads/attachment/docs/public/Public_Campaigns/Know_Your_Rights/Stop_and_Search_-_Nov_2010.pdf

Bigo, D., 2006. Internal and external aspects of security. *European Security,* 15 (4), 385–404.

Bowling, B., 2007. Fair and effective policing methods: towards 'good enough' policing. *Journal of Scandinavian Studies in Criminology and Crime Prevention*, 8 (1), 17–32.
Bowling, B., Parmar, A., and Phillips, C., 2008. Policing minority ethnic communities. *In*: T. Newburn, ed. *Handbook of policing*. 2nd ed. Cullompton: Willan, 528–555.
Bowling, B. and Phillips, C., 2007. Disproportionate and discriminatory: reviewing the evidence on police stop and search. *Modern Law Review*, 70 (6), 936–961.
Bramadat, P. and Wortley, S., 2008. *Religious youth radicalisation in Canada*. Canada: Department of Canadian Heritage, Multiculturalism and Human Rights Branch.
Brodeur, J.P., 2001. High and low policing in post 9/11 times. *Policing*, 1 (1), 25–37.
Dodd, V., 2010. Police demand new powers to stop and search terror suspects. *The Guardian*. Available from: http://www.guardian.co.uk/uk/2010/dec/29/police-stop-and-search-powers [Accessed 29 December 2010].
Goodey, J., 2001. The criminalization of British Asian youth: research from Bradford and Sheffield. *Journal of Youth Studies*, 4 (4), 429–450.
Hall, S., Critcher, C., Jefferson, T., Clarke, J., and Roberts, B., 1978. *Policing the crisis: mugging, the state and law and order*. London: Macmillan Education.
Hocking, J., 2003. Counter-terrorism and the criminalisation of politics: Australia's new security powers of detention, proscription and control. *Australian Journal of Politics and History*, 49 (3), 355–371.
Hocking, J. and Lewis, C., eds., 2007. *Counter-terrorism and the post-democratic state: Monash studies in global movements*. London: Edward Elgar.
Hudson, B., 2007. Diversity, crime and criminal justice. *In*: M. Maguire, R. Morgan, and R. Reiner, eds. *The Oxford handbook of criminology*. 4th ed. Oxford: Oxford University Press, 158–171.
Innes, M. and Thiel, D., 2008. Policing terror. *In*: T. Newburn, ed. *The handbook of policing*. 2nd ed. Cullumpton: Willan, 553–579.
Jefferson, T., 1993. The racism of criminalization: policing and the reproduction of the criminal other. *In*: L.R. Gelsthorpe, ed. *Minority ethnic groups in the criminal justice system*. Cambridge: Institute of Criminology, 553–579.
Kundnani, A., 2007. *The end of tolerance: racism in 21st century Britain*. London: Pluto Press.
Loader, I., 2009. Ice-cream and incarceration: on appetites for security and punishment. *Punishment and Society*, 11 (2), 241–257.
Mawby, R., McCulloch, J., and Batta, I., 1979. Crime amongst Asian juveniles in Bradford. *International Journal of the Sociology of Law*, 7, 297–306.
McCulloch, J. and Pickering, S., 2009. Pre-crime and counter-terrorism. *British Journal of Criminology*, 49, 628–645.
Ministry of Justice, 2009. *Statistics on race and the criminal justice system 2007/8. A ministry of justice publication under section 95 of the Criminal Justice Act 1991*. London: Crown Copyright.
Moeckli, D., 2008. The impossibility of terrorist profiling [online]. Available from: http://www.opendemocracy.net [Accessed 12 November 2009].
Mythen, G. and Walklate, S., 2008. Terrorism, risk and international security: the perils of asking what if? *Security Dialogue*, 39, 221–42.
Nagarajah, S., 2005. Mistaken identity. *The Guardian*. Available from: http://www.guardian.co.uk/world/2005/sep/05/religion.july7 [Accessed 5 September 2005].
Pantazis, C. and Pemberton, S., 2009. From the 'old' to the 'new' suspect community: examining the impacts of recent UK counter-terrorist legislation. *British Journal of Criminology*, 49, 646–666.
Parmar, A., 2010. Policing and ethnic profiling. *In*: K.P. Sveinsson, ed. *Ethnic profiling: the use of 'race' in UK law enforcement*. London: Runnymede, 8–10.
Parmar, A., 2007. *Crime and the Asian community: disentangling perceptions and reality*. Unpublished thesis (PhD), University of Cambridge.
Sen, A., 2007. *Identity and violence: the illusion of destiny*. London: Penguin Books.
Travis, A., 2009. Stop and search disproportionately targets black and Asian people. *The Guardian*, 1 May. Available from: http://www.guardian.co.uk/uk/audio/2009/may/01/stop-and-search-black-asian

Waddington, P.A.J., Stenson, K., and Don, D., 2004. In proportion: race and police stop and search. *British Journal of Criminology*, 44, 889–914.
Walker, C., 2008. 'Know thine enemy as thyself': discerning friend from foe under anti-terrorism laws. *Melbourne University Law Review*, 32, 276–301.
Webster, C., 1997. The construction of 'Asian' criminality. *International Journal of the Sociology of Law*, 25 (1), 65–86.
Zedner, L., 2007. Pre-crime and post-criminology. *Theoretical Criminology*, 11 (2), 261–281.
Zedner, L., 2009. *Security. Key ideas in criminology.* London: Routledge.

Cases and legislation
Dumbell v Roberts [1944] 1 All ER 326.
Gillan and Quinton v UK [2010] European Court of Human Rights.
Terrorism Act 2000 (UK) c11, s44.
Explanatory Memorandum to the Terrorism Act 2000 (Remedial) Order 2011 (UK) 631.
Terrorism Review 2011 (UK) Cm 8004.
Protection of Freedoms Bill 2011 (UK) 146.

Ethnic profiling in ID checks by the Hungarian police

Balázs M. Tóth and András Kádár

Hungarian Helsinki Committee

This paper provides an overview of the Hungarian legal norms regulating police identification (ID) checks, briefly elaborating on the legally permitted aims of the measure and on whether the relevant legal provisions restrict officers' decisions on whom to stop for this purpose. The paper also describes the methodology of two major research projects on 'ethnic profiling' of Roma from the past five years and presents their findings. In order to assess the effectiveness of the police practice and the patterns of ethnic profiling in the particular field, the paper provides an analysis of data based on more than 20,000 ID check forms. The research results show clear ethnic disproportionality and extremely low effectiveness in police ID check practice. The paper also offers some recommendations for the improvement of the present legal framework concerning ID checks.

The term 'ethnic profiling' refers to the use of race, ethnicity, religion, or national origin rather than individual behaviour as the basis for making law enforcement decisions about who may be involved in criminal activity. Ethnic profiling appears most frequently in law enforcement officers' decisions about who to stop and ask for identification (ID), question, search and sometimes arrest (OSI 2009a, p. 17). Ethnic profiling assumes that these characteristics will help to predict which people will be involved in particular crimes. The Hungarian police enjoy a significant amount of discretion in deciding whom to stop or question; nothing could be more telling than the title of a study on ethnic profiling, 'I Can Stop and Search Whoever I Want' – a quotation taken from an interview with a Hungarian police officer in 2005 (OSI 2007a, p. 52). The quotation implies that police officers in Hungary are authorised by law to stop and search people entirely arbitrarily, without any prior suspicion or later justification. Although the legal basis for this has been amended since 2005, the actual situation has not changed substantially. This practically unlimited discretion proves especially problematic when the ethnicity of the person concerned may play a role in the police's decision on whether to take action or not. In order to put the research findings in context, we briefly outline the situation of the Roma in Hungary and the legal norms regulating police ID check powers.

Social context

The Roma are Hungary's largest – and visible – ethnic minority. While they have been facing prejudices and hostility throughout their history, their situation turned particularly critical following the democratic transition of 1989, after which most large factories, having employed the majority of unskilled Roma workers, were closed down. The unemployment rate within the Roma community has been above 70% since the beginning of the 1990s (Kertesi 2005, p. 5). But Roma are not only disadvantaged in the field of employment. According to a recent study (Havas 2008, p. 123) approximately one-third of Roma pupils are educated in segregated classes, under sub-standard conditions. Moreover, at present there are 3000 segregated Roma classes in primary schools as opposed to 150 in 1980. Infant mortality rates are also twice as high among the Roma than among other groups (OSI 2007b).

The general public seems to be aware of the situation of the Roma minority. 90% of respondents in a 2009 survey stated that discrimination based on ethnic origin is widespread in Hungary (FRA 2009, p. 6). Furthermore, 62% of respondents belonging to the Roma minority stated that they were discriminated against in the preceding 12 months in various fields (FRA 2009, p. 9). A survey in 2009 showed that 29% of the respondents would not accept a Roma person as a co-worker, 43% would not accept a Roma as a neighbour and 76% would not accept a Roma person as a partner (Marketing Centrum 2009).

The marginalised situation of this group is also reflected in the proportion of Roma within the prison population. According to research on the representation of Roma in penitentiary institutions, prisoners regarding themselves as Romani amounted to 30% and 40% of the prison population in 1995 and 1996, respectively. This results slightly deviated from the data based on the ID of the interviewers (they regarded 44% of the respondents to be of Roma origin), while it differed greatly from the estimation of wardens, who thought 61% of the prison population to be Roma (Huszár 1997). According to estimations by penitentiary personnel and the Hungarian Helsinki Committee's (HHC) civilian monitors, these proportions have not changed significantly in the past decade. This is a significant overrepresentation, since according to reliable sociological research the estimated proportion of Roma is much lower: approximately 6% of the Hungarian population (Hablicsek 2007, p. 54).

In 2000, the HHC launched a pilot research project titled 'The prevalence in the Hungarian criminal justice system of the constitutional principle of equality before the law concerning Roma and non-Roma defendants' to examine the reasons for the disproportionately high percentage of Roma citizens in the Hungarian penitentiary system. After analysing 146 case files, the researchers found significant differences in the proportion of members of the minority and majority population entering the criminal justice system resulting from stop and search measures. Two factors may account for this difference: either ID checks against the Roma are more efficient or the Roma are more frequently controlled by the police. The answer can be found in the results of two thematic research projects focusing on ethnic profiling and ID checks described in detail below.

Legal context

In Hungarian legal terminology, there is no direct equivalent for 'stop and search'. According to the 1994 Police Act, an ID check (*igazoltatás*) is a police measure aimed at establishing the identity of a person by obliging him/her to present a document verifying who he/she is. Four types of ID checks can be differentiated. Under Article 29 of the Police Act, in force until January 2008, a police officer could check the identity of any person *whose personal identity needed to be established.* Since no further specification or qualification was added, the article gave officers unrestricted authority to decide whom to check. As of 1 January 2008, the law was amended. The new provision lists the legally permitted aims of the measure as: protection of public order, public safety, crime prevention and crime detection, establishing the lawful stay of the concerned person, and/or protection of the rights of the person checked or of others. The aim of amending the definition was to narrow police officers' discretion, but the change has not had a real impact on police practice.

The second type of ID check is when the measure is carried out in the course of traffic control and here no suspicion of unlawful behaviour is required. The third type of the measure is 'intensive control' which can be ordered by the head of a police unit in order to arrest a criminal suspect or to prevent or frustrate an action or incident posing a threat to public safety. In such cases, the officer conducting the check is not required to assess individual circumstances and is authorised to check every single person without further justification within the area and time defined in the order. Finally, there are so-called non-autonomous ID checks, the performance of which is not dependent on the officer's discretion. If the police officer catches a perpetrator or asks witnesses on the spot, he/she will necessarily have to identify the given individual. In this case, there will be a primary measure – such as interviewing a suspect or a witness – and the ID check will only be supplementary. In cases of such a non-autonomous ID checks, the aim of the primary measure becomes the lawfully permitted aim of the given check.

An ID check is often, though not always, accompanied by questioning the person checked. Under Article 32 of the Police Act, a police officer may pose questions to anyone who may have information that is necessary for carrying out police tasks. The person asked may be held up, or detained briefly on the street and he/she is obliged to provide any information requested. Under the Police Act, the police officer may search the ID checked person's clothing, luggage, or vehicle if that is necessary for establishing their identity, for averting a threat to public order or security, or due to the suspicion of a criminal or petty offence.

We do not have exact statistics, but based on the empirical evidence from these studies, we can say that a significant percentage of ID checks are accompanied by questioning. In essence, the measure can be compared to 'stop and account' measures in British police practice or 'on-street interrogation' in the USA. Furthermore, a relatively high percentage of ID checks carried out within the framework of traffic control involves the superficial checking of the boot of the car, and some ID checks (especially those initiated on the suspicion of some unlawful behaviour) involve a search element, which will not appear as a separate measure, but are handled in the statistics together with the ID check. This latter type of action can be said to be the equivalent of British 'stop and search' and similar measures discussed elsewhere in this volume.

For the coerciveness and intrusiveness of the measure to be assessed, it must be noted that under Hungarian law if a person is unable or unwilling to prove their identity, he/she may be taken into custody for a maximum of 24 hours and fined up to 50,000 HUF (approximately €180); if the fine is unpaid, a penalty of ten days imprisonment can be imposed.

According to the general provisions outlined by the Police Act, an officer shall take or initiate measures upon finding or being notified of a fact that requires police intervention. The Service Regulation adds to this rule that a police officer shall be under an obligation to act in situations where he/she discovers a crime or a petty offence or where the public order or citizens' person or property is threatened. This means that a minimal level of suspicion is required to justify an ID check that is not determined by law. According to Hungarian law, the existence of a so-called 'simple suspicion' (a concept not defined in detail in law, but clearly meaning a lesser degree of certainty than required to initiate criminal proceedings) is enough for any police measure to be applied.

In practice, the concept means that a person may be subjected to an ID check if a police officer suspects unlawful behaviour, whether or not this is based on information. It is often said that an ID check is the least restrictive police measure, so under the principle of proportionality, where there is any degree of suspicion is in place, checking identity will be an appropriate solution. Moreover, as outlined earlier, searches of clothing, luggage and vehicles may be applied simultaneously with ID checks, often without any specific suspicion as to the content of such belongings. In these cases, the person concerned may be forcefully subjected to a search without sufficient justification.

Given the extremely wide legal discretion enjoyed by police officers, the danger of selecting people to be ID checked on the basis of their ethnicity is always present. The higher the discretion is, the greater the danger of abuses of power, a danger also noted by the European Court of Human Rights (Gillan and Quinton v The United Kingdom, paras 83 and 85). The actual correlation was pointed out long ago in the field of police stops. In the USA, research carried out by the New Jersey Attorney General's Office showed that the disproportionate patterns in traffic stops increased when the discretion of the officer was higher (Harris 2002, pp. 59–60). UK research also shows that stop and search patterns become more disproportionate when the law does not require any ground to carry out a stop. In case of the former measures, blacks were 7.4 times more likely to be stopped in 2007, as opposed to 16.9 times in case of 'suspicionless,' discretionary measures in the similar period (OSI 2009b, p. 34). There is also evidence that ethnic elements in a profile result in higher disproportionality (and lower efficiency) even when lacking higher discretion (Ramirez *et al.* 2003, p. 1214). With this legal framework and the empirical data on the more frequent ID checking of Roma people, the need for an in-depth analysis of the actual practice was evident in 2005, when the first research into ethnic profiling by the Hungarian police was carried out.

The 2005 TÁRKI research

The research carried out by the Social Research Institute in 2005 was aimed at collecting information about the experiences and opinion of the public about police ID checks. The quantitative part of the research was questionnaire-based and consisted of a representative sample comprised of 1000 people, while the qualitative part was based on six focus group discussions each with seven or eight ethnically homogenous participants, 80 interviews of police officers and 20 interviews with members of the public. The main conclusions of the research (Balogi *et al.* 2006) were that Roma are more frequently ID checked than members of the majority; they are more frequently ID checked on the street, in bars and at public events, while members of the majority are more likely to be checked when driving; and Roma find the circumstances of ID checks much worse, perceiving them less likely to be conducted lawfully or politely.

The research also found overt racist stereotypes among police officers: 23% of the police officers surveyed admitted that they tend to stop members of certain groups – especially Roma persons – more often, and 47% believed other police officers tended to do so. They explained that this was because of the 'lifestyle' of members of the Roma minority and they tended to assume that Roma commit crimes more frequently. Similar stereotypes to classify people based on their ethnic origin are also documented in the UK and Canada (Bowling and Philips 2003, Satzewich and Shaffir 2009).

The methodological limits of the research meant that no conclusions could be reached as to possible justifications (or otherwise) of police ID-checking practice. To explore this in more detail, monitoring of police practice was required in which officers register the perceived ethnicity of the person stopped, as well as the aim of the ID check and its result. Lacking reasons for the more frequent control of the Romani people and the outcome of these measures, no inference could be drawn as to the reasons and justifications for the disproportionate nature of the practice. The OSI and the HHC therefore carried out another quantitative research project entitled *Strategies for Effective Stop and Searches* (STEPSS) in 2007 and 2008.

The research by the OSI and HHC in 2007–2008

The aim of the STEPSS project was – inter alia – to obtain reliable data about the number, reasons and outcome of ID checks according to the ethnicity of the people who were stopped and checked (Kádár *et al.* 2008). The STEPSS project was carried out in three pilot sites across Hungary: Budapest's 6th District, Szeged and Kaposvár. These three locations represent a range of different police districts with differing populations, crime profiles and resources. Budapest's 6th District covers a busy city-centre and includes the main railway station. Szeged, with the population of 200,000, is a medium-sized city close to the Romanian border. Kaposvár is a relatively rural police district with 120,000 inhabitants.

According to Hungarian law, police officers are not always required to fill out official forms after ID checks. In practice, however, officers usually do fill out ID check forms because they are obliged to do so according to internal order no. 22/2007 (OT 15) by the National Police Commander. Even when they do fill them out, the standard forms do not contain all the data relevant to the project and the official forms are not anonymous. Therefore, a new, so-called 'STEPSS form' was designed by the Police and the HHC and used alongside the official forms. The STEPSS form used in Hungary contained the following data:

- time of ID check;
- place of ID check;
- gender of concerned person;
- age of concerned person;
- grounds for ID check;
- results of ID check;
- perceived ethnicity of the person concerned, established by the officer;
- civil monitor's remark.

When asking about the result of the ID check, the researchers wished to know whether the check was followed by any further police measures, such as arrest or short-term arrest of the person checked or the initiation of petty offence proceedings. This question was included on the assumption that if a check was followed by any of the previous outcomes, the police action is more likely to have had a proper basis in intelligence or information. While a subsequent procedure does not necessarily indicate that a check was conducted on a proper basis, the research methodology (and the degree of detail provided by the officers on the forms) did not make it possible for the researchers to carry out the individual assessment of the checks whether preliminary information sufficiently justified the police action. Therefore, the qualification of checks on the basis of their subsequent results needs to be seen as an estimative method giving only an approximate picture of the degree to which ID checks were justified.

Analysis of project data

Numbers of stops

During the six months of STEPSS data collection (17 September 2007–17 March 2008), the three Hungarian police units participating in the project performed approximately 36,939 ID checks. Of these stops, 22,375 were recorded on the forms developed as part of the STEPSS project (Table 1).

The data show large differences in the numbers of stops conducted by the three police departments. The variation is especially conspicuous between Szeged and Kaposvár, since the latter produced a consistently higher number of checks even though its population is substantially smaller.

Table 1. Overall data of ID checks within the project period.

Area	Number of stops	Percentage of total	Number of forms completed	Percentage of total	Percentage of forms compared to total number of checks
Budapest	3033[a]	8	2015	8	66
Kaposvár	22,089[a]	60	13,506[b]	53	61
Szeged	11,817[a]	32	9934[b]	39	84
Total	36,939[a]	100	25,455[b]	100	69

[a]Adjusted figure (for explanation see project report).
[b]Hypothetical figure (for explanation see project report).

Overall, the numbers indicated represent a decrease in the number of ID checks from the previous year. In Budapest, there was a drastic 75.3% decrease in ID checks compared to the same period in the preceding year. In Szeged, the total number of such measures dropped by 17.5% compared to the same period in the previous year, while in Kaposvár there was a slight increase (4.7%).

It is likely that the decrease in overall stop numbers reflects a number of factors. One of these is the general loss of confidence on the part of the police, which, according to a number of officers asked during the project evaluation, started with the widely publicised instances of excessive use of force during the violent riots of October 2006 in Budapest. As a result, there was a decrease in police activity throughout the whole country. Low morale and lack of public trust in the police were repeatedly mentioned during the evaluation interviews for the project. The decrease in ID checks in Szeged and Budapest during the project period may also reflect the increased administrative workload on the officers (caused by being required to fill out the form). This is substantiated by the fact that in Budapest the decrease was radical (over 70%) compared to the same period in the previous year, but after the monitoring phase was over, the monthly average of ID checks increased by 25%.

When asked about the possible explanation for the trends and numbers, the interviewed police officers did not mention the January 2008 amendment of the Police Act (prescribing the conditions of ID checks with greater detail than before the modification). The following were identified as factors influencing the number of checks: (1) the use of personnel for other purposes (e.g. demonstrations), meaning that there were fewer officers on the streets; (2) intensive control around the Christmas holidays; (3) events attracting larger crowds; (4) ordering of specific actions; (5) the number of officers on leave in the given period; (6) the weather conditions; and (6) others tasks (e.g. shooting practice, training tasks, physical tests) (Table 2).

Table 2. The proportion of ID checks in relation to the population.

Place	Number of stops[a]	Estimated population	Number of stops per 1000 population per year
Budapest[a]	6065	65,000	93
Kaposvár[b]	44,177	122,000	362
Szeged[c]	23,633	203,000	116

[a]Estimated annual number (for explanation see STEPSS project report).
[b]KSH Népességtudományi Kutató Intézet, Eloreszámítási adatbázis, 2003 (http://www.nepinfo.hu/index.php?m = 830&id = 566).
[c]http://www.icicom.hu/teruletfo/csmhu15.htm.

As noted earlier, ID checks in Hungary involve not only discretionary stops on the street of those suspected of committing a crime, but also non-autonomous checks. When asked about the approximate proportion of such checks, different estimates were given by the competent police officers: 10% in Kaposvár, 20% in Szeged and 30% in Budapest. If we adjust the above numbers using this data, we still get very high numbers: 65 checks per 1000 people in Budapest, 325 in Kaposvár and 93 in Szeged.

Effectiveness

The effectiveness of ID checks was determined by examining the percentage of ID checks that were followed by further police measures. This is often referred to as the 'hit rate'. The research identified three main types of follow-up procedures: (1) short-term arrests, (2) arrests and (3) petty offence procedures initiated (including on-the-spot fines).

Overall, including traffic related checks, only 1% of ID checks led to an arrest, 2% to a short-term arrest and 18% to petty offence procedures. In the whole, it appears that ID checks are inefficient and may also be ineffective; large numbers of people are being inconvenienced by the police for ID checks, with little result. The data certainly do not support the argument that extensive checks are an efficient tool against criminality, and highlights the sheer amount of police time wasted conducting ID checks.

Police officers sometimes refer to the deterrent effect of ID checks by saying that if someone is going out to commit a crime and is 'interrupted' in doing so by an ID check, he/she will give up with the planned crime. However, this hypothesis has never been justified by a systemic analysis of the practice in Hungary. In the UK, research found that search 'has only a limited disruptive impact on crime' and that 'searches reduced the number of "disruptable" crimes by just 0.2%' (Miller *et al.* 2000, pp. v–vi; see also Bowling and Weber, this issue). As long as there is no credible evidence as to the significant deterrent effect of ID checks, we have no reason to assume it since it is more rational to hold that if someone planning to commit a robbery happens to be ID checked, they will accomplish their plans either later or away from where the police measure took place.

The question arises, why are so many ID checks are performed in light of their low effectiveness as an investigative tool? There are two likely explanations. One possible reason is the organisational culture originating from the socialist regime's aspiration to keep the citizens under as much control as possible. ID checks in this context were a tool enabling the State to know who is doing what and where. Without a conscious effort to break away from this culture, it is very difficult to change this deeply entrenched pattern. Probably not independent from this organisational heritage, patrol officers are informally required to carry out as many recordable activities during their shifts as possible. Simply put, they need to appear to be productive. There is anecdotal evidence that there are several units that require a minimum number of ID checks to be made per shift, and the number of ID checks is a relevant factor in officers' performance appraisal. These two elements together probably account for the widespread use of stop and check in Hungary.

Ethnic disproportionality

The data also show that Roma are disproportionately targeted for ID checks. Within the framework of the project, 22% of all persons checked by the police were of Roma origin (according to the perception of the officer performing the check), as opposed to 75% being identified as 'Caucasian' by the acting officer. Thus, the Roma, whose proportion within the population is around 6%, are more than three times as likely to be stopped when their percentage of the general population is taken as a comparative 'benchmark.' (Research in Toronto revealed similar disproportionality ratio, see

Wortley and Owusu-Bempah, this issue). Moeckli (2007) convincingly argues that patterns of stop and search that are disproportionate without being more efficient (i.e. with a higher than average 'hit rate') should be deemed a form of discrimination when judged by ECtHR standards. An ID check in Hungary will almost necessarily mean recording and processing personal data, which is a restriction of privacy according to the Court's well established practice (see. e.g. *Rotaru v Romania*, para. 43, and *S and Marper v United Kingdom*, paras. 66–67.). Therefore, Hungarian ID checks should be subject to the Convention's prohibition of unlawful discrimination.

Ethnicity and effectiveness of ID checks

The research data show that ID checks of Roma are no more likely to yield results than measures enforced in relation to non-Roma. It is often argued that disproportionately targeting of ethnic minority groups is justified by differential rates of criminal involvement. The hit rate of police checks, however, shows no significant differences by ethnic group. Roma are disproportionately subjected to ID checks, yet the hit rates calculated for the Roma and the non-Roma group are almost equal. On a national level, 78% of ID checks involving Roma were 'unsuccessful' in the sense that no further measure was taken after the check, while for non-Roma this ratio was 79%. The percentage of checks followed by a petty offence proceeding for Roma and non-Roma was 19% and 18%, respectively. Rates of arrests and short-term arrests are practically the same within the Roma and the non-Roma sample.

Almost identical hit rate does not mean that the practice is justified. In the UK the percentage of searches that result in arrest is 11% for both white and black people, in relation to which Bowling and Philips (2007) enumerate several arguments that the charge of discrimination cannot be rejected on the basis of equal hit rates. Some of these arguments apply equally well to the Hungarian case; for example, being guilty and being arrested are far from the same thing, arrests might result from confrontational police measures, arrests can be made for reasons unrelated to the suspicion for which the measure was initiated. It should be added, however, that equal efficiency can never justify unequal treatment of a minority group. Over-policing of a given community will necessarily result in more people from that group coming to the attention of the police and more innocent people being unreasonably ID checked and/or searched. This is definitely a form of discrimination against a social group, namely unequal treatment by the criminal justice system of individuals in comparable situations. The devastating consequences of the discriminatory practice on the African–American community have been documented in the US, where the method of racial profiling has had the direct impact on the social exclusion of the whole black community (Mauer 2006).

In addition, when ID checks are initiated upon the suspicion of a criminal offence (where in fact the overall hit rate is rather high), a significantly higher proportion of Roma are stopped without a sufficient ground than non-Roma (37% as opposed to 25%).

It must also be pointed out that within the group of persons stopped and checked on the suspicion of a criminal offence, the Roma are more likely than the non-Roma to end up with a petty offence procedure launched against them (13% as opposed to 5%). One possible explanation for this is that police officers sanction members of Roma community much more frequently than their peers from the majority, practically, this means that officers impose on-the-spot fines for every minor violation (e.g. riding a bicycle in an abandoned place in the daytime without lights or with tires in poor condition) while they are more lenient towards ethnic Hungarians. The possibility for abuse by using discretion to not enforce the law is always present and it is difficult – if not impossible – to effectively control the patrolling officers (Quinton *et al.* 2000, Waddington *et al* 2004). This hypothesis of selective law-enforcement is validated by the findings of one the leading Hungarian NGOs, the Hungarian Civil Liberties Union, whose Roma Program revealed such practices in Hungarian regions densely populated by Roma.

Conclusion

Although the amended legal definition of an ID check that came into effect on 1 January 2008 is more detailed than the previous one, the current regulation still confers almost unrestricted power on police officers to stop and check whomever they want. Reference to the rather abstract possible reasons for stop-checks listed in Article 29 of the Police Act (e.g. crime prevention) does not adequately explain why it was necessary to establish an individual's identity.

One possible solution to narrow police discretion would be to oblige officers to communicate to the person stopped and subjected to an ID check the specific, legal basis for the check and the factual grounds upon which this basis was decided. In addition, if the citizen so requests, the officer should have to provide them with a written certificate about the ID check which contains the justification for the measure. The provision of a certificate should also be obligatory if the stop is followed by a search. A search is such a deep intrusion into privacy, as confirmed by the ECtHR in *Gillan and Quinton v. The United Kingdom,* that it justifies the introduction of additional legal protection.

Processing data concerning ethnic affiliation is a sensitive issue. However, there is increasing professional consensus that strict data-protection rules (and their strict interpretation) do not always serve the best interests of the minority groups that they were originally designed to protect. In practice, the rules sometimes favour the discriminating parties, because groups suffering disadvantageous and discriminatory treatment cannot provide proof of unequal treatment without access to systemic data collection (De Schutter and Ringelheim 2010, Wortley and Owusu-Bempah, this issue). Therefore, it is essential that the law obliges officers conducting ID checks to record the person's perceived ethnic identity, yet it must be impossible to link the recorded data to a concrete person. An aggregate database not containing personal data is sufficient to prove the existence of racial profiling, at the same time it does not arouse concerns about the processing of sensitive personal data.

Interviews with higher-ranking police officers suggest very strongly that the number of ID checks is often used in assessing police officers' job performance and productivity. To improve the quality of ID checks, the value placed on quantity needs to be 'repositioned', i.e. regarded as merely one factor in performance management, rather than as a finite measure of police effectiveness. To achieve this goal, new and reformed performance assessment tools should be introduced. Evaluation of effective policing should not rely exclusively on factors such as the number of perpetrators caught, the number of fines imposed for committing a petty offence, or the number of ID checks conducted. The assessments should take into account citizen satisfaction with local police work (see Marks, this issue). Citizen input provides an incentive for under-performing police units to focus on community relations rather than, as in the current system, on data manipulation. Shifting the evaluation of officers' work from numerical performance indicators towards a more complex set of standards would be an important move to improving police legitimacy as well. When analysing possible ways of enhancing police legitimacy, Tyler's (2004, p. 96) review of the evidence concludes that 'while instrumental issues are important, it is difficult for legal authorities to sustain a viable legal system simply based upon performance.' Just as important are the values of procedural justice such as fairness, legitimacy and equity. These cannot be measured by quantitative data but are essential for good policing and the maintenance of a safe and peaceful society.

References

Balogi, A., et al., 2006. Vélemények és tapasztalatok a magyar rendőrség igazoltatási gyakorlatáról [Opinions and Experiences Concerning the ID Check Practice of the Hungarian Police]. TÁRKI Research Report.

Bowling, B. and Philips, C., 2003. Policing ethnic minority communities. *In*: N. Tim, ed. *Handbook of Policing*. Devon, UK: Willan Publishing, 528–555.

Bowling, B. and Philips, C., 2007. Disproportionate and discriminatory: reviewing the evidence on stop and searches. *The Modern Law Review*, 70 (6), 936–961.

De Schutter, O. and Ringelheim, J., 2010. Ethnic monitoring – the processing of racial and ethnic data in anti-discrimination policies: reconciling the promotion of equality with privacy rights. Bruxelles: Bruylant.

FRA (European Union Agency for Fundamental Rights), 2009. *European minorities and discrimination survey*. Available from: http://fra.europa.eu/fraWebsite/eu-midis/index_en.htm

Hablicsek, L., 2007. Kísérleti számítások a roma lakosság területi jellemzőinek alakulására és 2021-ig történő előrebecslésére [Tentative calculations relating to the formation of the territorial characteristics of the Roma population and future estimates until 2021]. *Demográfia*, I, 7–54.

Harris, D.A., 2002. Profiles in injustice. Why racial profiling cannot work. New York: The New Press.

Havas, G., 2008. Esélyegyenlőség, deszegregáció [Equal opportunities, desegregation]. *In*: K. Fazekas, J. Köllő and J.Varga, eds., *Green paper for the reform of Hungarian public education*. Budapest: Miniszterelnöki Hivatal, 121–138.

Huszár, L., 1997. Az "ethnical issue" – romák a börtönben [The ethical issue – Roma in prisons]. *In*: *A büntetés-végrehajtás néhány problémája a kutatások tükrében* [Some problems of the penitentiary system as reflected by research]. Budapest: BV. Szakkönyvtár – 1997/2. BVOP Módszertani Igazgatóság.

Kádár, A., *et al.*, 2008. *Control(led) group*. Budapest: Hungarian Helsinki Committee.

Kertesi, G., 2005. *Roma foglalkoztatás az ezredfordulón* [Roma employment at the millenium]. Budapest: The Institute of Economics of Hungarian Academy of Sciencies.

Marketing Centrum, 2009. Public opinion survey, 15–23 January 2009.

Mauer, M., 2006. *Race to incarcerate*. New York: The New Press.

Miller, J., Bland, N., and Quinton, P., 2000. *The impact of stops and searches on crime and the community*. London: Home Office, Police Research Series Paper 127.

Moeckli, D., 2007. Stop and search under the Terrorism Act 2000: a comment on R (Gillan) v Commissioner of Police for the Metropolis. *The Modern Law Review*, 70 (4), 654–679.

OSI, 2007a. *"I can stop and search whoever I want". Police stops of ethnic minorities in Bulgaria, Hungary and Spain*. New York: OSI.

OSI, 2007b. *Left out: Roma and access to health care in Eastern and South Eastern Europe (fact sheet)*. Available from: http://www.soros.org/initiatives/health/focus/roma/articles_publications/publications/leftout_20070420/leftout_20070423.pdf

OSI, 2009a. *Addressing ethnic profiling by the police: a report on the strategies for effective police stop and search project*. New York: OSI.
OSI, 2009b. *Ethnic profiling in the European Union: pervasive, ineffective and discriminatory*. New York: OSI.
Quinton, P., Bland, N., and Miller, J., 2000. *Police stops, decision-making and practice*. London: Home Office, Police Research Series Paper 130.
Ramirez, D.A., Hoopes, J., and Quinlan, T.L., 2003. Defining racial profiling in a post-September 11 World. *The American Criminal Law Review*, 40, 1195–1233.
Satzewich, V. and Shaffir, W., 2009. Racism versus professionalism: claims and counter-claims about racial profiling. *Canadian Journal of Criminology and Criminal Justice*, 51 (2), 199–226.
Tyler, R.T., 2004. Enhancing police legitimacy. *Annals of the American Academy of Political and Social Science*, 593, 84–99.
Waddington, P.A.J., Stenson, K., and Don, D., 2004. In proportion race, and police stop and search. *British Journal of Criminology*, 44 (5), 889–914.

Cases and legislation

Gillan and Quinton v The United Kingdom (Application no. 4158/15)
Rotaru v Romania (Application no. 2841/95)
S and Marper v United Kingdom (Application nos. 30562/04 and 30566/04)
Act XXXIV of 1994 on the Police (Hungarian Police Act)
Decree of Minister of Justice and Law Enforcement No. 62/2007 (Hungarian Police Service Regulation)

The usual suspects: police stop and search practices in Canada

Scot Wortley and Akwasi Owusu-Bempah

Centre for Criminology and Sociolegal Studies, University of Toronto, Canada

This paper explores police stop and search activities in Canada using data from a 2007 survey of Toronto residents. The paper begins by demonstrating that black respondents are more likely to view racial profiling as a major problem in Canada than whites or Asians. By contrast, white and Asian respondents are more likely to believe that profiling is a useful crime-fighting tool. Further analysis reveals that the black community's concern with racial profiling may be justified. Indeed, black respondents are much more likely to report being stopped and searched by the police over the past two years than respondents from other racial backgrounds. Blacks are also much more likely to report vicarious experiences with racial profiling. Importantly, racial differences in police stop and search experiences remain statistically significant after controlling for other relevant factors. The theoretical implications of these findings – and their meaning within Canada's multicultural framework – are discussed.

Introduction

Canada is one of the world's most active immigrant-receiving nations and has received international praise for its official policies of multiculturalism and inclusion. However, a closer examination of the historical record reveals that racial discrimination has long been an issue within Canadian society – particularly with respect to the operation of criminal justice system (Mosher 1998, Henry and Tator 2005, Walker 2010). In recent years, racial bias with respect to police stop and search practices has emerged as a particularly controversial issue. Canada's growing black community has been especially vocal in their complaints about what has come to be known as 'racial profiling'. By contrast, allegations of racial bias have, in most cases, been vehemently denied by Canada's major police services (see Tanovich 2006, Tator and Henry 2006).

Unfortunately, researching possible racial bias within the Canadian criminal justice system is particularly difficult because, with few exceptions, there is a complete ban on the collection and release of all race-crime data (see Owusu-Bempah and Miller 2010). This ban not only includes crime statistics, but all data related to the processing of racial minorities through the criminal justice system. In other words, unlike the United States and Great Britain, Canadian researchers do not have regular access to official data on the race of people stopped and searched by the police (or any other justice outcome for that matter). As a result, most of the research that has been conducted on this issue has been qualitative in nature (see James 1998, Neugebauer 2000, Ontario Human Rights Commission 2003, Eid *et al.* 2011). The results of such qualitative studies, however, have been vigorously attacked as 'anecdotal' or 'junk science' by police officials and some academics (Gabor 2004, Melchers 2006).

Although the qualitative studies described above may provide rich detail about how police activities impact the members of the black community, their results are often difficult to generalise because they are based on small, non-random samples. Furthermore, previous Canadian studies have also tended to focus on the black community in isolation and have not directly compared the experiences of black people with the experiences of whites or other racial minorities. In this paper we attempt to contribute to the literature on race and police stop and search practices in Canada by examining data from a recent survey of Toronto residents. Toronto is a prime location for such a study because it is Canada's largest and most ethnically diverse city and home to over half of the nation's black population (Chui *et al.* 2008). We use this survey data to address the following research questions:

1. To what extent do Canadians view racial profiling as a social problem? Do perceptions vary by racial background?
2. Are blacks and other racial minorities in Canada more likely to be stopped and searched by the police than members of the white majority? Do racial differences in police stop and search encounters remain after statistically controlling for other theoretically relevant factors?
3. How do Canadians interpret their encounters with the police? Do interpretations vary by racial group?
4. To what extent are Canadians indirectly exposed to racial profiling through the experiences of friends and family?

The paper concludes by reviewing the major theoretical implications of the survey results and discussing how Canada's ban on race-crime statistics may hinder future efforts to reduce racially biased policing and improve police-minority relations.

Methodology

The data used in this research were gathered in 2007 by the Hitachi Research Centre at the University of Toronto. A two-stage probability selection technique was used to select respondents and produce a representative sample of black, Chinese and white adults (18 years of age or older) living in Metropolitan Toronto. The first stage of the sampling procedure involved the random selection of residential telephone numbers within Toronto. The second stage involved selecting the adult member of the household who was approaching his/her next birthday. The birthday selection technique is commonly used by survey researchers because it gives each adult within the household an equal probability of being selected. Finally, a screening question was asked to ensure that respondents self-identified as either black, Chinese or white.

Interviews were conducted between October and December 2007. A response rate of 78% was achieved. The interviews were conducted in either English or Chinese (Mandarin or Cantonese dialects) and took on average 35 minutes to complete.

The final sample consisted of 1522 respondents who identified themselves as either black ($N = 513$), Chinese ($N = 504$) or white ($N = 505$). A review of sample characteristics reveals that black respondents are somewhat younger than their Chinese and white counterparts. Black respondents are also less educated, less likely to be married, more likely to be unemployed and report lower household incomes. Finally, the majority of white respondents were born in Canada, while the majority of both black and Chinese respondents are foreign born. Overall, the sample characteristics for this study's black, white and Chinese respondents are largely consistent with the demographic profiles for these groups produced by the Canadian Census (Chui *et al.* 2008).[1]

Results

Perceptions of racial profiling

Respondents were asked the following question: racial profiling is said to exist when people are stopped, questioned or searched by the police because of their racial characteristics, not because of their individual behaviour or their actions. In your opinion, is racial profiling a problem in Canada or not? The results suggest that black Canadians are much more likely to perceive racial profiling as a major social problem than their Chinese and White counterparts. Indeed, 6 out of 10 black respondents (57%) view racial profiling in Canada as a 'big problem', compared to only 21% of white and 14% of Chinese respondents.[2] Respondents were then asked: suppose that, in a particular neighbourhood, most of the people arrested for drug trafficking, gun violence and gang activity belong to a particular racial group. In order to fight crime in this area, do you think it would be okay or legitimate for the police to randomly stop and search people who belong to this racial group more than they stop and search people from other racial groups? Consistent with the above results, white (39%) and Chinese respondents (34%) are more likely to view racial profiling tactics as a legitimate crime-fighting strategy than their black counterparts (23%). Are these observed racial differences in opinion related to actual racial differences in contact with the police? This question is addressed the next section.

Direct contact with the police

Respondents were asked how many times they had been stopped and questioned by the police – while driving in a car or walking or standing in a public space – in the past two years. The results suggest that a third of the black respondents (34%) have been stopped by the police in the past two years, compared to 28% of whites and 22% of Chinese respondents. Blacks are especially likely to experience multiple police stops. Indeed, 14% of black respondents indicate that they have been stopped by the police on three or more occasions in the past two years, compared to only 5% of white and 3% of Chinese respondents. On average, blacks experienced 1.6 stops in the past two years, compared to 0.5 stops for whites and 0.3 stops for Chinese respondents.

Further analysis reveals that black males are particularly vulnerable to police stops (Table 1). One in four black male respondents (23%) indicated that they were stopped by the police on three or more occasions in the past two years, compared to

Table 1. Percent of respondents who have been stopped by the police in the past two years, by race and gender.

	Black		Chinese		White	
Number of stops	Male	Female	Male	Female	Male	Female
None	52.8	73.3	70.8	85.3	64.9	76.8
One	15.0	11.7	16.4	11.9	17.8	14.1
Two	8.9	5.7	6.6	2.2	9.1	6.4
Three or more	23.3	9.3	6.2	0.7	8.2	2.7
Sample size	180	333	226	278	208	297

only 8% of white males and 6% of Chinese males. On average, black males experienced 3.4 police stops in the past two years, compared to 0.7 stops for white males and 0.5 stops for Chinese males. Although black females are less likely to be stopped and questioned by the police than black males, they are significantly more likely to report police stops than white or Chinese females. In fact, black females (9%) are more likely to report three or more police stops than white (8%) or Chinese males (6%). On average, black females report 0.7 police stops in the past two years, compared to 0.4 stops for white females and 0.2 stops for Chinese females.

Respondents were also asked if they had been physically searched by the police in the past two years. Once again, the data reveal that black people – particularly black males – are more vulnerable to police searches than respondents from other racial backgrounds. Overall, 12% of black male respondents report being searched by the police in the past two years, compared to only 3% of white and Chinese males. Black females are also more likely to report being searched by the police (3%) than white or Chinese women (1%).

The data clearly indicate that black respondents are more likely to be stopped and searched by the police than white or Chinese respondents. However, there are factors, besides race, that may explain black over-representation in police encounters. For example, black Torontonians tend to be younger and less affluent than their white and Chinese counterparts. Thus, it may be youthfulness or poverty – not racial bias – that explains why black people are more likely to be stopped and searched. Similarly, black people may be more likely to be stopped because they are more likely reside in high crime neighbourhoods, often marked by aggressive police patrol strategies (see Parker *et al.* 2010). Furthermore, racial differences in behaviour, not race itself, might explain why black people receive greater police attention. For example, compared to people from other racial backgrounds, black people may be more vulnerable to police stops because they spend more time driving or hanging out in public spaces (see Fridell 2004). Finally, blacks may be more likely to draw the legitimate attention of the police because they are more likely to be involved in traffic violations or various forms of criminal activity (see Gabor 2004).

In order to address these competing hypotheses, we produced a series of logistic regressions predicting police stop and search experiences. In addition to race, these regressions statistically control for a variety of demographic variables including age, gender, education, household income and place of birth. Our analysis also controlled for level of crime within the respondents' neighbourhood, frequency of driving, level of involvement in public leisure activities, alcohol use, marijuana use and criminal history. A full description of both dependent and independent variables is provided in Appendix 1.

The results of the multivariate analyses indicate that black racial background remains a strong predictor of police stop and search activities after statistically controlling for other theoretically relevant variables (Table 2). Chinese racial background, on the other hand, is unrelated to the probability of being stopped and searched by the police. The results further suggest that, the more stringent the measure of police stops, the stronger the relationship with black racial background. For example, an examination of the odds ratios indicates that blacks are 1.9 times more likely than whites to experience one or more stops in the past two years, 2.3 times more likely to experience two or more stops and 3.4 times more likely to experience three or more stops. Furthermore, the results suggest that blacks are also 3.3 times more likely than whites to have been searched by the police in the past two years.

The results also indicate that males and younger respondents are more likely to be stopped and searched by the police than females or older respondents. Respondents living in high crime neighbourhoods are also more likely to be stopped and searched than those who reside in safer communities. Interestingly, alcohol use increases the likelihood of being stopped by the police, but it is unrelated to police searches. Marijuana use, on the other hand, increases the probability of being stopped at least once in the past two years, but it does not predict multiple police stops or the likelihood of a police search. The results also indicate that respondents with a criminal record are more likely to report police stops and searches than respondents with a clean criminal history. Although driving frequency is positively

Table 2. Logistic regressions predicting police stops and searches.

	Stopped one or more times		Stopped two or more times		Stopped three or more times		Searched by police	
Predictor variables	B	Odds	B	Odds	B	Odds	B	Odds
Black	0.633**	1.88	0.814**	2.26	1.232**	3.43	1.184*	3.27
Chinese	0.166	1.18	−0.106	0.90	0.056	1.06	0.359	1.43
Gender (1 = male)	0.562**	1.75	0.752**	2.12	0.905**	2.47	1.064**	2.89
Age	−0.021**	0.97	−0.039**	0.96	−0.048**	0.95	−0.054**	0.94
Place of birth	−0.263	0.77	−0.275	0.76	−0.157	0.85	−0.382	0.68
Education	−0.056	0.95	−0.075	0.93	−0.092	0.91	−0.203	0.82
Household income	0.109	1.12	0.036	1.04	0.095	1.10	−0.029	0.97
Marijuana Use	0.462*	1.59	0.389	1.48	0.224	1.25	0.262	1.29
Alcohol use	0.125**	1.13	0.124**	1.13	0.134*	1.14	0.033	1.03
Criminal record	−0.079	0.93	0.443	1.56	1.043*	2.84	1.209*	3.35
Community crime	0.085**	1.09	0.114**	1.12	0.137**	1.15	0.104**	1.11
Public activities	−0.034	0.96	−0.008	0.99	−0.039	0.96	0.012	1.01
Driving frequency	0.264**	1.30	0.282**	1.33	0.214**	1.24	0.129	1.14
Constant	−1.806**	0.16	−2.464**	0.09	−2.896**	0.05	−2.760**	0.06
Nagelkerke R square	0.200	0.261	0.297	0.272				

Sample size = 1522; $**p < 0.01$; $*p < 0.05$.

related to police stops, it is unrelated to police searches. Finally, according to the data, education, household income, place of birth and public activities are not significant predictors of police stop and search activities.

Respondent interpretations of police encounters

All respondents who reported that they had been stopped and questioned by the police in the past two years ($N=423$) were subsequently asked a series of questions about their most recent police encounter. The results clearly indicate that black respondents tend to interpret police stops more negatively than their Chinese and white counterparts (see Table 3). To begin with, respondents were asked if they thought their latest police stop was fair or unfair. Almost half of the black respondents (47%) felt that their last police stop was unfair, compared to only 17% of Chinese and 12% of white respondents. Compared to white and Chinese respondents, black respondents were also less likely to report that the police adequately explained the reason for the stop and were more likely to report that the police treated them in a disrespectful manner.

Finally, respondents were asked the following open-ended question: *The last time you were stopped by the police, why do you think they stopped you?* One out of every four black respondents (25%) specifically claimed that they were stopped because of their race. By contrast, only two Chinese respondents and two white respondents cited race as the reason that they were stopped. Interestingly, both of these white respondents claimed that they were stopped by the police because they were riding in a car with black people. With these results in mind, it is not surprising to note that black respondents were much more likely than Chinese or white respondents to report that they were 'very upset' by their last police encounter.

Indirect experiences with racial profiling

The data clearly suggest that black Canadians are much more likely to be stopped and searched by the police than their Chinese and white counterparts. This situation, of course, may help explain why black Canadians are more likely to perceive that racial profiling is a major social problem. However, direct experience is not the only way that individuals can learn about police practices. People can also learn indirectly through the experiences of friends and relatives. In order to explore this possibility,

Table 3. Respondent interpretations of their most recent police stop, by race.

Interpretations of most recent police encounter	Black %	Chinese %	White %
Respondent feels the stop was unfair	46.6	16.8	12.0
Police did not explain reason for the stop	29.9	10.3	6.3
Not treated with respect by the police	42.5	17.8	15.5
Respondent feels that they were stopped because of their racial background	24.7	1.9	1.4
Respondent was "very upset" by the stop	43.1	20.6	15.5
Sample size	174	107	142

respondents were asked if they knew of any close family or friends who had been the victim of racial profiling – by the police – over the past two years. The results suggest that black Canadians are much more likely to report friends or family members who have been racially profiled than the members of other racial groups. Overall, 46% of black respondents claim that they have at least a few friends who have been racially profiled in the past two years, compared to only 17% of white respondents and 10% of Chinese respondents. Indeed, almost one in ten black respondents (9%) claims that 'most' of their family and friends have been racially profiled by the police in the past two years, compared to only a fraction (0.2%) of both white and Chinese respondents.

The results of a logistic regression analysis (see Table 4) suggest that black racial background is a significant predictor of vicarious racial profiling even after statistically controlling for other relevant variables. By contrast, Chinese respondents are no more likely to report friends and family who have been racially profiled than their white counterparts. Overall, an examination of the odds ratios suggests that blacks are 6.5 times more likely to know of a family member or friend who has been racially profiled by the police than whites. The results also suggest that younger people are more likely to report vicarious exposure to racial profiling than their older counterparts. People who live in high crime neighbourhoods are also more likely to know someone who has been racially profiled, as have those who use marijuana and consume alcohol on a frequent basis. Interestingly, foreign-born respondents are less likely to report vicarious racial profiling than those born in Canada.

Discussion

Many scholars have argued that the influence of race on criminal justice outcomes, including police stop and search practices, is largely due to a systematic process of racialisation. Racialisation consists of the classification of people into groups by

Table 4. Logistic regression predicting vicarious exposure to racial profiling.

Predictor variables	B	Odds
Black	1.864**	6.45
Chinese	0.182	1.20
Gender (1 = male)	−0.193	0.83
Age	−0.012*	0.99
Place of birth	−0.443*	0.64
Education	−0.043	0.96
Household income	0.092	1.10
Marijuana use	0.686**	1.99
Alcohol use	0.125**	1.13
Criminal record	−0.186	0.83
Community crime	0.095**	1.10
Public activities	−0.007	0.99
Driving frequency	0.011	1.01
Constant	−1.654**	0.19
Nagelkerke R square	0.258	

Sample size = 1522; $^{**}p < 0.01$; $^{*}p < 0.05$.

reference to their skin colour or physical features and the process of stereotyping that emerges as a result of this classification system (Miles 1989). In a classic observational analysis of police patrol practices, Skolnick (1966) observed that the police in the United States tend to perceive young, black males as 'symbolic assailants' and thus stop and question them on the street as a means of 'crime prevention.' Anderson (1990) confirms this trend in his more recent ethnographic study of a multi-racial community located in a large American city. In documenting the general police tendency to stop, search and harass young black citizens as part of their routine patrolling activity, Anderson notes that:

> On the streets, colour-coding works to confuse race, age, class, gender, incivility, and criminality, and it expresses itself most concretely in the person of the anonymous black male. In doing their job, the police often become willing parties to this colour-coding of the public environment... a young black male is a suspect until he proves he is not. (Anderson 1990, pp. 190–191)

The survey results presented in this paper suggest that a similar process of racialisation exists within the Canadian police environment. According to our results, blacks are over three times more likely to experience multiple police stops than whites or Asians and are three times more likely to report being searched during these police encounters. Black males appear to be particularly vulnerable to police stop and search practices. Black respondents are also six times more likely than respondents from other racial backgrounds to report that they have close friends or family members who had been a recent victim of racial profiling. Importantly, racial differences with respect to both direct and indirect police contact remain statistically significant after controlling for other relevant variables including age, income, education, driving habits, community-level crime, alcohol and marijuana use and criminal history. These findings suggest that race matters. Indeed, black racial background appears to be a master status that attracts police attention and significantly contributes to police decisions to conduct street interrogations. To the police, young black males represent the usual suspects.

It is also important to note that Chinese respondents are no more likely to be stopped and questioned by the police than their white counterparts. This finding suggests that not all minorities are subject to racial profiling in Canada. This result is also consistent with the argument that, in contemporary Canadian society, Chinese immigrants are often seen as a 'model minority' and have avoided the negative, crime-related stereotypes often associated with blacks (see Zong and Perry 2011). The Canadian situation, however, may be unique as Chinese immigrants have clearly not been able to escape negative police attention in all immigrant-receiving countries (see Namba inpress).

Additional analysis reveals that although blacks are more likely to be stopped by the police, they are even more likely to interpret these stops as unfair. This result has two possible explanations: (1) blacks are, in fact, treated worse than others during police stops; or (2) many blacks already perceive the police as racially biased and thus interpret all police encounters through the lens of discrimination. This second argument is consistent with police complaints that blacks frequently 'cry racism' even when they have been stopped for legitimate reasons (Barlow and Barlow 2002, Ioimo *et al.* 2007). It is possible that both explanations have some validity. Blacks may justifiably perceive police bias because they are – as the data above suggest – more likely to experience multiple police stops and searches. However, perceptions of bias may also contribute to how black people interpret their future encounters with the police. Thus, while white people usually view the police stops they experience as legitimate – blacks may question the motives of the police and treat such encounters with great suspicion. Furthermore, black distrust of the police could impact their demeanour during police encounters. A negative demeanour towards the police could lead to less respectful treatment by the police. Such poor treatment, in turn, could further reinforce black perceptions of police bias (see Engel *et al.* 2010). In other words, the relationship between police stops, perceptions of bias and how police encounters are interpreted may be reciprocal.

Overall, the results of this study are consistent with survey results produced in the United States and Great Britain (see Bowling and Phillips 2002, Engel and Canlon 2004, Alpert *et al.* 2005, Skogan 2006, Weitzer *et al.* 2008, Bradford *et al.* 2009). The results are also similar to other data emerging from Canada. For example, a recent survey of Toronto high school students found that black youth are much more likely than youth from other racial backgrounds to be subjected to police street interrogations and that racial differences in being stopped and searched cannot be explained by racial differences in self-reported criminal activity, gang membership, drug and alcohol use or public leisure activities (Wortley and Tanner 2005). Unfortunately, due to Canada's ban on race-crime statistics, survey results have not yet been supplemented with official data.

What are the major implications of these findings? First of all, logic dictates that there is a direct relationship between how closely people are monitored by the police and how likely they are to get caught for breaking the law. In other words, if black people are systematically stopped and searched more frequently than others, they are also more likely to be to be detected and arrested for illegal activity than people from other racial backgrounds who *engage in exactly the same behaviour*. Thus, consistent with the major principles of conflict criminology, racial differences in police stop and search activities directly contribute to the over-representation of black people in the Canadian criminal justice system (Wortley and Owusu-Bempah 2011).

Police stop and search experiences can also undermine the legitimacy of the criminal justice system. Indeed, a number of studies have now confirmed that people who are frequently stopped and searched by the police have less trust in the justice system and are more likely to view criminal justice institutions as biased (see review in Wortley and Owusu-Bempah 2009, Bowling this volume). Importantly, additional research suggests that people with a poor perception of the justice system are less likely to cooperate with police investigations (Brown and Benedict 2002). Furthermore, a number of theoretical perspectives, including Tyler's theory of Legitimacy and Compliance (Tyler 1990) and Sherman's Defiance Theory (Sherman 1993), have clearly shown that people with poor perceptions of the justice system are less likely to obey the law. Thus, racial differences in stop and search activities could ultimately contribute to racial differences in criminal behaviour.

In conclusion, as Phillips and Bowling (2003, p. 277) point out, the structural context of life within minority communities – and by extension the nature of policing in these communities – cannot be fully understood without historical contextualisation. This is particularly important for a nation such as Canada which seems to suffer from amnesia when it comes to its historical treatment of racialised peoples. For example, in a recent address to G20 leaders, Prime Minister Stephen Harper declared that Canada has no history of colonialism (Ljunggren 2009). This comment completely ignores Canada's deep roots in both English and French colonialism and its legacy of blatant discrimination against Aboriginals, blacks and other racial minorities (see Mosher 1998, Henry and Tator 2005).

It is also important to note that Canada's much lauded policy of official multiculturalism may actually facilitate the racialisation of blacks and other minorities. Opposition to multiculturalism has been voiced by those who view the policy as one that further accentuates differences between racial groups rather than promoting inclusiveness. It has also been argued that the true intent of multiculturalism is to provide a counter argument to charges of racism and the increasing demands of minorities to equal access to all sectors of Canadian society (Knowles 2007). Thus, while supposedly embracing 'other' cultures, Canadian multiculturalism may actually provide a veil behind which discrimination flourishes and the cultural hegemony of the dominant group is secured.

This view is well captured in the theory of 'democratic racism'. Democratic racism is an ideology that permits the emergence of two seemingly conflicting sets of values: a public commitment to racial justice and equality on one hand, but a refusal to seriously investigate and address racial inequalities and potential racial bias when these issues emerge (Henry and Tator 2005, p. 349). In our opinion, the Canadian government's unofficial ban on the collection and dissemination of race-based criminal justice statistics provides an excellent example of democratic racism in action. At the same time that the police and other criminal justice agencies claim to provide equitable service to all Canadians, they systematically withhold vital information that is essential to the examination and ultimate elimination of any racial disparities that may exist. Indeed, it must be recognised that the ban on race-crime and race-based statistics has actually helped the Canadian justice system deflect allegations of racial bias. For example, the Canadian courts have often dismissed allegations of racial profiling due to a lack of empirical data (see Tanovich 2006). The fact is, without proper data, it is impossible to truly monitor the activities of criminal justice decision-makers, document the extent of racial discrimination and determine whether anti-racist policies are having an impact. Thus, the current ban on race-crime statistics serves to reduce accountability within the Canadian justice system and prevents Canadians from honestly investigating the true impact that the police and other justice institutions have on the lives of minority citizens.

Notes

1. For more details about the study methodology (see Wortley and Owusu-Bempah 2009).
2. All of the racial differences highlighted in the text are significant at the $p > 0.01$ level.

References

Alpert, G., MacDonald, J.M., and Dunham, R., 2005. Police suspicion and discretionary decision making during citizen stops. *Criminology*, 43, 407–434.

Anderson, E., 1990. *Streetwise: race, class and change in an urban community*. Chicago: University of Chicago Press.

Barlow, D. and Barlow, M.H., 2002. Racial profiling: a survey of African American police officers. *Police Quarterly*, 5 (3), 334–358.

Bowling, B. and Phillips, C., 2002. *Racism, crime and justice*. Britain: Pearson Education Ltd.

Bradford, B., Jackson, J., and Stanko, E., 2009. Contact and confidence: revisiting the impact of public encounters with the police. *Policing and Society*, 19, 20–46.

Brown, B. and Benedict, W.R., 2002. Perceptions of the police. *Policing*, 25 (3), 543–580.

Chui, T., Tran, K., and Maheux, H., 2008. *Canada's ethnocultural mosaic: the 2006 census.* Catalogue no. 97-562-X. Ottawa: Statistics Canada.

Eid, P., Magloire, J., and Turenne, M. 2011. *Racial profiling and systemic discrimination of racialized youth: report of the consultation on racial profiling and its consequences.* Montreal: Commission des Droits de la Personne et des Droits de la Jeunesse.

Engel, R. and Canlon, J., 2004. Examining the influence of drivers' characteristics during traffic stops with police: results from a national survey. *Justice Quarterly*, 21, 49–90.

Engel, R., Klahm, C., and Tillyer, R., 2010. Citizens' demeanor, race and traffic stops. *In*: S. Rice and M. White, eds. *Race, ethnicity and policing: new and essential readings.* New York: New York University Press, 287–308.

Fridell, L., 2004. *By the numbers: a guide for analyzing race data from vehicle stops.* Washington: Police Executive Research Forum.

Gabor, T., 2004. Inflammatory rhetoric on racial profiling can undermine police services. *Canadian Journal of Criminology and Criminal Justice*, 46, 457–470.

Henry, F. and Tator, C., 2005. *The colour of democracy: racism in Canadian society.* Toronto: Nelson.

Ioimo, R., *et al.*, 2007. The police view of bias-based policing. *Police Quarterly*, 10, 270–287.

James, C., 1998. 'Up to no good': black on the streets and encountering police. *In*: V. Satzewich, ed. *Racism and social inequality in Canada: concepts, controversies and strategies of resistance.* Toronto: Thompson, 157–176.

Knowles, V., 2007. *Strangers at our gates: Canadian immigration and immigration policy 1540–2006.* Toronto: Dundurn Press.

Ljunggren, D., 2009. *Every G20 nation wants to be Canada, insists PM.* Reuters. Available from: http://www.reuters.com/article/GCA-G20Pittsburgh/idUSTRE58P05Z20090926 [Accessed 27 July 2011].

Melchers, R., 2006. *Inequality before the law: the Canadian experience of racial profiling.* Ottawa: Research and Evaluation Branch, Royal Canadian Mounted Police.

Miles, R., 1989. *Racism.* New York: Routledge.

Mosher, C., 1998. *Discrimination and denial: systemic racism in Ontario's legal and criminal justice systems: 1892–1961.* Toronto: University of Toronto Press.

Namba, M., in press. War on illegal immigrants, national narratives and globalization: Japanese policy and practice of police stop and question in the global perspective.

Neugebauer, R., 2000. Kids, cops, and colour: the social organization of police-minority youth relations. *In*: R. Neugebauer, ed. *Criminal injustice: racism in the criminal justice system.* Toronto: Canadian Scholars Press, 46–59.

Ontario Human Rights Commission, 2003. *Paying the price: the human cost of racial profiling.* Toronto: Ontario Human Rights Commission.

Owusu-Bempah, A. and Millar, P., 2010. Research note: revisiting the collection of justice statistics by race in Canada. *Canadian Journal of Law and Society*, 25 (1), 97–104.

Parker, K., Lane, E., and Alport, G., 2010. Community characteristics and police search rates: accounting for the ethnic diversity of urban areas in the study of black, white and hispanic searchers. *In*: S. Rice and M. White, eds. *Race, ethnicity and policing: new and essential readings.* New York: New York University Press, 309–348.

Phillips, C. and Bowling, B., 2003. Racism, ethnicity and criminology: developing minority perspectives. *British Journal of Criminology*, 43 (2), 269–290.

Sherman, L., 1993. Defiance, deterrence and irrelevance: a theory of criminal sanction. *Journal of Research on Crime and Delinquency*, 30, 123–135.

Skogan, W., 2006. Asymmetry in the impact of encounters with the police. *Policing and Society*, 16 (2), 99–126.

Skolnick, J., 1966. *Justice without trial: law enforcement in a democratic society.* New York: John Wiley and Sons.

Tanovich, D., 2006. *The colour of justice: policing race in Canada.* Toronto: Irwin Law.

Tator, C. and Henry, F., 2006. *Racial profiling in Canada: challenging the myth of a few bad apples.* Toronto: University of Toronto Press.

Tyler, T., 1990. *Why people obey the law*. New Haven, CT: Yale University Press.
Walker, B., 2010. *Race on trial: black defendants in Ontario's criminal courts 1858–1958*. Toronto: University of Toronto Press.
Weitzer, R., Tuch, S., and Skogan, W., 2008. Police-community relations in a majority-black city. *Journal of Research on Crime and Delinquency*, 45, 398–428.
Wortley, S. and Owusu-Bempah, A., 2009. Unequal before the law: immigrant and racial minority perceptions of the Canadian criminal justice system. *Journal of International Migration and Integration*, 10, 447–473.
Wortley, S. and Owusu-Bempah, A., 2011. Crime and justice: the experiences of black Canadians. *In*: B. Perry, ed. *Diversity, crime and justice in Canada*. New York: Oxford University Press, 127–150.
Wortley, S. and Tanner, J., 2005. Inflammatory rhetoric? Baseless accusations? Responding to Gabor's critique of racial profiling research in Canada. *Canadian Journal of Criminology and Criminal Justice*, 47 (3), 581–609.
Zong, L. and Perry, B., 2011. Chinese immigrants in Canada and social injustice: from overt to covert racial discrimination. *In*: B. Perry, ed. *Diversity, crime and justice in Canada*. New York: Oxford University Press, 106–134.

Appendix 1. Description of independent variables used in all regression analyses

Race: Two dummy variables were used to denote race. Black (1 = black; 0 = other) and Chinese (1 = Chinese; 0 = other). White is the default category left out of the analysis.

Age: Age is an interval variable ranging from 18 to 89 years. Mean age = 45.1 years.

Gender: Gender is dummy coded (1 = male; 0 = female).

Education: Education is an ordinal variable coded: 1 = elementary or less; 2 = some high school; 3 = completed high school; 4 = some post-secondary; 5 = completed college; 6 = bachelor's degree; 7 = professional or graduate degree.

Household Income: Income is an ordinal variable ranging from 1 (<$10,000 per year) to 12 ($200,000 or more).

Place of Birth: Dummy variable: 1 = Born outside of Canada; 0 = Born in Canada.

Number of Times Stopped by the Police: Respondents were asked how many times in the past two years they had been stopped and questioned by the police. Contact with the police was coded: 0 = no stops; 1 = one stops; 2 = two stops; 3 = three or more stops.

Marijuana Use: We asked the respondents whether they had used marijuana in the past two years. Marijuana use is dummy coded: 0 = has not used marijuana in past two years; 1 = has used marijuana in past two years.

Alcohol Use: All respondents were asked how often they had consumed alcohol in the past twelve months. Response options ranged from 0 (never) to 7 (Every day or almost every day).

Criminal record: Respondents were asked if they had ever been arrested by the police at some point in their life. Criminal record was dummy coded: 1 = has a criminal record; 0 = no criminal record.

Vicarious Police Contact: Respondents were asked if any family members had been the victim of racial profiling by the police in the past two years. This variable was dummy coded: 1 = family/friends have been profiled in the past 2 years; 0 = family and friends have not been profiled.

Driving Frequency: All respondents were asked how often they usually drive in a motor vehicle as either the driver or as a passenger. Response options ranged from 0 (never) to 6 (every day).

Public Activities: Respondents were asked how often they engaged in four different types of public activity: a) used public transit; b) visited shopping malls or theatres; c) hung out on the street or in parks; and d) went to bars or nightclubs. Response options ranged from 0 (never) to 6 (every day). Answers to these four questions were combined into a single variable measuring frequency of engaging in public activities (alpha = 0.66). This variable ranges from 0 to 24 (mean = 8.55).

Community Crime and Disorder: Respondents were asked how often the following problems occurred in their neighbourhood: a) homeless people on the street begging for money; b) prostitution; c) drug trafficking; d) gun violence; and e) violence between rival gangs. Response options ranged from 0 (never) to 4 (very often). Responses to these five questions were eventually combined into a Community Crime and Disorder Index (alpha = 0.77). Scores on this index range from 0 to 20 (mean = 2.54).

The fantastical world of South Africa's roadblocks: dilemmas of a ubiquitous police strategy

Monique Marks

Community Development, University of KwaZulu-Natal, Durban, South Africa

Roadblock operations are a very prominent feature of the policing landscape in South Africa. They are increasingly being employed as a tactic for crime reduction and as a mechanism for reassuring the public that police are 'out there', providing a visible service. The paper draws on limited observation of police roadblocks in Durban and on interviews with police operational leaders and lower ranking police officers who have been involved in roadblock operations. In this paper I try to answer the following questions: How do police conduct roadblock operations within a framework of community-oriented service delivery? Who do the police target/profile in conducting such stop and search operations? What do the police understand as the real deliverables of such operations? How do the public view and respond to roadblock operations?

Introduction

By most standards, South Africa is considered a country with a serious crime problem. Some even refer to South Africa as the crime capital of the world. In regard to regular crime, this is probably an exaggeration, but it is certainly true in regard to violent crime. However, South Africa's high level of violent crime sets the country apart from other crime-ridden countries. This reality fuels citizens' general fear of crime, and the police are constantly under the public spotlight to do something visible to reduce crime levels. Public confidence in the police remains low across all population groups, and there remain many questions about distributive and procedural fairness of the police in South Africa (Roberts and Struwig 2010).

It is no surprise then that the police in South Africa are under pressure to present 'new' strategies. Recently, in October 2010, General Bheki Cele, the National Police Commissioner, announced in Parliament that during the December festive season a 'new' policing strategy was to be implemented. 'Super roadblocks' were to be set up in all parts of the country, and both drivers and passengers would be checked when a vehicle was stopped. Through a 'multi-agency' approach to doing roadblocks, people stopped would be checked for a range of offences, including drunk driving, driving an unlicensed vehicle, transporting of illegal and dangerous goods, transportation of illegal persons (for example, undocumented migrants) and tax evasion. General Cele warned South Africans to 'brace themselves for difficult times' over the festive season (Mjekula 2010). These multi-purpose roadblocks brought together a spread of regulatory agencies, including the South African Police Service (SAPS), the various metropolitan police forces, the Road Traffic Inspectorate, the Assets Forfeiture Unit and the South African Revenue Services (Mthethwa 2010).

On 4 November 2010 the operation was formally launched by the Police Minister and the Police Commissioner, with the 'super roadblocks' incorporated into the national 2010/2011 Operation Duty Calls Festive Season Crime-fighting Campaign (see unabridged speech by Minister of Police, Nathi Mthethwa, 2010). In 'Operation Duty Calls', the Minister promised, South Africans would see their police vigorously fulfilling their contractual obligation to fight crime and make communities safer. In a heightening of police visibility, the campaign would offer public reassurance, and in pushing systematic hard strategies it would make sure that criminals 'feel the bite' of the police.

In launching Operation Duty Calls, the Minister of Police used hard-hitting rhetoric to simultaneously instil feelings of reassurance and fear in the South African public. While super roadblocks are a recent 'innovation' to the South African policing landscape, roadblocks (along with other forms of stop and search operations) have become the backbone of much visible policing in South Africa. On 24 December 2010, journalist Michelle Jones reported that during the festive season there were 'roadblocks every day, in every town, and at all times of night and day'.

Roadblock operations in general are directed towards road safety checks, especially over the festive periods. This should come as no surprise given how unsafe the South African roads are: over the 2010 festive period alone, more than 1100 people died in road accidents. According to the South African Department of Transport, between December and March 2010, more than 5.5 million vehicles were checked, 2.3 million fines issued, at least 10,000 drunken drivers arrested and more than 24,000 un-roadworthy vehicles discontinued from use.

This paper begins with a recollection of a night spent on a (police centred) roadblock with the Durban Metropolitan Police. The roadblock I describe mainly focused on drunken or unlicensed drivers as well as un-roadworthy or unlicensed vehicles. I recount this story to give the reader some insight into the operation of roadblocks in South Africa and to frame some key questions about the use of roadblocks as a police strategy. These questions resonate with corresponding concerns in regard to stop and search operations in other parts of the world. This paper might read as somewhat impressionistic given the limited empirical research (including my own) on roadblock operations in South Africa. However, many of the ideas shared in this paper are drawn from a fairly long history that I have in researching police in South Africa, mostly as an ethnographer.

A view from the street: generating questions from observation

Picture the scene. It is 6 pm on Christmas Eve, 2011. The Durban Metropolitan Police are setting up a roadblock in Umlazi Township. Umlazi is the second-biggest township (home to more than 750,000 people) in South Africa, established in 1967 to house urban South Africans classified as 'Black African'. Later in the night, the Metropolitan Police (who have limited authority to investigate, lay charges and make custodial arrests) are joined by the SAPS who are responsible for conducting more extensive searches on vehicles that have been stopped.

The police officer in charge of the operation is a black woman, Captain Rylands. Captain Rylands is evidently very experienced, and the police officers under her command are receptive to her operational planning and her instructions. The team of police working under Captain Rylands' command comprised, according to South African race classification, 'Black African', 'Indian' and 'Coloured' (mixed race) officers. The roadblock is set up with great efficiency; within 45 minutes the scene is set so that every vehicle entering Umlazi via the main road can be stopped. By 7 pm there are already thousands of cars streaming into the township – residents heading home to their families to celebrate Christmas Eve, or visitors from other parts of Durban coming to see friends and relatives. The drivers and the passengers of the cars are all 'Black African'.

My role in joining the Metro Police in Umlazi on Christmas Eve was to simply observe how roadblocks are conducted. I was looking out for any indications of profiling, and I wanted to see how the public and the police responded to one another in roadblock encounters. I also wanted to gain some insight as to what is achieved in such operations.

The commander of the roadblock and her officers were welcoming me and seemed to be little influenced of me being an observer. I have learned over the many years, working as a participant observer of the police, how to conduct myself in a manner that makes the police feel at ease. I dress as a non-uniformed police officer would, and I am often assumed to be a police officer by those that are being 'policed'. I am fluent with 'police speak' and officers engage with me in an open and relaxed manner, often reflecting on operational dilemmas and controversies.

Shortly before the roadblock was fully in place, two female police officers spotted a car doing a slight zig-zag as it came down the street. The driver was belligerent, refusing to take a breathalyser test. It turns out that he was a SAPS officer. He pleaded with the officers conducting the roadblock to take pity on him because he was a fellow police officer. The two officers refused to give him any special treatment. In their view, he was endangering the lives of others on the road, and the fact that he was a police officer made the offence even more serious. He was removed from his car and was instructed to phone a friend or a relative to come and fetch his vehicle, as he would be spending the night in a police cell while his case was being processed.

This prompted me to find out more about whether any kind of profiling was taking place in the roadblock operation. Umlazi being a 'Black African' township, racial profiling was highly unlikely; the relatively homogeneous demographics of the area simply do not invite racial profiling. I asked the officer in charge of the operation what briefing her team had been given about who to stop. Her answer was that in all roadblock operations the instruction is to stop every vehicle that comes through the roadblock to avoid acting in prejudicial ways. I observed that for the first hour of the roadblock, every car was stopped, whether the driver was young or old, male or female, or accompanied by children. Nor did it matter whether the car was new or old, expensive or cheap.

However, by 9 pm the line-up of vehicles waiting to come into Umlazi stretched for about a kilometre. Recognising that it would be impossible to stop every single car, Captain Rylands decided to let cars pass through freely for about 20 minutes before resuming the roadblock in full again. This of course meant that some 'guilty' drivers 'got away', but it was an unavoidable risk, said the commanding officer, because 'people needed to get home at some point on Christmas Eve'.

During this 'free' time, I noticed that a few minibus taxis[1] were stopped, and the drivers were asked to show their licenses and take the breathalyser test. Two taxi drivers, with about 15 passengers in each taxi, were found to be driving under the influence. They were removed from their taxis and the 'customers' were asked to get out of the taxis. I was interested to see if the police would be concerned that innocent passengers still wanted to get home, and I was very impressed by their innovative solution and their care shown to 'innocent' passengers. What the officers did was to watch out for minibus taxis that were empty. They then took the money collected by the drunken taxi driver and gave it to a sober taxi driver; the passengers climbed into the empty taxi and were on their way home again with just a brief delay.

The courtesy shown by the police to the minibus passengers was extended to all persons stopped in the roadblock. Despite the inconvenience that the roadblock presented to commuters, there was a general congenial interaction between the police and the people caught up in the roadblock, with very few instances of antagonism towards the police. Even those arrested, aside from the first 'offender', responded in a way that could best be described as resigned. Most members of the public that I spoke with informally during the roadblock indicated that they appreciated the roadblock because they felt that roadblocks prevented road accidents and provided reassurance of a police presence.

Captain Rylands officially closed the roadblock at about 2 am on Christmas morning. Altogether 12 people had been arrested that night, in the course of a seven-hour roadblock. The SAPS did not find any illegal substances, weapons or people in their vehicles search. I wondered whether the level of resources that had been put into the roadblock – human, physical, logistic – had 'paid off'. I asked a number of police officers, both rank-and-file and supervisory, for their assessment of the roadblock. Most of them whom I spoke to felt that the roadblock had been a success, despite the low number of arrests. As they saw it, awareness of roadblocks deters people from driving over the limit or in cars that are unlicensed or unroadworthy. But more importantly they believed that the very obvious presence of police in a roadblock operation indicates that a policing service is being delivered. And this is particularly important to those who live in areas that are perceived, or officially categorised, as high crime areas such as Umlazi.

Being part of this the Umlazi roadblock operation helped me to frame questions that I believe are important in understanding the workings of roadblocks in South Africa. The following questions came to mind: How does profiling 'work' in South African roadblock operations? How is 'success' understood and measured in regard to roadblocks? What are the limitations of roadblocks as a policing strategy? What are the limits of roadblocks as a crime prevention/combat tactic? These questions will be addressed in the rest of the paper.

Finding ways to answer questions about police roadblocks

Much of my research on policing over the past 10 years has been conducted using an ethnographic approach. My inclination as a researcher is to immerse myself in the policing landscape I am trying to understand, so as to feel, see, hear and imagine the lived reality of the actors whose declared objective is to create a safer environment.

Surprisingly perhaps, the police have usually created the space for me to observe and participate in their working world (see Marks 2005).

I was optimistic about my chances of joining up with the police (both the SAPS and the Durban Metropolitan Police) in their 2010/2011 festive season roadblock operations. I share the view of Gould and Mastrofski (2004) in that direct observation enables a clearer sense of what really goes on during roadblocks – how police use their discretion in stopping and searching, the manner in which police and public relate to one another the roadblock operation outcomes, and the lack of fit between officers' words and action and between law and practice.

But I quickly discovered that access as (participant) an observer was far more difficult 16 years after the transition to democracy than it had been in the early years of democratic transformation (when I conducted my first police ethnography). A new era has dawned in the world of the South African police in recent years. A new National Commissioner has assumed the police throne, and with him has come a sharp reversion to highly militarised policing and a very hierarchical organisational structure (see Marks and Wood 2010). Accompanying this has been an obvious reversal of many of the goals of 'transformation' that were set in place in the early years of democratic transition when the police committed themselves to a reform process directed at demilitarisation, transparency, accountability and community-oriented practice.

Given this reversion, doors that were once open to direct observation of police operations are now shut. At every turn, I came to realise that my once relatively free access to the police was now seriously curtailed. A new political order and a more insular command and control structure now present formidable obstacles to doing policing ethnography (or observation) in South Africa.

Having realised this changed context, I had to contemplate an alternative research design. I decided that I would still try to do some participant observation. I managed to do this on two occasions – once informally with members of the Public Order Police unit and once with the Durban Metro Police on Christmas Eve. I supplemented my observations with interviews with senior police officers from both the Durban Metropolitan Police and the SAPS who have been involved in the design and command of roadblocks for many years, as well as with more informal conversations with rank-and-file police from both police organisations. The result is a paper whose research data is much thinner than I had anticipated. Nonetheless, I hope it provides a glimpse into the South African roadblock topography.

Roadblocks as a policing strategy: a form of community policing?

Across the world, stop and search operations, including roadblocks, are seen as 'an important tactic in the police crime reduction armoury' (Qureshi and Farrell 2006, p. 83), and this remains the case despite the controversy about stop and search, particularly when directed at minorities (see, for example, Bowling and Phillips 2002).

In South Africa, roadblocks and stop and search operations in general are integral to police operational planning. As part of the visible policing strategy, the police in South Africa have becoming increasingly dependent on their use (Institute for Security Studies 2010). In a submission by the Institute for Security Studies to the parliamentary portfolio committee on police in October 2010, it was noted that in the period 2009/2010 the number of roadblocks increased by 22.6% compared to the previous year, the number of cordon and searches increased by 86%, stop and search operations increased by 53% and the number of people searched increased by 30.6%. In each case, these tactics are intended to escalate and enhance *visible* policing, thereby improving police legitimacy and preventing crime.

Making sense of this statistical data is complicated. It could be claimed that an increase in stop and search operations indicates a shift toward more 'hard' policing tactics. This would fit with arguments that the police in South Africa are becoming increasingly militarised in their 'war' against crime and disorder (Rothmann 2004).

Yet simply to see increased dependence on stop and search operations as a shift toward more hard-nosed policing leaves too much out of the picture. Specifying the super roadblocks as a component of Operation Duty Calls suggests that the architects of this strategy perceive roadblocks as mechanisms for delivering a meaningful public service. Conversations with both police managers and with rank-and-file police officers revealed a common sensibility that the public 'appreciate' roadblocks because they function as both preventative and reassuring. In this way of thinking, roadblocks are viewed by the police as integral to a broader community policing strategy. This resonates with research on stop and search operations in other parts of the world, such as America, where aggressive order maintenance is integral to broader problem-solving strategies (Gould and Mastrofski 2004).

Most of the senior police officers I spoke with claimed to be committed to a 'community policing' philosophy in which stop and search operations play a vital role in achieving crime reduction and safety goals. As the highest ranking officer in the Durban Metropolitan Police informed me, 'for the most part, roadblocks have a psychological impact; the public thinks we are on the look-out and that we are concerned with rooting out crime and disorder problems, particularly over the festive season'. In his experience, members of the public, despite being inconvenienced by roadblock operations, often thank the police for holding roadblocks. I observed this response from the public in Umlazi on Christmas Eve.

There were, however, high-ranking and rank-and-file SAPS officers who did not share this view. One of the SAPS provincial heads of operational policing in KwaZulu-Natal unreservedly stated that roadblocks are generally ineffective as a crime reduction or prevention strategy. He also asserted that police often disregard procedural fairness in conducting stop and search operations, contributing to negative perceptions of police. A small number of rank-and-file police officers declared that police resources are wasted in roadblock operations since they yield limited outcomes and are a short-term approach to policing and safety problems.

Regardless of what individual police officers have to say, in South Africa, roadblocks are here to stay. And two simultaneous logics underpin police reliance on this tactic: roadblocks are favoured because they offer visible manifestation of (1) zero tolerance for disorderly and illegal conduct and (2) demonstrate a commitment to the duty of the police to protect. How citizens really feel about these police proclamations is hard to establish since there are no existing public opinion surveys in regard to roadblock operations.

Profiling and roadblocks

Perhaps the biggest controversy around stop and search operations – whether in roadblocks or building raids or checkpoints – is the exercise of discretion by police officers which results in selective policing. Police discretion in such operations often occurs with little direct supervision from police managers or commanders who might be more cautious of the problems of apparent or inconsistent profiling (Fitzgerald and Sibbit 1997, Skolnick and Caplovitz 2001, Bowling *et al.* 2004, p. 1). Profiling might be part of a strategy or it might be the result of the individual prejudices and basic assumptions (Dixon *et al.* 1989). Contributing to the prevalence of individual (often prejudiced) profiling by individual police officers is that police officers often carry out their search practices without an accurate knowledge of legal and constitutional requirements (Gould and Mastrofski 2004). I have observed this frequently in my observations of police patrols where police discriminately stop and search members of the public who appear indigent or fearful of the police. Police generally fail to inform citizens of their rights. They disregard documented police procedures in regard to stop and search operations that stipulate how search and seizure powers are exercised, including prescriptions of fairness and equality of treatment of citizens (see Marks 2005). Police in South Africa, as elsewhere, make creative use of legal ambiguities and gaps (Gould and Mastrofski 2004).

The much noted profiling of minority groups in stop and search operations across the world is as much the result of the possible police officer and organisational discrimination as it is a reflection of rates of crime committed by particular social groupings. Gelman *et al.* (2007) refer to this 'natural profiling' (p. 813). Police tend to justify their disparate patterns of stop and searches on the grounds that minorities disproportionately commit more crimes (Kennedy 1997). For South Africa – historically, and possibly presently – racial profiling that links 'blackness' with criminality translates to majority profiling.

In the Christmas Eve roadblock I observed in Umlazi, I noted that the police made conscious attempts to treat all drivers with uniform care and wariness. In my conversations and observations I tried to determine whether any form of 'natural profiling' was present in roadblock operations. In truth, I found it very difficult to establish what kind of profiling was taking place on the night I spent in Umlazi, in part because all the drivers and passengers were 'Black Africans'. The officer in charge had very clearly briefed her 'troops' to avoid any overt discrimination in selecting which drivers to stop, and the principle of stopping each and every vehicle was implemented as far as possible. The only drivers who did seem to be singled out were the minibus taxi drivers. With their general reputation for risky driving and involvement in road accidents, this was not a surprise.

Formal interviews held with senior police leaders in Durban who were involved in the design and command of roadblocks indicated two very different strands of thinking. The Head of the Durban Metropolitan Police was insistent that profiling does not occur and that in a roadblock operation his officers are instructed, where possible, to stop every vehicle without prior prejudice. His instruction seemed to have been adhered to by the officers manning the roadblock in Umlazi on Christmas Eve. A similar position was expressed by other veteran police commanders who are aware of the possible political consequences of racial profiling. These police were acutely aware of the need to 'break with past [apartheid driven] practices' and are outwardly committed to policing routines governed by equity and fairness considerations.

Yet some senior officers openly admit that profiling determines how the police conduct roadblocks and other stop and search operations. One of Durban's most seasoned Brigadiers stated bluntly that when he conducts roadblocks he is 'not concerned with fairness'. According to him, police have a 'sixth sense' about which groups of people are most likely to be offenders and what kind of behaviour should raise suspicion (such as displays of awkwardness, of being personally unkempt and driving vehicles which do not 'fit' the appearance of the driver).

This, perhaps politically incorrect, view was echoed by a number of lower ranking police officers that I spoke with. In general, most police avoided discussing race as a signifier. Class, however, was almost consistently a signifier – 'scruffy' appearance signals potential trouble. One senior officer went as far as saying that he targets youth from a working class (predominantly white) suburb who have tattoos on their bodies.

This is important to note since, as Bethan Loftus (2007) points out, the diversity agendas of the police drive some aspects of police culture underground, obscuring the classist character of police culture and police work. Aggressive and discriminatory policing and attitudes towards the growing ranks of poor, unemployed (and, in Loftus's UK-based study, predominantly white) young males are almost completely taken for granted, accepted and ignored by the higher-ups.

Loftus's insights resonate with the policing of roadblocks and other stop and search operations in South Africa. Yet the relative invisibility of class profiling means that it is not often brought under public, or even academic, scrutiny. It should be borne in mind, however, that although explicit racial discrimination may not be immediately evident, with the inextricable link in South Africa between race and class, race profiling still remains a factor – the vast majority of poor people in South Africa are black. Race and class thus intersect to provide a profile of suspicion.

Another (fairly observable) group which has been clearly targeted in stop and search operations in South Africa are African foreign nationals. These (black) foreign nationals do not speak the local languages, they often dress and behave in ways which make them distinct from locals and police are well attuned to these differences. Senior officers interviewed claimed that it is a statistical 'reality' that foreign nationals (particularly those that are undocumented) are likely to be involved in criminal activities. As a result they are viewed as 'legitimate' targets of stop and search operations.

Targeting of African foreign nationals in stop and search operations has received a fair degree of media attention. In November 2010, human rights groups expressed outrage at stop and search operations (incorporated into Operation Duty Calls) which were aimed at foreign nationals. In inner-city Johannesburg, large contingents of police raided buildings believed to be occupied mainly by foreign nationals (Bega 2010). Human rights groups accused the police of feeding popular paranoia towards foreign nationals and creating trauma for foreign nationals whose livelihood in South Africa is already precarious (Bega 2010).

It is equally important to bear in mind that profiling occurs not just in relation to individual or group characteristics. Also targeted for stop and search operations, including roadblocks, are geographical localities (Smith 1986). Gelman *et al.* (2007) and Gould and Matrofski (2004) refer to this as neighbourhood profiling in stop and search policing. While roadblocks are regularly mounted on the major highways, they have also become an everyday feature of the exit and entry points of places like Umlazi and Phoenix, considered to be impoverished, unregulated and criminogenic. This seldom occurs in elite (mostly white) residential areas.

Residents from Phoenix (a lower-middle-class and working-class Indian area) and KwaMashu (a working-class African township) complain about the regularity of roadblocks in non-elite areas. Listeners on East Coast Radio regularly phone in to complain about the 'unfairness' of certain residents being stopped so frequently – even that people from poorer Durban communities are in danger of losing their jobs because the police so often delay them while they are trying to get to work. Ubiquitous roadblocks may have been applauded during the festive season, but citizens are now annoyed by the inconvenience they cause and sceptical about their effectiveness and the fairness of policing planning. We should thus be alerted to the fact that the public have mixed feelings about stop and search operations. While they indicate visible police action, they also curtail rights to freedom and privacy. A tension clearly exists between the 'right to security' and the 'securitisation of rights' (Lazarus 2011).

Assessing success in roadblock operations

When the Christmas Eve roadblock in Umlazi drew to a close, I wondered what had really been achieved that night, and how one should try to assess the effectiveness of such an exercise. Twelve people had been arrested. Was that a good or a bad indicator? In my conversations with police officers I tried to establish what they regarded, from the police perspective, as an effective roadblock operation. More visionary senior officers interviewed recognised that arrest rates should not be viewed as an indicator for roadblock 'success'. A SAPS General remarked that the police should take a long-term view which focuses on decreases in the prevalence of crime and risky behaviour, as well as community satisfaction. The Head of the Durban Metro Police asserted that a worthy, but difficult to measure performance indicator, is a shift in public awareness, such as around issues of road safety. These views are somewhat at odds with national police priorities which stipulate that roadblock effectiveness is best measured through what Bayley (1994) would refer to as 'indirect indicators', such as arrests and recoveries.

Strangely what makes police roadblocks most effective – their visibility – is simultaneously what renders them somewhat defective. For example, if police operating a roadblock are unable to close off all exit points, it is possible for a driver who spots a roadblock in time to switch to another route – and those with reason to evade roadblocks will make every effort to do so. The overall effectiveness of roadblocks is also compromised by the reality that the police are simply unable to check every vehicle that passes through. However vigilant and streetwise the police may believe themselves to be, officers from all ranks acknowledged that the chance of failing to spot lawbreakers is pretty high. And, as we have seen from the Umlazi story, heavy traffic makes roadblocks difficult to manage in a fair and equal manner.

The effectiveness of roadblocks in crime prevention is increasingly compromised by the creative use of information technology and social networks by citizens. It is no secret to the police that people quite commonly phone one another to warn about a roadblock and to suggest alternate routes. What took *me* by surprise was how the social network, more particularly Facebook, is now widely used by South Africans to pass on information about roadblocks. For KwaZulu-Natal there is now a Facebook page called 'Road Blocks KZN' where anyone can do an up-to-the-minute check – or give warning of – roadblocks around the province, their location and sometimes also their purpose and the particular police agency operating the roadblock. As of 23 December 2010, more than 6200 people had signed on as 'liking' Road Blocks KZN.

In assessing the effectiveness of roadblocks it is important to take account of the objective of particular roadblocks; broad policing objectives; public confidence measures; reduction of crime and risk behaviour and even arrests and seizures. However, ultimately it is important to bear in mind that what police really do is engage in 'a set of routines intended to produce a degree of certainty in managing fundamentally problematic yet recurrent situations' (Manning 2010, p. 190); the police dramatise order and allocate blame. Roadblock operations in South Africa are principally staged events with symbolic significance; they give some citizens a sense of relief that something positive is being done by the police, while others are left feeling targeted, scrutinised and restricted in exercise of their basic rights.

Conclusion

Many of the findings in this paper resonate with the conclusions drawn by Belur (in this issue) in her paper on Indian police roadblocks (nakabandis) in Mumbai. As is the case in Mumbai, police roadblocks in South Africa are here to stay. Police leaders in South Africa and India seem to believe that roadblocks and patrols are one of the most effective crime prevention strategies available to the police. Whether they truly are is hard to say. It all depends how one measures police effectiveness and how one assesses whether the resources put into such operations (especially the heavily resourced super roadblocks) 'pay off'. The very high levels of crime in South Africa make it extremely difficult to reach conclusions on this matter. There are, however, police officers at all ranks who remain sceptical about their value.

The roadblock tactic is being increasingly resorted to because it is perceived as simultaneously a community approach and a strong-arm line of attack. South Africa is in serious danger of becoming more and more securitised, where the focus is on reinforcing a 'right to security' at the expense of 'securitising rights' (see Lazarus 2011). The long-term impact of this securitisation is hard to gauge, but over time the South African public are likely to become less tolerant of roadblocks because they are extremely intrusive, and because there will always be suspicion of profiling, regardless of the policy and legal frameworks that insist on fair and equal police conduct. Ultimately, we need to take heed of Jean-Paul Brodeur's reminder that the police never have been able to create order. Rather, they are 'agents authorized to use diverse means prohibited to the rest of policed society in order to uphold a particular kind of socio-political order' (Brodeur 2010, p. 139). For now, police leaders and politicians are beholden to the fantasy that roadblocks play a significant role in creating order and decreasing crime rates. The 'new' super roadblock police stratagem is the clearest indication of this.

Note

1. Minibus taxis are an important form of 'public' transport in South Africa. Minibus taxis, privately owned, are often the only form of transport available to people who do not have vehicles of their own. About 15 people can fit comfortably into a minibus taxi. People wait for minibus taxis at a taxi rank, usually in town. The line to get onto a minibus taxi in the evenings, especially on public holidays, is generally very long and commuters may have to wait for hours. The minibus taxi industry is a continuing headache for the South African government. The industry is very difficult to regulate and minibus taxis are often responsible for serious road accidents.

References

Bayley, D., 1994. *Police for the future*. New York: Oxford University Press.

Bega, S., 2010. Fury as police round up foreigners. *Iolnews*, 6 November, Available from: http://www.iol.co.za/news/south-africa/fury-as-police-round-up-foreigners-1.722641 [Accessed 20 January 2011].

Bowling, B. and Phillips, C., 2002. *Racism, crime and justice*. London: Longman.

Bowling, B., Phillips, Cl., and Campbell, A., 2004. *Policing and human rights: eliminating discrimination, xenophobia and, intolerance and the abuse of power from police work*. Identities, Conflict and Cohesion Programme Paper Number 4. Switzerland: United Nations Research Institute for Social Development.

Brodeur, J., 2010. *The policing web*. New York: Oxford University Press.

Constitution of the Republic of South Africa No. 108, 1996. National Gazette No. 17678. Date of promulgation, 18 December 1996. Pretoria: The Government of South Africa.

Dixon, D., *et al.*, 1989. Reality and rules in the construction and regulation of police suspicion. *International Journal of the Sociology of Law*, 17 (3), 345–362.

Fitzgerald, M. and Sibbit, R., 1997. *Ethnic monitoring in police forces: a beginning*. Home Office Research Study 173. London: Home Office.

Gelman, A., Fagan, J., and Kiss, A., 2007. An analysis of the NYPD's stop-and-frisk policy in the context of claims of racial bias. *Journal of the American Statistical Association*, 102 (479), 813–823.

Gould, J. and Mastrofski, S., 2004. Suspect searches: assessing police behaviour under the US Constitution. *Criminology and Public Policy*, 3 (3), 315–362.

Institute for Security Studies, 2010. *Submission by the Institute for Security Studies to the Parliamentary Portfolio Committee on police: the South African police services annual report for 2009/2010*. Pretoria: Institute for Security Studies, 13 October 2010.

Jones, M., 2010. Roadblocks everywhere you go. *Iolnews*, 24 December.

Kennedy, R., 1997. *Race, crime and the law*. Cambridge: Harvard University Press.

Lazarus, L., 2011. The right to security – securing rights or securitizing rights. Paper presented at the *Criminology at the edge workshop*, 8–10 April, Centre for Criminology University of Cape Town.

Loftus, B., 2007. Policing the irrelevant: class, diversity and contemporary police culture. *In*: M. O'Neill, M. Marks and A. Singh, eds., *Police occupational culture: new debates and directions*. Oxford: Elsevier, 181–204.

Manning, P., 2010. *Democratic policing in a changing world*. Boulder: Paradigm.

Marks, M., 2005. *Transforming the Robocops: changing police in South Africa*. Durban: University of KwaZulu-Natal Press.

Marks, M. and Wood, J., 2010. South African policing at a crossroads: the case for a 'minimal' and 'minimalist' public police. *Theoretical Criminology*, 14 (3), 311–329.

Mjekula, L., 2010. Super roadblocks on the way. *Iolnews*, 20 October.

Mthethwa, N., 2010. *Unabridged statement: Minister of Police: Operation Duty Calls* [online]. Available from: http://www.defenceweb.co.za/index.php?option=com_content&view=article&id=10438:unabridged-statement-minister-of-police-operation-duty-calls&catid=3:Civil%20Security&Itemid=113 [Accessed 3 March 2011].

Qureshi, F. and Farrell, G., 2006. Stop and search in 2004: a survey of police officer views and experiences. *International Journal of Police Science and Management*, 8 (2), 83–103.

Roberts, B. and Struwig, J., 2011. Shooting blanks? South Africa's confidence in police. *HSRC Review*, 9 (2).

Rothmann, S., 2004. Expectations of, and satisfaction with, the South African Police Service in the North West Province. *Policing: An International Journal of Police Strategies and Management*, 29 (2), 211–225.

Skolnick, J. and Caplovitz, A., 2001. Guns, drugs and profiling: ways to target guns and minimize racial profiling. *Arizona Law Review*, 43 (2), 413–437.

Smith, D., 1986. The neighborhood context of police behavior. *In*: A.J. Reiss and M. Tonry, eds. *Crime and justice: an annual review of research*. Chicago : University of Chicago Press, 314–332.

Police stop and search in India: Mumbai *nakabandi*

Jyoti Belur

Department of Security and Crime Science, University College London, London, UK

The Indian police have wide discretionary powers of stop and search. One peculiar and regular manifestation of this power is '*nakabandi*' (meaning blockade), where the police set up road blocks on important road junctions and conduct stop and search operations. This paper is the first attempt of its kind to describe the way the Mumbai police exercise these powers in the form of *nakabandi* and what is achieved from these operations. The conditions under which the police conduct stop and search operations in Mumbai and their effectiveness are discussed. While police *nakabandi* do not ostensibly raise allegations of racial discrimination and controversy like police stop and search operations in the West, nevertheless several questions regarding their purpose and efficacy arise, especially in relation to the amount of time and resources devoted to these operations.

Introduction

Policing the city of Mumbai, the financial capital of India, with a population of 21 million, poses challenges on a scale that few other metropolitan police forces in the world have to contend with. The rise of organised crime in the 1980s and an unprecedented rise in terrorist activities from the 1990s have led to rising fear of crime and public insecurity (Belur 2010). The police have responded in creative ways to deal with these problems while handicapped by poor working conditions, an inefficient criminal justice system, politicisation of the police, combined with a serious lack of resources and infrastructure (Verma 2000, Dhillon 2005).

For example, since the 1990s in response to fervent public and political demands to tackle organised crime, the Mumbai police responded, amongst other measures, by using deadly force in elaborately constructed scenarios known as *encounters*. Police use of such rough and ready 'justice' has received political and social approval in Mumbai (Belur 2010). The Indian police have been accused of abusing power and being violence prone. Part of this is attributable to serious institutional and organisational problems (Krishnamurthy 1996) and part resulting from the legacy of colonial policing that continues to affect present day policing practices and culture (Verma 1999). The two-pronged threat of serious crime and terrorism to public security has meant that often fundamentals of 'due process' and guiding principles of 'reasonable suspicion' have been disregarded by the police and public alike. There is pressure on the police to do something or at least appear to be proactive, regardless of whether their actions are particularly effective or not.

The Mumbai police have long used stop and search operations in the form of *nakabandi* or roadblocks as a crime control measure, but these have gained an added urgency in the period following the terror attacks in November 2008. While the police in several countries use roadblocks to stop and search in different contexts, such static checkpoints have seldom been included in the wider literature on police stop and search. However, this research revealed that the police in Mumbai necessarily use road blocks as a form of stop and search because of the sheer impossibility of conducting effective foot stops, given the sheer size of population in crowded public places and the layout of main streets and roads.

Academic literature on police stop and search in the West primarily focuses on the socio-legal aspects of these operations and mainly revolves either around police stereotyping and racism, or its adverse impact on minority ethnic communities in different countries (see this issue). The current study was sensitised by this research and explored the question of whether the Mumbai police use some form of stereotyping, and to what extent it was determined by race, ethnicity or class, or was specifically prejudicial to ethnic minorities. It was also concerned with exploring the effectiveness of stop and search in Mumbai. It therefore contributes to the small body of literature on operational productivity and the effectiveness of stop and search operations on crime, either preventing or detecting it (e.g. Miller *et al.* 2000, Havis and Best 2004, Skogan and Frydl 2004, Delsol and Shiner 2006, Trone 2010).

This paper is the first attempt of its kind to examine police powers to stop and search as practiced by the police in India. The paper is necessarily descriptive and tentative in nature. It is only the first step in the process of analysing and then explaining police use of stop and search powers conducted in a non-Western context. The first short section of the paper discusses methodological issues. The second section introduces police *nakabandi* in Mumbai to illustrate how police powers to stop and search are exercised in India. The next section discusses the effectiveness of police stop and searches. The concluding section presents recommendations for further research and policy implications for police stop and search in Mumbai.

Methodology

The paucity of overall police research in India means that stop and search has received little if any attention, especially since it is not the subject of controversy that it is in many Western countries nor it is widely perceived as problematic or discriminatory. There are also limited data on police stop and search that are publicly available. Consequently, primary data for this paper were gathered through personal observation of police stop and searches in four different locations in Mumbai and informal interviews with eight police officers of various ranks conducted in January 2011. The sample was selected on the basis of personal contacts in one of Mumbai's five policing regions. Whilst recognising that the sample size is small and non-random, the data provide the basis for making some general observations and comments about the way police exercise the power to stop and search in Mumbai. It is a preliminary research on which future research might follow.

Secondary data sources include publicly available official statistics, government documents and media reports. My background as an ex-police officer in India and personal contacts with the police force in Mumbai meant that I had some knowledge of operational details and access to departmental documents not publicly available.

The Mumbai metropolitan area is one of the most densely populated regions with an estimated population of 21 million in 2011 concentrated on a stretch of land extending 42 kilometres north to south and 17 kilometres east to west (Baker *et al.* 2005). The island of Mumbai has a poorly structured road network with only three main roads connecting the north–south corridors and poor east–west links to the suburbs (Patankar 1998). Rapid growth of the city's population matched by a huge spurt of growth in road traffic has created considerable challenges for the setting up of effective security checkpoints. The locations observed represented a diversity of contextual settings for the police road blocks. The first observed location was on a main road adjoining a mixed residential complex; the second, a busy east–west link road near an industrial estate; the third, a rather crowded and chaotic intersection bordering a huge slum area that, according to officers interviewed, was notorious for harbouring criminals and terrorists or their accomplices; and the final observed location was at an approach road to a highly sensitive vital installation.

Police officers interviewed included officers on duty at the observed locations and senior supervisory officers of the area. The observations were conducted during the evening sessions – between 5 and 7 pm during peak traffic time. There was a mix of cyclists, auto rickshaws, two-wheelers, cars, taxis, buses, trucks, mini vans, occasional hand-carts and pedestrians in three of the four areas. Only the approach road skirting the vital installation had a lower volume of traffic.

Legal powers of stop and search

The Mumbai police draw their powers of stop and search from section 100 (3) of the Code of Criminal Procedure (CrPC) 1973 which specifies:

> Where any person in or about such place is reasonably suspected of concealing about his person any article for which search should be made, such person may be searched and if such person is a woman, the search shall be made by another woman with strict regard to decency.

Thus the national legal provision allows for the search of any article 'for which a search should be made' giving the police very broad powers to stop and search persons. The Mumbai police also draw on section 65(2) of The Bombay Police Act 1951 which empowers the police to specifically stop and search on the streets or public places:

> When in a street or a place of public resort a person has possession or apparent possession of any article which a Police officer in good faith suspects to be stolen property, such Police officer may search for and examine the same and may require an account thereof...

Additionally, several Minor Acts also set out provisions allowing the police to stop and search, for example, The Motor Vehicles Act 1988, The Indian Arms Act 1959, The Narcotics and Psychotropic Substances Act 1985, the Terrorist and Disruptive Activities (Prevention) Act 1985 (repealed in 1995) and the Prevention of Terrorism

Act 2002 (repealed 2004). However, there are no specific directives or legal provisions that empower the police to exercise the powers to stop and search in the form of *nakabandi*. The latter variation of police powers has been regularly used in Mumbai for many years and for which the public appear to accept ungrudgingly.

The CrPC 1973 empowers the police to stop and search a person on 'reasonable suspicion' of possession of stolen property. However, the Bombay Police Act softens this fuzzy requirement even further by specifying that police stop and searches done in 'good faith' are permissible. Thus, the standard of 'reasonable suspicion', which itself has not been defined by law or policy, is further diluted by the caveat introduced by the Bombay Police Act defining searches done in 'good faith' to be legitimate, regardless of the manner of their execution. Moreover, the legal expectation that the public are bound to 'conform with reasonable orders of the police' as per the provisions of section 68 of the Bombay Police Act makes compliance with police requests to search almost mandatory. Refusal to comply would attract the penal provisions of section 187 of the Indian Penal Code which can be in the form of either a fine or imprisonment for up to six months.

The attitude of the courts towards police exercise of their powers to search persons and places is also quite lax in that they have ruled that 'violations of provisions of section 100 CrPC strictly per se does not vitiate the prosecution case' (State of Punjab Vs Balbir Singh 1994) and further held that failure to comply with requirements of search would only amount to an 'irregularity' and would not 'per se be illegal', nor would it 'vitiate the trial' (Verma 1997, Tek Chand Vs State of Rajasthan 2009). Thus, the conduct of stop and search operations is not subject to any significant legal or departmental scrutiny giving the Indian police greater discretion, unlike the systemic review that similar police operations are subject to in the Anglo-American context.

Officers interviewed asserted that there have been few, if any, complaints regarding police stop and search in Mumbai. However, even if there were any allegations, there is little legal recourse for the complainant. In its Report on the Law of Arrests, the Law Commission of India noted that even in the case of a wrongful arrest:

> Nothing happens to the police officer who has unlawfully or unjustifiably interfered with the liberty of a citizen and/or has wrongfully confined the person, whether in police custody or elsewhere... any wrongful or illegal act on their behalf would not affect them, their careers or their prospects in service; all that would happen is, the person arrested would be let off by the courts. (Law Commission of India 2001, pp. 32–33)

Thus, if there is systemic protection for police officers in the case of something as serious as wrongful arrests, one can reasonably conclude that there would be little legal redress for police stop and searches that are perceived as unjustified or unfair.

Nakabandi

'*Nakabandi* means prohibiting all movements into or out of the town' (Kundu and Basu 1999). There is no definitive evidence of when the exercise of police stop and search in this form was first introduced in Mumbai, although there are media references to *nakabandi* from the early 1980s. Traditionally, *nakabandis* were held in the immediate aftermath of a high profile crime; as a preventive measure before any anticipated public disorder or big event; or routinely as a crime prevention measure. The situation, however, changed in the aftermath of the Mumbai terror attacks of 26–29 November 2008. These atrocities, committed by 10 terrorists in several public locations, left 165 dead and 304 persons injured (Ministry of External Affairs 2009).

A Special Memo issued by the Commissioner of Mumbai in August 2009 states that while the main aim of *nakabandi* following the terrorist attacks is to prevent them, the prevention and detection of crime in general is just an important goal. The memo further cautions against the observed police practice of focusing on fining petty traffic violations, which should not be the main aim of *nakabandi*. Currently, *nakabandi* operations are set up as per the instructions contained in an internal memo issued by the office of the Commissioner of Police, Mumbai (January 2009) issued against the background of the terror attacks and to remedy erstwhile *nakabandi* operations that were unsystematic and ineffective.

An ideal-type *nakabandi* involves a minimum of 13 personnel (one Inspector, one or two Sub-Inspectors, two Head Constables and eight Constables) divided into four parties. The physical layout of the operation involves the setting up of two barricades in a zig-zag pattern manned by armed personnel from the first party on a designated main road or intersection. The checking zone consists of an area beside the road where the stopped vehicles can be checked by five officers from the second party. Two police check-posts should be set up on either side of the road behind the checking party manned by the third party. A mobile vehicle comprising the fourth party brings up the rear of the blockade in order to pursue those who ignore requests to pull over. Not every vehicle is to be stopped and searched; officers standing behind the barricades identify and indicate vehicles that must pull over for checking, thus ensuring that other traffic can pass unimpeded.

Interviews with police officers revealed that all 89 police stations in Mumbai must daily conduct at least one two-hour *nakabandi*. The times and places are either determined centrally by the Commissioner's office or regionally by the Additional Commissioner's office in each of the five regions in Mumbai.

It is evident from Figure 1 that the police in Mumbai devote considerable time, manpower and resources on *nakabandi*, which is incorporated into routine policing. Following the terror attack in November 2008, the city saw nearly a doubling of *nakabandi* operations in 2009. These reduced marginally in 2010, but were nonetheless at a much higher level than previous years. The growing number of

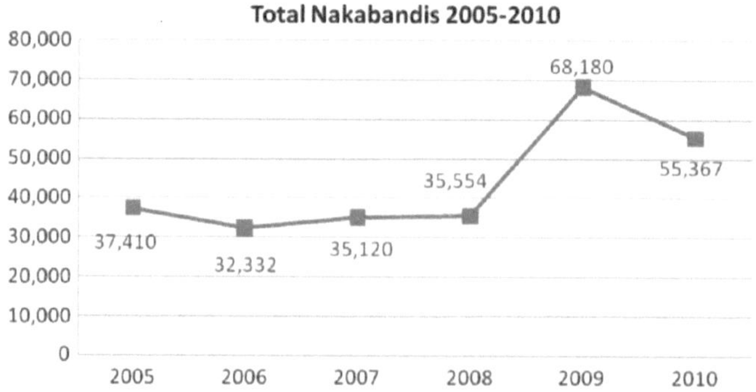

Figure 1. Total *nakabandi* in Mumbai, 2005–2010.
Source: Mumbai Police Website: http://www.mumbaipolice.org.

nakabandi conducted and conversations with officers clearly indicate that the city police consider *nakabandi* an effective deterrent to terror attacks.

The Mumbai police undertake huge numbers of vehicle stop and searches but conduct fewer foot stops. The main reason for this might be the impracticality of conducting individual stop and search actions in very crowded locations. *Nakabandis* are usually conducted in crowded areas, on narrow roads that witness heavy traffic flows,[1] which include legal and unregistered vehicles such as cycles, handcarts and even occasional bullock carts. A traffic count conducted by private consultants at some of the busiest road junctions in Mumbai in 2009 showed that on an average around 20,000 people in around 5000 vehicles pass through a junction per peak hour. However, this does not include cyclists and pedestrians who spill over from the pavements onto the streets.

The topography of the city is such that suitable check points can potentially be set up at only a few locations. These check points are largely fixed and I was informed by police officers that *nakabandis* follow a fairly regular temporal and spatial pattern. Standing orders mandate setting them up either in the mornings (around 11 am when the banks open and there are large cash deposits or withdrawals by businesses) or in the evenings between 5 and 7 pm. Occasionally late night *nakabandis* are conducted based on specific intelligence, as a preventive measure during festivals, or preceding VVIP visits and public meetings. One senior officer interviewed said that *nakabandis* were set up with the twin objectives of preventing crime, especially chain snatching[2] and/or disrupting potential terrorist attacks. Despite this, the three cases in which I saw the police take any further action after stopping and searching a person resulted in the issuance of a ticket for violating the Motor Vehicle Act.

Furthermore, there is no legal obligation to record the reasons for each stop. It was observed that there is no systematic method of recording the stops. In some locations only the vehicle registration was noted; in others, the name of the person driving the vehicle or the make of the vehicle. There was a lack of consistency, not only across the locations but even within the same location – a result of being individually rather than systemically determined. Additionally, all information was recorded on a loose sheet of paper and I was told there was no system of filing them or maintaining systematic records. The only official record of a *nakabandi* operation is recorded in the Station General Diary.[3] A typical entry relating to *nakabandis* only includes information relating to the duty personnel; the time, location and duration of the *nakabandi* and whether the supervisory officer visited the *nakabandi* site. This is quite unlike the recording practices in the UK and USA where in recent years extensive paperwork has become the norm following each police stop and search; either as a result of an organisational initiative or a legal obligation.[4] Maintaining a detailed database makes it amenable to analysis and to draw conclusions on why, when and who the police stop and search.

The lack of similar data precluded any formal analysis of who the Mumbai police stop and search and why. Observation and interviews revealed that the police focus on stopping one or two young men on a two-wheeler, of a certain build and age, generally carrying a backpack. The CCTV footage of the terrorists involved in the Mumbai 2008 terrorist attack revealed that they were physically fit young men carrying a backpack filled with explosives and armament which they subsequently deployed in the attacks. Consequently, the police concentrate on stopping and searching youths of similar appearance. Additionally, the modus operandi of chain and bag snatchers included a two-wheeler as the most flexible mode of transport to make a quick getaway in crowded areas, thus the focus on two-wheelers.

Other objects of police attention are taxis or private cars carrying all male passengers. I also observed that officers conducted a cursory check of the stopped person's backpack or the vehicle storage area; they occasionally asked the person to produce vehicle documents or a licence; but rarely conducted a personal search or pat down. It was not always clear on what basis they were making the decision to stop someone and let others go. When asked, officers replied that they were looking for persons with the profile and appearance described above. Officers claimed that it was their experience that this 'type of person' was more likely to be involved in criminal or terrorist activities. Such construction of typifications is not unusual in this type of police work (Schutz 1967, Quinton, this issue).

In two observed locations, some women police constables were part of the *nakabandi* teams. They helped in checking the bags of the few women co-passengers stopped. I inferred that the presence of women police in these operations was wholly dependent on availability of staff at any given time. Also, since none of the persons stopped was subject to a pat-down, the presence of women police (who comprise a mere 2.5% of the Mumbai police force) was not felt to be absolutely essential. Vehicles carrying women and children were hardly stopped and officers seemed convinced that terrorists or criminals rarely involve families; a misconception that persists despite the fact that a woman was one of the three persons convicted in the twin car bombing in Mumbai in August 2003 (*Times of India* 2009). This loophole in the way the Mumbai police practice stop and search has been and could potentially be exploited by criminals (*Times of India* 2005).

Effectiveness of police stop and search

The outcomes of police stops and searches in the West, mainly arrests, tend to demonstrate the disproportionate and discriminatory nature of the arrests based on ethnicity (Bowling and Phillips 2007, Gelman *et al.* 2007) or class (Allen and Monk-Turner 2010). Those who dispute the claim that police stops and searches are racially discriminatory, when other factors are taken into account (Waddington *et al.* 2004) they seldom comment on whether the outcomes of stop and search are particularly robust indicators of their effectiveness.

Some studies have found that stop and search operations contribute significantly to detection and prevention of certain crimes, such as possession of an offensive weapon (Fitzgerald 1999). Recent reports on knife crime in the UK indicate that while knife-related offences have gone up, knife-related injuries have decreased because thousands of knives were taken off the street through stop and search operations like Operation Blunt (*BBC* News 2010, Davenport 2011). However, these claims have been disputed (Travis 2010). Exceptions apart, on balance, the relevant literature tends to conclude that police stops and searches are not very effective in increasing arrests (Miller *et al.* 2000, Delsol and Shiner citing Home Office 2005) or disrupting crimes. However, some researchers do acknowledge that the effect of police presence on crimes not committed or disrupted cannot be measured (Reid 2009, Miller 2010). Finally, despite accusations of discrimination and racism, police stop and searches nevertheless command police and public support as they provide reassurance and are considered effective if used appropriately (Miller *et al.*2000, Skogan and Frydl 2004, Reid 2009, Ellis 2010).

Nakabandi as a peculiar manifestation of stop and search highlighted the issues of efficiency and productivity, but racial discrimination was not a major concern. However, my observations indicated that the police focused on specific targets, which might be considered discriminatory if not in terms of race but appearance and type of vehicle. The times, places and conditions under which the police impose *nakabandis* are predictable enough to make it easier for criminals to alter their modus operandi to avoid being stopped. A reported instance of car thieves who lay low for a while after stealing a vehicle to avoid the inevitable police *nakabandi* that followed (*Hindustan Times* 2007) should therefore come as no surprise, as criminals have been known to alter behaviour in response to law enforcement efforts to stop them (Ekblom 1999).

Routinising *nakabandi* has resulted in more emphasis on monitoring the process rather than its outcomes. Access to internal departmental data indicated that supervisory officers were expected to visit each *nakabandi* site to oversee operations, but they were expected to only report whether nominated officers were present at the location. There is little or no incentive at senior levels to ensure that *nakabandis* are more result oriented. As long as there were no public complaints of police misbehaviour, senior officers seemed content with the status quo.

Officers interviewed were convinced that *nakabandi* reassures the public and reduces fear of crime. They believed that for the public, presence of police officers on the street evidences their commitment to serve. Within hours of the latest Mumbai bomb attacks on 13 July 2011, the Mumbai Police Commissioner was announcing that *nakabandis* were in place in the city. Here it seemed that *nakabandi*, a post-catastrophe reaction, was framed as theatre, representing both control and reassurance. Regardless of whether it yielded tangible results, the police characteristically driven by what Bittner (1974, p. 30) referred to as 'someone had better do something *now*' urgency, set up a public presence in the form of *nakabandi*. But in the total absence of public opinion surveys on public confidence in policing or fear of crime, whether this 'performance' actually fulfils its aim remains unexplored.

While the police officers I spoke to were convinced that *nakabandi* operations have reduced crime, especially at the stipulated times and in the designated areas, there are little or no data to support their conviction. Mumbai police continue to emphasise on *nakabandi* as an important part of regular policing. Informal interviews highlighted police belief that the absence of further terror attacks is a clear indication of the operational effectiveness of *nakabandi*. Some may argue that 'stop and search reassures the public because of its visibility and may deter or disrupt crimes that are therefore never committed' (Reid 2009, p. 173). However, given the predictability and regularity of *nakabandi* there is little to prevent criminals from committing offences outside of these times and away from the *nakabandi* checkpoints. Thus, as a situational crime prevention intervention, the efficacy of *nakabandi* appears to be based purely on police perception of the deterrent effect of these operations.

The police can use stop and search to disrupt crime in three ways: apprehend people equipped with tools or weapons for committing crimes before they commit them; search for stolen goods and prevent escape post-commission of crime; and deter crime by sheer presence in the area (Jordan 2000). How do *nakabandis* perform on all three counts?

Data for the number of *nakabandis* conducted and their outcomes for the period 2006–2010 for one region (which includes 16 of a total of 89 police stations for the city) in Mumbai are shown in Table 1.

If all these were ideal-type *nakabandis* as described earlier, then the estimated total investment in man hours would be 1,093,066 man hours[5] spent over a period of five years in this region alone. However, concrete recoveries over that period were meagre. While data for recoveries from *nakabandi* for the whole city were unavailable, it is perhaps not unreasonable to expect a similar relationship between resources invested and outcomes achieved from *nakabandi* in general. It suggests that police policy-makers and senior officers need to rethink investment in *nakabandi* more strategically to produce higher tangible outcomes. They would also have to establish systems of measuring the intangible impact they are said to have on disrupting crime, terrorism and increasing public confidence.

Let us take the specific example of chain snatching to examine whether police presence does in fact have any deterrent impact. According to my interviewees and departmental memos, preventing and detecting chain snatching is an explicit goal during *nakabandi*. However as Table 2 shows, chain snatching has been steadily increasing even though overall crime recorded has fluctuated over the years. Admittedly, the number of chain-snatching cases detected has also been increasing, but this increase has been far lower than the increase in crimes recorded. The figures are not supportive of the argument that *nakabandis* are effective.

Lack of detailed data on the locations and timing of police *nakabandi* operations and occurrence of chain-snatching incidents mean that any conclusions drawn are imperfect at best. It might well be the case that in the absence of *nakabandi* chain snatching would have been at a much higher level. However, more rigorous research and perhaps randomised controlled trials would be required to evidence this better.

Conclusion

This first attempt to explore police *nakabandi* in India flags up concerns of proportionality and efficacy of manpower and effort invested in *nakabandi* compared to the observable results they produce. While admittedly stop and search operations

Table 1. *Nakabandi* in one region, 2006–2010.

Year	Total nakabandis for one region**	Firearms seized	Other weapons seized	Wanted persons arrested	Absconders arrested	Stolen vehicles recovered	Drugs and alcohol seizures	Stolen property recovered
2006	4483	1	0	0	0	0	0	0
2007	5017	0	2	0	0	1	0	0
2008	7341	0	0	0	0	0	0	0
2009	12,858	0	2	0	0	0	0	0
2010	12,342	0	2	2	0	0	0	0
Total	42,041	1	6	2	0	1	0	0

Courtesy: Office of the Regional Additional Commissioner of Police.

Table 2. Annual chain snatching and total registered IPC[a] crime statistics.

Year	Registered IPC offences	Difference (from previous year)	Registered chain snatching	Annual change in chain snatching registered	Annual change in chain snatching detected
2005	31,094	Not available	1036	Not available	Not available
2006	30,759	−335	1295	+259	+96
2007	30,197	−562	1422	+127	+169
2008	32,520	+2323	1442	+20	+3
2009	30,987	−1533	1600	+158	+107
2010	33,645	+2658	2044	+444	+40

Courtesy: Mumbai Police Website.
[a]IPC crimes refer to crimes registered under the Indian Penal Code.

have unobservable effects and those that cannot be measured in terms of the numbers of crimes prevented or deterred by sheer presence on the streets, professional policing demands some attempt to quantify and evaluate the benefits of the policy. Lack of opinion polls that measure the level of public confidence in police operations and police presence on the streets during *nakabandi* has meant that officers' belief in public appreciation for police *nakabandi* is based on anecdotal and hearsay evidence. Clearly, this is a gap that needs to be filled with more research on the impact of *nakabandi* on public confidence in the police and on fear of crime and terrorism.

Furthermore, available evidence is insufficient to support police officers' belief that the policy has had a definite impact on crime. The absence of further terrorist attacks until very recently had strengthened their conviction that *nakabandis* does have a deterrent impact on terrorist activities. However, the Mumbai Commissioner's reaction in the immediate aftermath of the latest terror attacks in July 2011 (*BBC* 2011) showed that *nakabandi* is presented as much for reassurance, as a security imperative, for public consumption.

Police officers' general belief that police presence on the streets enhances their credibility in the eyes of the public has provided an impetus for the organisation to continue *nakabandi* without reflecting on their utility in operational terms. It remains to be seen whether the latest terror attacks will lead to a rethink about their effectiveness or whether the police will continue time-honoured knee-jerk responses to crisis situations.

Unless the Mumbai police have to produce a cost–benefit analysis to justify *nakabandi*, there will be little incentive to improve their systems of data collection and analysis. Professionalising the police demands evidence-based approach to investing manpower and resources in *nakabandi* as a security measure, a strategy that the top echelons of police leadership appear to be giving little thought to. Providing a visible response, which appears to be a priority for the police, need not preclude either efficiency or economy.

Acknowledgements

Grateful thanks to the anonymous police officers who participated; Prof. Richard Wortley for his support; Aiden Sidebottom, Prof. Ben Bowling and peer reviewers for their insightful comments on earlier drafts.

Notes

1. Mumbai has a vehicle population of approximately 1,938,000 according to the Mumbai Traffic Police Website.
2. The modus operandi in chain-snatching crimes usually involves two motorcycle borne riders speeding towards a woman walking alone in a desolate area, yanking off her neck chain and speeding away. Alternatively, the perpetrator approaches the victim on foot, snatches her chain and escapes on a waiting motorcycle ridden by an accomplice (Times of India 2010).
3. A Station General Diary is a running record of major incidents, important events and police station activities, maintained in every Indian police station.
4. For example, the UF-250 forms that the New York Police Department (NYPD) are obliged to fill out (Gelman *et al.* 2007), and Police and Criminal Evidence (PACE) regulations for police forces in England and Wales.
5. Number of operations (42,041), multiplied by the number of men on duty in each operation (13), multiplied by the time allotted for each operation (2 hours).

References

Allen, J. and Monk-Turner, E., 2010. Citizens perception of the legitimacy of traffic stops. *Journal of Criminal Justice*, 38, 589–594.

Baker, J., *et al.*, 2005. *Urban poverty and transport: the case of Mumbai.* Washington D.C.: World Bank, World Bank Report 3693.

BBC News, 2010. *Met police stop-and-search powers 'not effective'* [online], 25 January 2010, Available from: http://news.bbc.co.uk/1/hi/england/london/8479124.stm [Accessed 31 March 2011].

BBC News, 2011. *Mumbai: explosions shake India's financial hub* [online], 13 July 2011. Available from: http://www.bbc.co.uk/news/world-south-asia-14141454 [Accessed 18 August 2011].

Belur, J., 2010. *Permission to shoot? Police use of deadly force in democracies.* New York: Springer.

Bittner, E., 1974. Florence Nightingale in pursuit of Willie Sutton: a theory of the police. *In*: H. Jacob, ed. *The potential for reform of criminal justice.* Beverly Hills, CA: Sage, 17–44.

Bowling, B. and Philips, C., 2007. Disproportionate and discriminatory: reviewing the evidence on police stop-and-search. *The Modern Law Review*, 70, 936–961.

Davenport, J., 2011. Knife crime and muggings rise but police hail stop-and-search. *The Evening Standard*, 18 Jan.

Delsol, R. and Shiner, M., 2006. Regulating stop-and-search: a challenge for police and community relations in England and Wales. *Critical Criminology*, 14, 241–263.

Dhillon, K., 2005. *Police and politics in India- colonial concepts, democratic compulsions: Indian police 1947–2002*. New Delhi: Manohar.

Ekblom, P., 1999. Can we make crime prevention adaptive by learning from other evolutionary struggles? *Studies on Crime and Crime Prevention*, 8 (1), 27–51.

Ellis, D., 2010. Police stop-and-search: disproportionality, discretion and generalisations. *Police Journal*, 83, 199–216.

Fitzgerald, M., 1999. *Final report into stop and search.* London: Metropolitan Police.

Gelman, A., Fagan, J., and Kiss, A., 2007. An analysis of the New York City Police Department's "stop-and-frisk" policy in the context of claims of racial bias. *Journal of the American Statistical Association*, 102, 813–823.

Havis, S. and Best, D., 2004. *Stop-and-search complaints (2000–2001). A police complaints authority study.* London: Police Complaints Authority.

Hindustan Times, 2007. Gang of four steals Qualis at gunpoint. *Hindustan Times*, 4 Feb.

Jordan, P., 2000. *Stop-and-search: impact on crime and impact on public opinion.* London: Police Foundation.

Krishnamurthy, S., 1996. *Human rights and the Indian police.* 2nd ed. Bangalore: R.R. Publishers.

Kundu, A. and Basu, S., 1999. *Words and concepts in urban development planning in India*. Most City Words Project, Inde du Nord/Northern India, Working Paper No. 4, December 1999, UNESCO.
Law Commission of India, 2001. *One hundred and seventy seventh report on law relating to arrest*. New Delhi: Government of India.
Miller, J., Bland, N., and Quinton, P., 2000. *The impact of stops and searches on crime and the community*. London: HMSO.
Miller, J., 2010. Stop and search in England: a reformed tactic or business as usual? *British Journal of Criminology*, 50 (5), 954–974.
Ministry of External Affairs, 2009. *Mumbai terror attacks: dossier of evidence*. New Delhi, India: Ministry of External Affairs.
Patankar, P., 1998. Financing transport infrastructures in megacities: Mumbai experience. *In*: K. Verma, ed. *Readings in Indian railways*. Delhi: Academic Foundation Publication, 170–191.
Reid, K., 2009. Race issues and stop-and-search: looking behind the statistics. *The Journal of Criminal Law*, 73, 165–183.
Schutz, A., 1967. *The phenomenology of the social world*. Evanston IL: Northwestern University Press.
Skogan, W. and Frydl, K., 2004. *Fairness and effectiveness in policing: the evidence*. Committee to Review Research on Police Policy and Practices, National Research Council. Washington DC: National Academy of Sciences.
State of Punjab Vs Balbir Singh, 1994. *Supreme court ruling* [online]. Available from: http://www.courtjudgments.org/balbir-singh-vs-state-of-punjab [Accessed 8 April 2011].
Tek Chand Vs State of Rajasthan, 2009. *Rajasthan high court ruling* [online]. Available from: http:/indiankanoon.org/doc/1683831 [Accessed 8 April 2011].
Times of India, 2005. Gangster girlfriends walk the edge. *Times of India*, 5 Nov.
Times of India, 2009. Three get death for Gateway, Zaveri Bazar blasts. *Times of India*, 7 Aug.
Times of India, 2010. City, chain-snatching capital of India. *Times of India*, 23 Aug.
Travis, A., 2010. Police stop-and-search 'not cutting knife crime' new figures suggest. *The Guardian*, 24 Jan.
Trone, J., 2010. *The New York Police Department's stop and frisk policies: are they effective? Fair? Appropriate?*. New York: John Jay College.
Verma, A., 1997. Maintaining law and order in India: an exercise in police discretion. *International Criminal Justice Review*, 7, 65–80.
Verma, A., 1999. Cultural roots of police corruption in India. *Policing: an International Journal of Police Strategies and Management*, 22 (3), 264–279.
Verma, A., 2000. Politicisation of the police in India: where lies the blame. *Indian Police Journal*, 47 (4), 19–37.
Waddington, P.A.J., Stenson, K., and Don, D., 2004. Race, and police stop-and-search. *British Journal of Criminology*, 44, 889–914.

'War on Illegal Immigrants', national narratives, and globalisation: Japanese policy and practice of police stop and question in global perspective

Mitsuru Namba

Tokyo Surugadai Law Offices, Tokyo, Japan

Policing, even stop and account, despite being tied to the local, has been confronted with the current pervasiveness of global interconnectedness. The complicated interaction between the global and local in the field of policing, however, is always the result of political and cultural assumptions in each society. This article firstly offers a brief description of recent Japanese policy and practice of police stop and account as part of a 'War on Illegal Immigrants'. While reflecting on the global trend of criminalisation of immigration, it then explains political and cultural implications which have brought about this extraordinary policy and practice in the context of modern Japanese society. It concludes that recent development of Japanese police stop and account policy and practice can be best understood as the site for interaction between the national narratives in relation to crime and ethnicity, and the corresponding apparatus of globalisation.

A police officer on duty at a *koban*[1] (an urban neighbourhood office), when patrolling on foot, stopped and questioned a Japanese woman walking on the street as she had averted her eyes and appeared to keep away from him. As he thought by appearance she was a Southeast Asian national, he asked her 'Are you Japanese?' Although she replied 'I am Japanese', he ascertained her nationality again. As she remained silent, he asked her to accompany him to the police station...(Asahi Shinbun 2006)

Introduction

If a case is shown as a visible 'event' in a society, there is an assumption that an invisible 'part of pattern' would lie behind the case. As Bauman (2004, p. 19) puts it, '[s]tories are like searchlights and spotlights; they brighten up parts of the stage while leaving the rest in darkness'. While the account above, excerpted from a Japanese quality paper, appears to show an unfortunate 'event' resulting from recent police stop and account in Japan, it reveals at the same time that intensive stop and account targeting of foreign nationals[2] became normalised in Japanese society. Nevertheless, a case is never merely an event or part of pattern in itself but always the result of political and cultural assumptions in a society. One of the aims of this article is to explain political and cultural assumptions which not only produce the event like the case above but also reduce countless cases behind it to mere parts of an accepted pattern in the contemporary context of Japan. In other words, following Bauman (2004), this article is an attempt to examine how immigrants are being transformed into a 'superfluous' population, namely, 'wasted lives', as an outcome of modernisation in the context of Japanese policing.

In the meantime, the task of explaining these assumptions is being confronted with a significant difficulty in the currently pervasive global interconnectedness. Policing, even stop and account,[3] despite mostly being tied to the local, is not the exception. This social transformation, as Giddens (1990, p. 64) notes, inevitably directs our attention to 'the complex relations between local involvements and interaction across distance'. Therefore, in order to tackle the challenge brought about by this trend of globalisation, as Aas notes (2007, p. 6), one may not '[simply map] the emerging global interconnections, but also [examine] how people and social institutions adjust to these developments locally, through cultural specific strategies'. The article also aims to reveal this complicated interaction between the global and local through the lens of Japanese police stop and account policy and practice.

In what follows, I firstly offer a brief description of recent Japanese policy and practice of the police stop and account behind the event above by reviewing relevant materials. While reflecting on the global trend of criminalisation of immigration, I then explain the political and cultural implications which enabled to establish and implement this stop and account policy and practice. I conclude that recent development of Japanese police stop and account policy and practice can be best understood as the site for interaction of national narratives in relation to crime and ethnicity, and the corresponding apparatus of globalisation.

Police stop and account as part of the 'War on Illegal Immigrants'

The case at the outset happened in the course of an intensive crackdown against irregular immigrants by the Japanese government, admittedly dubbed the 'War on Illegal Immigrants', implemented through the 'Five-Year Plan to Halve the Number of Illegal Foreign Residents' (hereinafter, Five-Year Plan). This Five-Year Plan was launched in late 2003, with the publication of the 'Action Plan for the Realisation of a Society Resistant to Crime' in December 2003 (hereinafter, Action Plan) (Ministerial Conference against Crime 2003, p. 4). The Action Plan boldly stated:

> In recent years, the crimes committed by foreign nationals have worsened. Among others, violent crimes such as break-in robberies are increasing, and there can be seen a great number of crimes operated in cooperation with *Bouryokudan* (traditional organised crime groups in Japan). While the number of foreign nationals illegally staying in Japan is estimated at approximately 250,000, it is necessary to halve in five years the number of these people who have become the hotbed of crime so that nationals may live in peace.

While numerous immigration and criminal measures were proposed to achieve the seemingly ambitious target above, a strengthening of police stop and account was vigorously emphasised. The measures proposed in the 'Joint Declaration on the Strengthening of Measures against Illegal Immigrants in Tokyo Metropolis' (hereinafter, Joint Declaration) (Ministry of Justice *et al.* 2003, p. 1), declared two months prior to Action Plan, clearly reveals this:

> In order to reinforce the crackdown on illegal immigrants, the cooperation between Tokyo Immigration Bureau and the Metropolitan Police Department should be strengthened. Among others, while joint detection of immigration bureau and police office shall be normalised, the effort should be made to intensify police stop and account against illegal immigrants by the Metropolitan Police Department.

Following the publication of the Action Plan and the Joint Declaration, police officers have engaged with intensive stop and account against irregular immigrants. This policy, however, inevitably brought about an insolvable dilemma to police officers who actually carry out stop and account. To be sure, Japanese police stop and account is legally regulated by Article 2(1) of the Police Official Duties Execution Act 1948, and this provision provides that police officers must have 'sufficient ground to suspect that a person has committed or is likely to commit a crime judging reasonably from surrounding circumstances'. Whereas this reasonable suspicion is interpreted to require an objective basis based on facts, police officers cannot usually have reasonable suspicion against 'illegal immigrants' without asking for their nationality and checking the passport or the alien registration certificate of the person. In order to implement the policy of the Action Plan and the Joint Declaration under these circumstances, police officers in patrol appear not to have any other choice but to stop and question foreign-looking people even without any reasonable suspicion of the having committed crimes. In this sense, it might be said that the Action Plan and the Joint Declaration *de facto* justified 'illegal' police stop and account.

In any event, with the authorisation of the Action Plan and the Joint Declaration, police officers throughout the country, mainly in urban districts, extensively carried out stop and account against foreign-looking people. Although the comprehensive statistics of police stop and account comparable to that under Section 95 of the Criminal Justice Act 1991 in Britain (see Bowling and Phillips 2007) are not available in Japan, a number of police statistics relating to immigration offences appear to show a dramatic change in this police activity. For example, the number of foreign nationals detected by the police for immigration offences had increased dramatically from 7783 persons in 2002 to 16,364 persons in 2005, then significantly decreased to 6843 persons in 2009. Among them, the number of foreign nationals directly transferred from police office to immigration bureau under a fast track procedure also increased significantly from 1043 persons in 2002 to 6647 persons in 2006, then significantly decreased to 2793 in 2009 (National Police Agency 2010). Taking into account the vigorous emphasis on the crackdown against 'illegal immigrants' in the Action Plan and the Joint Declaration, these figures at least suggest, on the one hand, that police stop and account against foreign nationals has immensely intensified since 2003 in order to achieve the goal of halving the number of 'illegal immigrants', and on the other, that the number of irregular immigrants in public places has significantly decreased since 2006, presumably as a consequence of the removal and deterrence of 'irregular immigrants' by means of comprehensive immigration and criminal measures, and the avoidance of public places by irregular immigrants themselves.

Apart from considerably limited statistics, a survey on police stop and account against foreign nationals, carried out by the Tokyo Bar Association between December 2006 and January 2007, might reflect this extraordinary nature of stop and account practice (Tokyo Bar Association 2007).[4] The number of total respondents was 122, which consisted of Chinese (49%), Taiwanese (9%), Malaysian (7%), Korean (5%), Indonesian (4%), Bangladeshi (3%) and others. Main findings from this survey are:

1. 52% of the respondents experienced being stopped and questioned by the police in the past three years. The number of times stopped and questioned was once for 35%, twice for 19%, three times for 10%, four times for 6% and five times or more for 28%.
2. Of the respondents being stopped and questioned, Chinese accounted for 43%, followed by Malaysian for 8%, Taiwanese and Bangladeshi for 6%, Korean, Indonesian and Burmese for 5%, Singaporean and Ethiopian for 3%.
3. In terms of the situation of being stopped and questioned, the most common situation was 'in a railway station'. This was followed by 'on the road', 'on the way home' tied with 'on the way to school or working place', and 'riding bicycles or driving cars'.
4. With regard to the reason for being recognised as foreign nationals, 40% of respondents attributed to their colours or appearance. Meanwhile, 28% put it down to the use of foreign language conversation, 20% to clothing, and 10% to the possession of foreign newspaper or magazines.

These findings show that, firstly, a significant number of foreign nationals were stopped and questioned by the police after the beginning of the 'Five-Year Plan', and many of them were repeatedly stopped and questioned. Secondly, the proportion of nationality of the respondents stopped and questioned was more or less proportionate to that of the total number of respondents. Thirdly, police stop and account against foreign nationals was widely conducted in the midst of their everyday life such as 'in a railway station'. Finally, police officers were judging 'foreignness' of people not only by their colour or appearance but also by other factors such as conversation, clothing, newspaper or magazines.

Consequently, by January 2009, this policy and practice of stop and account against irregular immigrants, effectively combined with various immigration and criminal measures, brought about the almost complete achievement of the target articulated in the Five-Year Plan. According to the announcement of the Ministry of Justice in February 2009, the number of 'illegal immigrants' was reduced by 48.5% in five years, from approximately 220,000 persons in January 2004 to around 113,000 persons in January 2009 (Ministry of Justice 2009). In the following part, the significant nature of this police stop and account policy and practice, which partly but essentially contributed to the accomplishment of the Five-Year Plan, will be examined in a broader perspective.

'War on Illegal Immigrants' as globalisation of criminalisation of immigration

While recent Japanese police stop and account policy and practice is characterised by its abhorrence of 'illegal immigrants', the introduction of extraordinary hostile measures against irregular immigrants is not peculiar to Japan. As many commentators note, most Western countries, especially in the aftermath of September 11, have more or less strengthened the enforcement of immigration law and increased their reliance on incarceration and expulsion of 'illegal immigrants' and asylum seekers (see van der Leun and van der Woude, Weber, Provine and Sanchez, this issue). For example, in the US, as Cole (2005, p. 26) described, immigration law was transformed from 'an administrative mechanism for controlling entry and exit of foreign nationals into an excuse for holding suspicious persons without meeting the constitutional requirements that ordinarily apply to preventive detention'. In many European countries, as Fekete (2005) shows, the concerted managerial enterprises of setting the targets of the deportation of failed asylum seekers have displayed the institutions compared to 'deportation machine' at the expense of the protection of asylum seekers under the Refugee Convention and various human rights.

This phenomenon of criminalisation of immigration can be characterised by its exclusionary, preventive and transnational nature, and thus be situated in line with the concepts of 'criminology of the other' (Garland 2001) or what German professor Gunther Jakobs terms 'enemy penology'. Garland depicts the emergence of criminology of the other as the response to the social transformation of late modern society, echoing the neo-conservative politics marked by 'the upholding of order and authority, the assertion of absolute moral standards, the affirmation of tradition and common sense'. Faced with ontological insecurity in late modernity, this 'new culture of control' advocates social defence against these dangerous enemies rather than concern with their welfare and prospects for rehabilitation (Garland 2001, pp. 184–186). Meanwhile, as Krasmann (2007) shows, enemy penology has the tendency to transgress the boundary between exception and rule, and inside and outside, and thus provokes the transformation of the constitutional state based on the rule of law into a preventive state predicated upon 'the logic of risk calculation'. It then assumes itself as a strategy for solving contemporary problems in the national as well as in the international area of criminal justice and security policy, being exemplary of a prevailing tendency of the globalisation of securitisation.

In the context of Japan, various criminal and immigration measures introduced in the course of the 'War on Illegal Immigrants' also seem to be associated with the global tendency of criminalisation of immigration. This phenomenon is exemplified by the recent Japanese stop and account policy and practice described above, indicating the epistemological transformation of irregular immigrants into criminalised 'illegal immigrants'. Beyond stop and account policy and practice, the trend of criminalisation of immigration has prevailed over the entire process of Japanese immigration and residential control of foreign nationals in the name of tackling with the reduction of 'illegal immigrants'. In terms of immigration control, in addition to the implementation of the Advance Passenger Information System (APIS) and the dispatch of liaison officers since 2005, new immigration procedure has been introduced since November 2007 that requires foreign nationals to submit their biometrical identification information such as fingerprints and a facial photograph at immigration control (Ministry of Justice 2008). Turning to residential control, following the strengthening of the punishment against employers of irregular immigrants in 2004, immigration bureau eagerly denounced and reported these employers to the police (Ministry of Justice 2006). Furthermore, the new system of residence management of foreign nationals is expected to be introduced in July 2012, which will enable the Minister of Justice to continuously collect and keep extensive personal information of foreign nationals (Ministry of Justice 2010).

While these various criminal and immigration measures in Japan can be situated in the globalisation of what Weber and Bowling (2004) term 'sites of enforcement' for migration policing, there appears to be a significant local character in the context of how this new culture of social control is invoked in Japan. As seen above, in the US and European countries, the recent phenomenon of criminalisation of immigration has been mainly displayed in the context of the counterterrorism and the deterrence of the increase of immigrants and asylum seekers. In contrast, the 'War on Illegal Immigrants' in Japan was principally invoked in the context of ordinary crime control rather than as part of the 'War on Terror' or the 'problem' of immigration. Accordingly, in attempting to explain recent Japanese police stop and account as part of the 'War on Illegal Immigrants', we should uncover the political and cultural implications which enabled to establish this extraordinary policy and practice in the context of ordinary crime control. Studies to address this question will consider the complicated interaction of national narratives in relation to crime and ethnicity in Japan, and the corresponding apparatus of globalisation.

Stop and account as the site for the interaction between national narratives and the apparatus of globalisation

Conventionally, policing of ordinary crime in Japan, especially the patrol work of *koban*, has long been favourably displayed as an ideal of community policing (Bayley 1991). Although the effectiveness of the *koban* system has been questioned with the thinning of social relations since the late 1980s, the National Police Agency has been continuously promoting *koban* as the local patrol centres for community safety (Leishman 1999). This unique style of Japanese policing has been frequently linked to the specific cultural explanation of the Japanese low crime rate, exemplified by what Braithwaite terms 'reintegrative shaming', namely that shaming in Japan occurs enough to prevent repeat offending, but is not sufficient to stigmatise offenders (Braithwaite 1989). The following account of an interview with an irregular immigrant, despite the experience of police stop and account in the wake of the Sarin Gas Attack in Tokyo in 1995, appears to resonate with this characterisation of Japanese policing:

> Just after Shoko Asahara [then the leader of the Aum Shinrikyo] did something evil on the train, I was questioned by a police officer in the Tokyo station. He asked me, 'Excuse me. Where are you from? Do you have a visa?' When I replied, 'I don't have a visa', he just told me, 'Why don't you go back to your country? Please return there'. (Suzuki 2010, p. 70)

Recent Japanese policy and practice of stop and account against irregular immigrants, however, seems to be at least partly contradictory to this conventional explanation of policing in Japan. Rather, this policy and practice appears to suit the alternative explanation of Japanese policing elaborated by Japanese professor Setsuo Miyazawa. According to Miyazawa (1992), Japanese police officers are less interested in reintegration than in operating in a highly 'enabling' legal environment, namely, extending the already considerable legal resources available to them as much as possible. From this perspective, recent police stop and account in Japan can be seen as an extensive response by the Japanese police to the changing environment of the policy regarding irregular immigrants rather than to a change of style or culture of policing itself. Following Miyazawa, in what follows, the political and cultural implications which led to the establishment of this environment will be examined.

Interaction between the national narrative of a most secure society and the apparatus of global penal populism

The policy of 'War on Illegal Immigrants' was established in the midst of allegations of rising fear of crime and increasing punitiveness in Japan, arguably comparable to the phenomenon of the 'reassurance gap' in Britain displayed by Innes (2004). Although Japan has long enjoyed the crime-related privilege as being one of the safest industrialised countries since the Second World War, this punitive trend of Japanese criminal policy has significantly developed since the late 1990s, with the public losing confidence in the safety and trust of the criminal justice system. For example, a survey conducted in 2004 by the Cabinet Office (2004) showed that 86.6% of respondents replied that public security had worsened over the past 10 years. As a number of commentators note, this phenomenon has been shaped through the media coverage of crime and the influence of the victim's movement, and thus reveals rising populism in Japan (Hamai and Ellis 2006, Johnson 2007, Miyazawa 2008). For example, according to Hamai and Ellis (2006), in the late 1990s, press coverage of police scandals fundamentally changed the way the press reported on policing issues, and then led to policy reactions that ensured more 'trivial' crimes were reported and recorded. This change, they argue, brought about the rise of the crime rate and the fall of the detection rate, and thus resulted in a hardening of the public attitude to crime and punishment through promotion by the media and victim support movement.

This rising populism in Japanese criminal justice policy can be situated in line with the global trend of what Pratt calls 'penal populism', along with many Western countries, especially with Anglo-American countries (Pratt 2007). According to Pratt (2007), the development of strong relationships between governments and extra-government forces such as 'law and order' groups, victim's rights activists and mass media which claim to speak on behalf of the public can be seen. As a result, he argues, such representations of public opinion have become more embedded in policy development, and the criminal justice 'establishments' have become less influential on government policy. Whereas Pratt points out that this has led to the development of a 'penal language of populism' articulated in commonsensical and easily understandable phrases, he posits that populist responses to crime are strongest when they are concerned with 'a common enemy, a group of criminals who seem utterly different from the rest of the population', as it increases the sense of anxiety and tension which characterises everyday life in late modernity (Pratt 2007, p. 5).

While this global trend of penal populism appears to reflect the social and cultural changes prevailing in modern societies, the modalities of the shift can differ in each society. In the context of Japan, it seems that penal populism can be best understood as the political movement for the restoration of a 'most secure society', as shown in the subtitle of the Action Plan, namely, 'To Restore Japan as the Most Secure Country in the World'. This understanding of Japanese penal populism appears to be able to explain its significant characteristics, that is, the preservation of a low crime rate and extraordinary hostility against 'illegal immigrants'. In terms of the preservation of the low crime rate, as a number of recent surveys show, the crime rate in Japan, especially for violent crime, still remains significantly lower than industrialised countries. As Hamai and Ellis posit (2006), from a comparative perspective, it is possible to see that the increase in fear of crime in Japan is disproportionate to the relatively low level of risk. They explain this discrepancy between the low crime rate and increasing fears of crime among the Japanese public in terms of what Cohen (1972) terms 'moral panic', and argue that this moral panic has been almost institutionalised in Japan (Hamai and Ellis 2006). In the meantime, this institutionalisation of crime-related moral panic seems to be prompted by the national narrative of a most secure society which is deeply rooted in the public imagination. As Japanese sociologist Kawai (2004) describes, the general sense of 'collapse of secure society' has led to a more specific and personalised fear that crime is occurring in the area where they live. This personally internalised fear, in turn, has been aggregated into punitiveness in Japanese criminal policy through the political movement for restoration of a most secure society.

Against this backdrop of development of penal populism in Japan, extraordinary hostility against 'illegal immigrants' has been surging, with the prevalence of discourse of 'illegal immigrants as hotbed of crime' as appeared in the aforementioned Action Plan. Critically it is this discourse that has brought about the 'enabling' legal environment in which the recent Japanese policy of stop and account as part of the 'War on Illegal Immigrants' has been established. In fact, the number of irregular immigrants detected by the police for criminal offences was only 1403 in 2003, occupying a trivial 0.4% of the total. In terms of felonious offences such as homicide, robbery, arson and rape, the number of detected irregular immigrants was just 175 in 2003, accounting for only 2.1% of the total (National Police Agency 2010). Nevertheless, irregular immigrants have been rapidly regarded as the most probable criminal offenders among the public. For example, the aforementioned survey by the Cabinet Office (2004) revealed that of those who replied that public security had worsened over the past 10 years, 54.4% believed that the deterioration in public security was caused by an increase in 'illegal immigrants'. While the emergence of this seemingly unsound crime-related hostility against irregular immigrants appears to be situated in line with global penal populism and the trend of creating a 'common enemy' (Pratt 2007), this exclusionary tendency seems to have been magnificently stimulated by the political movement for the restoration of a most secure society. By excluding irregular immigrants as a threat to the exceptional crime-related privilege of living in safe Japan, Japanese society has been making painstaking efforts to revive the national narrative of a most secure society.

Interaction between the national narrative of homogeneous nation and the apparatus of global population movement

Whereas the national narrative of a most secure society has played a significant role in establishing the policy of police stop and account as part of the 'War on Illegal Immigrants', the almost complete achievement of this policy can be attributed to another national narrative in Japan, namely, the 'homogenous nation'. It has long been said that Japan is an ethnically homogenous society as a consequence of historical and cultural peculiarities, largely through the experience of many centuries of 'closed country policy'. Although it has been recently argued that the myth of Japanese homogeneity as a self-contained, unique and ethnically pure nation was created only after the Second World War (Oguma 2002), it has rapidly acquired the greatest acceptance among the Japanese public. A number of commentators addressed this xenophobic culture of the Japanese to the extent that they believed that 'the requirement of preserving a culture is the total exclusion of persons belonging to other ethnic groups' (Anderson 1996, p. 128). This perception of a homogenous nation, combined with the effect of the international order at times of the Cold War, greatly supported tight immigration and residential control of foreigners in Japanese immigration policy in the post-war era (Morris-Suzuki 2010).

While the myth of a homogenous nation has been gradually threatened by the indigenous people movement and the phenomenon of gradual inflows of foreign workers since the 1980s, it appears to have remained firmly among the Japanese public, including criminal justice 'establishments'. It is possible to see that this national narrative deeply rooted in public imagination has led to the lack of discourse of ethnicity in Japanese criminology, and the creation of category of 'crimes committed by foreigners' by Japanese criminal officials. In terms of the absence of discourse of ethnicity, until the 1980s, most immigrants in Japan had been the Korean and the Chinese who entered Japan by force and voluntarily before and during the Second World War. These ethnic minority groups, however, as Kawai (2004) posits, have almost never been the subject of studies of criminology, as the subject of ethnicity has been cautiously avoided through the reflection on discriminatory treatment against these groups in the pre-war era. This self-reflective attitude of Japanese criminal justice 'establishments' towards ethnicity, arguably supported by the enduring public imagination of a homogenous nation, has continued even after the development of global population movement to Japan mostly from Asian countries since the 1980s. This absence of discourse of ethnicity in Japanese criminology can be exemplified by the phenomenon that it is almost impossible to see any reference to ethnicity in official criminal reports and policy papers, including the aforementioned Action Plan, despite the trend towards multi-culturalisation in Japanese society (Ministry of Internal Affairs and Communications 2006).

Instead of the discourse of ethnicity, Japanese criminal officials have created the category of 'crimes committed by foreigners' against the increase of foreign workers since the 1990s. For example, the White Paper on the Police 1993 emphasised the increase of 'crimes committed by foreigners', along with their characteristics such as being committed by an organisation, the increase of vicious crime, and the spread towards regional cities (National Police Agency 1993). This implicit characterisation of foreigners as potential criminal offenders has gradually taken hold in the Japanese public during 1990s, through the implied differentiation from the rest of the population by the national narrative of homogenous nation. With the development of penal populism promoted by the media and victims support movement since the late 1990s, this categorisation of 'crimes committed by foreigners' has acquired a status of ordinary phrase in Japanese society.

These lack of discourse of ethnicity and creation of the category of 'crimes committed by foreigners' as the derivation of the national narrative of homogenous nation appear to have greatly contributed to the policy and practice of police stop and account against irregular immigrants. In the phase of the establishment of police stop and account policy, the absence of discourse of ethnicity in criminology made it possible for policy makers to utterly ignore the risk of discrimination against foreign-looking people. It appears that they wrongfully maintained the image of Japan as a homogenous nation, and thus oversaw the possibility of Japanese with foreign appearance being the subject of police stop and account. Meanwhile, the categorisation of 'crimes committed by foreigners' has led to the justification of foreigners being the subject of police stop and account regardless of their immigration status, as they are regarded as suspicious people solely on the basis of their nationality. In the stage of implementation of police stop and account practice, with the justification of discourse and categorisation, police officers in patrol are allowed to freely stop and question any persons with foreign appearance without any reasonable suspicion of having committed crimes. More accurately, patrolling police officers are forced to conduct discriminatory stop and account against foreign-looking people solely on the ground that these people have a foreign appearance. In this way, Japanese stop and account against irregular immigrants has been utilised as a tool for the reinforcement of the national narrative of homogenous nation against the apparatus of global population movement.

Conclusion

Returning to the account cited at the outset, after being arrested for the non-possession of a passport, this foreign-looking Japanese woman was finally released as her mother could confirm her identity. In contrast, numerous police stop and account cases against foreign nationals have been continuously dumped into the dark where these cases are turned into mere parts of an accepted pattern in Japanese society. In the context of Japan, while the normalisation of exclusionary stop and account reflects the global trend of criminalisation of immigration, this 'local solutions to globally produced problems' (Bauman 2004, p. 6) was shaped through the interaction between the national narratives of a most secure society and homogeneous nation, and the globalisation of penal populism and population movement. On reflection, faced with the anxiety and tension in late modernity, every form of policing might more or less reflect an idealised 'imagined community' in each society (Anderson 1983). If this is the case, Japanese policy and practice of police stop and account might reflect the chillingly idealised community among the Japanese public against global population movement, namely, 'zero undesirable immigrants on our soil'.

Notes

1. See Yoshida and Leishman (2006) for the examination of recent activity and function of the *koban* system in Japan.
2. As of the end of 2009, the total number of foreign national residents in Japan is 2,186,121, accounting for 1.71% of the total population, approximately 127,510,000. Of these registered foreign nationals, Chinese marked the largest number at 680,518, accounting for 31.1%, followed by North and South Korean (578,495 for 26.5%), Brazilian (267,456 for 12.2%), Filipino (211,716 for 9.7%), and Peruvian (57,464 for 2.6%). See Ministry of Justice (2010).

3. In Japan, whereas police power of stop and account is set out in primary legislation, stop and search is not a legally defined power, though police officers have been exercising the power of stop and search subject to the consent of the person.
4. This survey was conducted by way of distributing questionnaires among foreign nationals who visited a legal consultation centre in Tokyo Bar Association, and among those who linked to a number of NGOs for immigrants.

References

Aas, K., 2007. *Globalization and crime.* London: Sage Publications.

Anderson, B., 1983. *Imagined communities.* London: Verso.

Anderson, M., 1996. *Frontiers: territory and state foundation in the modern world.* Cambridge: Polity Press.

Asahi Shinbun, 2006. Mistakenly arrested a Japanese women For the non-possession of passport. *Asahi Shinbun*, 28 Feb,

Bayley, D., 1991. *Forces of order.* Berkeley: University of California Press.

Bauman, Z., 2004. *Wasted lives: modernity and its outcasts.* Cambridge: Polity Press.

Bowling, B. and Phillips, C., 2007. Disproportionate and discriminatory: reviewing the evidence on police stop and search. *Modern Law Review*, 70 (6), 936–961.

Braithwaite, J., 1989. *Crime, shame and reintegration.* Cambridge: Cambridge University Press.

Cabinet Office, 2004. *Report on the national survey of public security.* Available from: http://www8.cao.go.jp/survey/h16/h16-chian/index.html [Accessed at 29 July 2011].

Cohen, S., 1972. *Folk devils and moral panics.* London: MacGibbon and Kee.

Cole, D., 2005. *Enemy aliens: double standards and constitutional freedoms in the war on terrorism.* New York: New Press.

Fekete, L., 2005. The deportation machine: Europe, asylum and human rights. *Race and Class*, 49 (1), 64–91.

Garland, D., 2001. *The culture of control.* Oxford: Oxford University Press.

Giddens, A., 1990. *The consequences of modernity.* Cambridge: Polity Press.

Hamai, K. and Ellis, T., 2006. Crime and criminal justice in modern Japan: from re-integrative shaming to popular punitivism. *International Journal of the Sociology of Law*, 34 (3), 157–178.

Innes, M., 2004. Signal crimes and signal disorders: notes on deviance as communicative action. *British Journal of Sociology*, 55, 335–355.

Johnson, D., 2007. Crime and punishment in contemporary Japan. *Crime and Justice*, 36 (1), 371–423.

Kawai, M., 2004. *Paradox of the collapse of myth of secure society.* Tokyo: Iwanami Shoten.

Krasmann, S., 2007. The enemy of the border: critique of a programme in favour of a preventive State. *Punishment and Society*, 9 (3), 301–318.

Leishman, F., 1999. Policing in Japan: east Asian archetype? *In*: R.I. Mawby, ed. *Policing across the world: issues for the twenty-first century.* London: University College London Press.

Ministerial Conference Against Crime, 2003. *Action Plan to create a society resistant to crime.* Available from: http://www.kantei.go.jp/jp/singi/hanzai/kettei/031218keikaku.html [Accessed 29 July 2011].

Ministry of Internal Affairs and Communications, 2006. *Report on the promotion of multicultural coexistence: towards the promotion of multicultural coexistence in community.* Available from: http://www.soumu.go.jp/kokusai/pdf/sonota_b5.pdf [Accessed 29 July 2011].

Ministry of Justice, 2006. *2006 Immigration control.* Available from: http://www.moj.go.jp/content/000007279.pdf [Accessed 29 July 2011].

Ministry of Justice, 2008. *2008 Immigration control.* Available from: http://www.moj.go.jp/content/000007317.pdf [Accessed 29 July 2011].

Ministry of Justice, 2009. *On the result of implementation of the Five-Year Plan to Halve the Number of Illegal Immigrants.* Available from: http://www.moj.go.jp/nyuukokukanri/kouhou/press_090217-1.html [Accessed 29 July 2011].

Ministry of Justice, 2010. *2010 Immigration control*. Available from: http://www.moj.go.jp/content/000058064.pdf [Accessed 29 July 2011].

Ministry of Justice, Tokyo Immigration Bureau, Tokyo Metropolis and the Metropolitan Police Department, 2003. *Joint declaration on the strengthening of measures against illegal immigrants in Tokyo Metropolis*. Available from: http://www.seisyounen-chian.metro.tokyo.jp/chian/gaikokujin/kyoudousengen.htm [Accessed 29 July 2011].

Miyazawa, S., 1992. *Policing in Japan: a study on making crime*. Albany: State University of New York Press.

Miyazawa, S., 2008. The politics of increasing punitiveness and the rising populism in Japanese criminal justice policy. *Punishment and Society*, 10 (1), 47–71.

Morris-Suzuki, T., 2010. *Borderline Japan: Foreigners and frontier controls in the postwar era*. Cambridge: Cambridge University Press.

National Police Agency, 1993. *White paper on police*. Available from: http://www.npa.go.jp/hakusyo/h05/h05index.html [Accessed 29 July 2011].

National Police Agency, 2010. *Situation of the cleared offences committed by foreign nationals visiting Japan*. Available from: http://www.npa.go.jp/sosikihanzai/kokusaisousa/kokusai/H21_K_RAINICHI.pdf [Accessed 29 July 2011].

Oguma, E., 2002. *A genealogy of 'Japanese' self-images*. Melbourne: Trans Pacific Press.

Pratt, J., 2007. *Penal populism*. London: Routledge.

Suzuki, E., 2010. Irregular migrants and Japanese society. *In*: A. Kondo, Y. Shiobara, and E. Suzuki, eds. *Irregular migrants and the special permission to stay*. Tokyo: Nippon Hyoronsha.

Tokyo Bar Association, 2007. *Report on questionnaire on stop and account against foreign nationals*. Tokyo: Tokyo Bar Association.

Weber, L. and Bowling, B., 2004. Policing migration: a framework for investigating the regulation of global mobility. *Policing and Society*, 14 (3), 195–212.

Yoshida, N. and Leishman, F., 2006. Japan. *In*: T. Jones and T. Newburn, eds. *Plural policing: a comparative perspective*. Oxford: Routledge.

Ethnic profiling in the Netherlands? A reflection on expanding preventive powers, ethnic profiling and a changing social and political context

Joanne P. van der Leun and Maartje A.H. van der Woude

Department of Criminal Law and Criminology, University of Leiden, Leiden, The Netherlands

Over the past decades the Netherlands has developed into a culture of control in which criminals and immigrants are mainly seen as 'dangerous others'. Tying in with this emergence of the culture of control is the development of a more preventive criminal justice system. By means of expanding preventive powers the criminal justice system is more and more aimed at detecting risky (groups of) persons as soon as possible. This so-called actuarial justice is accompanied by a great deal of discretionary power on the hands of those who have to enforce the law, bearing the risk that such powers may be carried out (in part) on the basis of generalisations relating to race, ethnicity, religion or nationality instead of on the basis of individual behaviour and/or objective evidence. The leading assumption in this article is that recent social, political and legal developments have increased the possibility for ethnic profiling in the Netherlands. Being a country of immigration, mostly immigrants tend to fall victim to these practices. Illustrated by the stop and search powers that have been introduced at municipal level in 2002 and in 2006 in the context of counterterrorism, the authors not only aim to provide insight into the complexity of actuarial justice in relation to ethnic profiling in the Netherlands but also aim to fuel the scientific debate on empirically researching ethnic profiling.

Introduction

Racial and ethnic profiling have been primarily linked to characteristics of police culture in the existing, rather Anglo-American-centred, literature. The present article on the Dutch case takes a different stance by linking issues of profiling to changing social, political and legal developments. Over the past decades, the Dutch criminal justice landscape has changed. Whereas Adler (1983) indicated the Netherlands as a country not obsessed with crime, and Kommer (1994) referred to it as a 'beacon of enlightenment and tolerance' with regard to its penal climate, neither of these statements will hold anymore nowadays. Crime and fear of crime have become important spearheads of Dutch governmental policy. Despite dropping crime rates since 2002, incarceration rates are high, the penal system is sober and the public and political discourse on crime and potential 'dangerous others' is far from tolerant (Downes and Van Swaaningen 2007). Although the impact and aftermath of the

9/11 terrorist attacks have contributed to these changes, in fact, the attacks fertilised an already lush breeding ground. Lingering apprehensions of the Dutch multicultural society were raised, and issues of immigration, integration and the overrepresentation of non-western ethnic minorities[1] in registered crime statistics were given a hitherto unknown acuteness (van der Woude 2010).

As Eijkman (2010, p. 2) also observes, the supposed relationship between ethnicity and social problems, especially crime and nuisance, has progressively become a political issue, resulting in extreme political statements including the calls for the 'deportation of convicted criminals with Moroccan nationality' and 'special stop and searches for Antillean youths in Rotterdam' (Maasstad Pers 2010). The development of a discourse in which minority groups are increasingly seen and addressed as 'dangerous others', comparable to criminals, is part of a broader process of crimmigration – the merging of migration policy and crime control – in the Netherlands (Stumpf 2006, Van der Leun 2010).

This has put an increasing pressure on law enforcement officials to profile on the basis of race or nationality. Dutch police, for instance, carried out targeted 'stop and searches' questioning the identity of specific groups of aliens, such as West Africans, as well as extra alcohol controls for foreign drivers, especially those coming from Poland (Nationale Ombudsman 2009, KLPD 2010). Moreover, countless policy measures – and special funds have been introduced to deal specifically with crime problems and disorder amongst youngsters with an Antillean and Moroccan background, the main 'symbolic suspects' at the moment. Despite the growing complexity of the relationship between crime and ethnicity and the therewith connected pressure on law enforcement officials, until now, there has been little systematic research on ethnic profiling in the Netherlands (Van der Leun *et al.* 2010). The leading assumption in this article is that recent social, political and legal developments have increased the possibility for ethnic profiling in the Netherlands. As the Open Society Justice Initiative concluded in an extensive report on ethnic profiling in the European Union (OSJI 2009), ethnic profiling is not only impermissible under international law but can also contribute to feelings of polarisation and stigmatisation among those who are subjected to it. On the other hand, police and other services that are increasingly expected to work intelligence-led have much better computerised data at their disposal than in earlier times, and profiling techniques in general have become widely used. This in combination with political and public pressure to solve issues in which migrants are involved – and sometimes overrepresented almost inherently creates tensions which cannot be ignored. Theoretically, this also sheds a different light on the traditional explanations for ethnic profiling.

We will first discuss some important social and political changes that have contributed to the securitisation of Dutch society, creating a climate in which criminals and immigrants are often seen and framed as potentially 'dangerous'. Tying in with these changes, we will go into the development of a more preventive criminal justice system, particularly focusing on expanding preventive law enforcement powers. Furthermore, we will address the issue of ethnic profiling in relation to the aforementioned developments. Due to the lack of solid empirical research, we will conclude with recommendations with respect to a future research agenda.

The emergence of a Dutch culture of control

The government paper *Crime and Society* (Ministry of Justice 1985) is generally taken to be the decisive point of change in Dutch criminal justice policy. Gradually a more business-like, centralised, bureaucratised and efficiency-oriented criminal justice policy was implemented with the goal to counter the rising crime rate as efficiently as possible (Rutherford 1996, pp. 60–61). Due to steeply rising crime rates combined with an increasingly 'liquid' and individualistic society (Bauman 2000, Boutellier 2004), concerns among the population grew and government officials feared for the public's the loss of confidence in the government (Roethof Commission 1984, p. 1).

Since then, criminal law was, and still is, seen as one of the most important means to counter the perceived loss of social control. The developments have clearly resulted in a more managerial conception of criminal law and the criminal justice system (Rutherford 1996, pp. 65–72). Despite widely shared criticism among academics, slowly but securely a rather Garlandian culture of control (Garland 2001) has emerged with almost predictable consequences, such as rising prison rates, a massively expansive criminal justice machinery and a firm 'law and order' discourse in order to protect the public (Pakes 2004, Van Swaaningen 2005, Downes and Van Swaaningen 2007). One of the key indices of the Dutch version of the culture of control concerns growing negative sentiments about immigration policy and immigrants, both in public and political discourse (Pakes 2004, Cavadino and Dignan 2006, Engbersen *et al.* 2007).

The Netherlands as immigration country

From the early 1960s on, the Netherlands can be considered a country of immigration, albeit a reluctant one. In this 'Golden Age' of the Dutch welfare state, 'guest workers' were recruited from the Mediterranean in order to fill the job surplus. Only much later when they started bringing their families over it began to dawn that many of them were going to stay. In the 1970s, almost half of the non-Dutch immigrants to the Netherlands came from Turkey, Morocco, Surinam, Netherlands Antilles and Indonesia. In the 1990s, the percentage of these five immigrant groups steadily declined. Since then, the share of immigrants from other countries increased from 30% in the early 1980s to more than 55% in the first years of the twenty-first century (Engbersen *et al.* 2007). This includes a sizable asylum immigration and contemporary labour migration. The Dutch government started easing its immigration rules concerning the highly-skilled aliens in October 2004 (IND 2004). At the same time, immigration from other EU countries persists and has recently been rising, particularly since Poland, Bulgaria and Romania joined the EU respectively in 2004 and 2007 (Engbersen *et al.* 2011). Next to that a significant number of undocumented migrants reside in the country who are increasingly viewed through a crime control lens (Van der Leun and Ilies 2010).

A changing public and political discourse on migration, integration and (fear) of crime

For a long time the dominant policy model was based on multiculturalism. In line with the Dutch tradition of 'pillarisation', compartmentalisation along socio-political lines, there were special arrangements for immigrants, financed by the state (WRR 2007, p. 15). Incorporation policies aimed at 'mutual adaptation in a multicultural society with equal' (WRR 1979). Although there appeared to be consensus because migration problems were rarely openly discussed, discontent with failing integration in particular of groups with a Muslim background simmered.

The 2002 governmental elections in the Netherlands are often seen as a 'watershed' moment in the discussions surrounding immigration. Worries suddenly came to the fore in a very loud and open way. The rise in prominence on the Dutch political spectrum of Pim Fortuyn, an outspoken critic of 'multiculturalism' revealed a sense of uncertainty, insecurity and dissatisfaction among the population (Geddes 2003, p. 118). The issues are not exclusively claimed by right-wing parties and the fine-tuning of migration and integration still takes place within the present coalition. Three 'key' events strongly contributed to this development: the 9/11 attacks, Pim Fortuyn and the murder of movie maker Theo van Gogh (Engbersen *et al.* 2007). Pakes, who also points out these three events, speaks of a 'cultural-security complex' (2004, p. 293). The described paradigm shift in migration and integration policies is accompanied by an increased negative and often openly xenophobic 'us versus them' discourse by national and local politicians and the media (Zedner 2005, see also Namba, this issue).

Researching crime and disorder

Over the years, many studies found an over-representation of certain groups of immigrants and their offspring in official crime statistics, also when controlling for demographic and socio-economic differences (Haen Marshall 1997, Engbersen *et al.* 2007). At present Antilleans and second generation Moroccans stand out in a negative way (Blom *et al.* 2005). In the 1980s and 1990s most available studies pointed to the issue of selectivity: the fact that police data, crime registrations and data of the judicial system are inherently biased because they depend on police policies and routines and complex decision-making processes (Sampson and Lauritsen 1997). Crimes which are relatively often committed by immigrants are highly visible types of crime.

The Dutch Aliens Act and the Identification Act were explicitly designed to prevent discrimination of foreigners. According to some this aim has succeeded (Junger-Tas 1997, Boekhoorn *et al.* 2004), others doubt that. For instance, early studies reported that negative stereotyping of non-western immigrants is not uncommon among police officers (Bovenkerk 1991). Junger (1990) maintained that ethnic selectivity by the police often arises from the desire to optimise the 'organizational output' given limited police resources rather than from discrimination. Yet, Bowling (1990) argued that she overlooked influential filtering processes by the police which are shaped by institutional police practices and beliefs.

Junger (1989) maintained that because no study showed clear evidence of police discrimination in the Netherlands and because the country had a 'liberal tradition', ethnic bias was not a plausible explanation for group differences in crime figures. In a review study of two decades ago, Rovers also concluded that at the stage of arrest there was no ground to assume a selective approach towards individuals from a migrant background (Rovers 1999, cf. Wittebrood 2004). Since then, Dutch criminological literature usually accepts that selective law enforcement influences but not causes or explains ethnic differences in criminal involvement. Empirical studies on the aliens police and the immigration control task of the general police carried out in the 1990s demonstrated that the police at that time were very reluctant to stop and question allegedly illegally residing immigrants. This had to do with preventing discrimination but also with maintaining good community relations within neighbourhoods (Van der Leun 2003). At the moment it is not clear if or to what extent recent anti-immigration sentiments in the Netherlands have affected relations between immigrants and the police, which were traditionally relatively good. Moreover, legal and administrative changes and the increased availability of computerised data may also have changed the scene.

Actuarial justice and the urge to pursue collective security

Over the past two decades, fighting crime and fears has become prominent on the Dutch political agenda. The name change of the Ministry of Justice into the Ministry of Security and Justice in October 2010 by the current government is telling in that sense. It reflects the emergence of a culture of control, in which collective security and shielding society from possible security risks are seen as the most important goals. Less attention is paid to individual rights especially since the public also seems willing to accept restrictions upon their individual rights and liberties if that is what it takes (Muller *et al.* 2007). The answer to the perceived increase in crime and insecurity is mostly found in a more preventive criminal law, also referred to as actuarial justice (Feeley and Simon 1994, De Roos 2007, pp. 129–149). The term refers to the increasing focus on the early detection and prevention of possible crime threats and risks (Moerings 2003). By using risk assessments, by broadening criminal liability by means of criminalising behaviour in preliminary stages before a harmful act has taken place, by introducing new and harsher penalties and by introducing new potentially intrusive investigatory powers, everything is aimed at detecting and 'disarming' risky and possibly dangerous (groups of) persons as soon as possible (Feeley and Simon 1992, pp. 452, 457).

The introduction of stop and search powers at municipal level in 2002 and in 2006 in the context of counterterrorism is one of the (many) concrete manifestations of actuarial justice in the Netherlands. In the following section, we will first discuss the legal context, before reflecting on actuarial justice in relation to ethnic profiling.

The legal context of stop and search powers in the Netherlands

Many of the previously mentioned changes in the Dutch criminal justice system can somehow be related to high crime figures for violent crimes in the 1990s, and the subsequent public and political unrest. This also holds for the introduction of preventive stop and search powers in 2002. The answer was found in the possibility to perform preventive security searches amongst citizens in designated areas that were seen to be more prone to attract violence or public order problems. Before 2002, law enforcement officials could carry out searches if there was a reasonable suspicion of a criminal offense and in order to establish one's identity (art. 55b Code of Criminal Procedure). Preventive searches were limited to airports only (art. 52 lid 3 Weapons and Ammunitions Act).

The legal basis for the 2002 expansion of preventive searches can be found in both the Municipalities Act and the Weapons and Ammunitions Act. After having consulted the municipal council and the public prosecutor, the powers to stop and search are vested in the mayor, by means of a by-law. The mayor decides which areas can be designated as 'security risk zones' in which anyone can be subjected to a 'preventive search' by police officers during a period of 12 hours. The police are empowered by the authority of the public prosecutor to search any individual as well as goods and vehicles, without having grounds for suspicion. The fact that these areas have been the stage of violent weapon-incidents in the past is sufficient to designate them as 'security risk zones' (*Kamerstukken II* 2000/2001, 26 865, nr. 7, pp. 2–3). Preventive searches can also be carried out as part of large scaled traffic controls, also known as 'phishing actions'. During these actions, bearing illustrious names such as 'Operation Dawn' and 'Operation Twilight', roadblocks are raised on parts of the highway in order to randomly check the cars that are present (see also Marks and Belur, this issue). Motorists are checked for their drivers-licenses, insurances, but also for outstanding fines, tax debts and residence permits. Besides all this, occupants as well as their luggage might also be subjected to preventive searching. The legal context of these actions has been disputed: questions have been raised about the legitimacy as well as the effectiveness (Salet 2009). All this has not contributed to a reserved attitude with regard to exercising stop and search powers: Over the years 2003, 2004, 2005 and 2006 both in Amsterdam and Rotterdam together, respectively, 47.409, 48.406, 29.786 and 18.005 preventive searches were carried out (COT 2007, p. 68). Over the year 2007 data are missing, but in Amsterdam 15.973 preventive searches were carried out in 2008 (COT 2009, p. 6).

Stop and search in the context of counterterrorism

Another body of law fitting within the trends described is Dutch counterterrorism legislation. Shortly after the 9/11 attacks in the United States, the then Dutch government announced a comprehensive action plan against Terrorism with the Action Plan Counter-Terrorism and Security (*Kamerstukken II* 2001/2002, 27 925, nr. 10). The plan contained a sizeable range of (inter)national measures for the intensification of the fight against terrorism (De Boer 2007). Besides a vast array of policy and institutional measures, a wide range of legislative measures has been taken. In this article, we will specifically focus on the Act on expanding the scope for investigating and prosecuting terrorist crimes (*Kamerstukken II* 2004/2005, 30 164). Under this act, the threshold triggering special investigative powers, such as observation, infiltration, undercover purchase and wire-tapping, is lowered. It is no longer required to have a reasonable suspicion of a criminal offence, mere 'indications' that a terrorist attack is being prepared are sufficient. Such indications are deemed to exist when the facts and circumstances *suggest* that a terrorist offense is being prepared. When there are indications of terrorist activity, the public prosecutor can give a verbal order to exercise stop and search powers during a 12 hour period in designated 'terrorist risk areas', a period which may be extended indefinitely (Art. 126zq, 126zr and 127zs Code of Criminal Procedure). Within the context of counterterrorism it is also possible for police officers to perform preventive searches without a preceding order by the public prosecutor in specific permanent security areas. Examples are: the Houses of Parliament, all airports, the train stations of the four major cities Amsterdam, The Hague, Rotterdam and Utrecht, the Media Park in Hilversum and the nuclear power station in Borssele (Art. 126 zq-zs Code of Criminal Procedure).

Ethnic profiling as a lurking danger of expanding preventive powers

The development of actuarial justice has resulted in an increase of discretionary powers for law enforcement officials. There is a risk that such activities may be carried out (in part) on the basis of generalisations relating to race, ethnicity, religion or nationality instead of on the basis of individual behaviour and/or objective evidence. This may be expressed directly or indirectly in the decisions of supervisory and/or investigative officials, regarding matters such as who they detain for identity checks, interrogation, security searches and sometimes arrest. Focal concerns and attribution theory in relation to sentencing research have shown that when faced with time and information restraints, judges tend to resort to a 'perceptual shorthand' to make decisions about the dangerousness and risk of recidivism of an offender (Tillyer and Hartley 2010). This shorthand is based on stereotypes and attributions linked to personal characteristics thereby providing an explanation for extralegal factors such as gender, race, ethnicity and social class being influential in sentencing outcomes (Steffensmeier *et al.* 1998). Recent research by Weenink (2009) supports the notion of perceptual shorthand influencing Dutch prosecutorial decision-making in juvenile justice cases. It is equally conceivable that police officers may develop similar shorthands. Especially while exercising investigative powers without the necessity of there being a reasonable suspicion or concrete indications one has to resort to something other than concrete offender-information to base one's decision on. Categorisation and stereotyping are inherent to police work (Wilson 1989, Bridges 1999, Philips and Bowling 2003, Bowling and Philips 2007, Miller 2010).

From a theoretical perspective it thus seems fair to seriously consider the possibility of ethnic profiling in relation to actuarial justice in the Netherlands, especially against the background of the development of a cultural-security complex. Ethnic profiling can be defined as 'the use by police, security, immigration or customs officials of generalizations based on race, ethnicity, religion or national origin – rather than individual behavior or objective evidence – as the basis for suspicion in directing discretionary law enforcement actions. It can also include situations where law enforcement policies and practices, although not themselves defined either wholly or in part by reference to ethnicity race, national origin or religion, nevertheless do have a disproportionate impact on such groups within the population and where this cannot otherwise be justified in terms of legitimate law enforcement objectives and outcomes' (OSJI 2009, p. 2). Although there is no explicit prohibition of ethnic profiling in Dutch legislation or regulations, it is a form of direct discrimination and therefore in defiance of the right to equal treatment and the ban on discrimination as included in the first article of the Dutch Constitution as well as in several international treaties that are directly applicable in the Netherlands (Eijkman 2010).

In recent years a couple of reports showed that the risk of ethnic profiling is not just a theoretical 'threat' for the Netherlands anymore: From the 2009 European Union Minorities and Discrimination Survey (EU-MIDIS) it appeared that 25% of Dutch Muslims of Turkish origin interviewed had been stopped by the police at least once in 12 months prior to the survey and that of these individuals 25% had the impression that the stop was based on ethnicity. The corresponding figures for Dutch Muslims of North African origin were 26% and 39%, respectively (EU-FRA 2009, pp. 13–14). A 2010 survey by EU-MIDIS shows that in the Netherlands both North-African (66%), Turkish (61%) and Surinamese (67%) respondents feel that discrimination based on ethnicity is very or fairly widespread. Comparable figures for autochthonous 'white' Dutch people are unavailable. Yet, the outcomes match the results of the Special Eurobarometer 296 in which a similar question was asked: for the Netherlands 79% of the respondents were of the opinion that discrimination based on ethnicity is very or fairly widespread (EU-MIDIS-5: EU-FRA 2010). After persistent complaints of minority and migrant groups in European countries about their treatment by the police and other criminal justice partners, the *Open Society Justice Initiative* made an inventory of police stereotyping in the Netherlands, France, Germany, Italy and other EU-states. According to this report, ethnic profiling is not only exercised on a large scale within continental Europe (OSJI 2009). The *European Commission against Racism and Intolerance* is also highly critical towards the situation in the Netherlands. The Commission expresses its worries about the increase of ethnic profiling in relation to preventing and fighting terrorism but also gives a more general warning about the changed tone in political and public discourse regarding minorities (ECRI 2008).

Stop and search and ethnic profiling

During the drafting of the stop and search powers outside the context of counterterrorism, the danger of a selective use of these powers was occasionally addressed, but overall not highly disputed in parliament. Most critics of the bill were reassured by the legislator who referred to the professionalism of law enforcers and the randomness of checks. In practice, it turns out that law officials tend to pick their subjects mostly based on their own intuition and experience. Clear indications or objective criteria are difficult to deduce. During the parliamentary procedure of the counterterrorism legislation, the danger of selectively applying investigative powers and therewith contributing to feelings of stigmatisation among the targeted (minority) groups, possibly even fuelling processes of radicalisation, was pointed out (van der Woude 2009). However, the standard response by the Minister of Justice would be that 'it wouldn't come to a misuse or a prejudiced use of discretionary powers'. Unsurprisingly, this was also his response to the parliamentary debates about the counterterrorist stop and search powers as well as to the highly critical report of the Dutch Council of State in which the Council explicitly warned about the danger of religious and ethnic profiling of Muslims in the aftermath of 9/11 and Madrid (*Kamerstukken II* 2005–2006, 30 164, nr. 5, p. 6; nr. 7, p. 21–22). Although the Minister was of the opinion that the professional and objective expert opinion of law enforcement officials should be trusted, he also stated that is not unthinkable that skin colour and traditional (religious) attire can play a certain role in this selection (*Kamerstukken II* 2005/2006, 30 164, nr. 7, p. 23). Despite the explicit recommendation of the Suyver Committee in 2009, which had examined the necessity of an integral evaluation of the Dutch counterterrorism legislation, to evaluate the powers' (un)foreseen negative side effects such as, for instance, ethnic profiling, this topic remains unexamined still (van der Woude 2011).

Obviously there are several more specific powers as exercised by police officers or by other law enforcement officials, which may have repercussions in the area of ethnic profiling. Cases in point are identification checks and immigration controls. Expanded powers in these areas may very well affect the position of (alleged) irregular migrants. For instance, the most recent Aliens Act 2000, which came into force in 2001, includes several renewed and expanded provisions (artt. 50 and 53) for immigration authorities to carry out house searches for irregular migrants and also broadened the scope for stopping people in the street to ask for their identity and nationality. An independent evaluation in 2004 of the use of these powers under the renewed Aliens Act 2000 showed that the new powers were increasingly being used, which was indicated by rising numbers of immigrants being stopped and questioned (Boekhoorn *et al.* 2004). In addition, the amendment of the Identification Act by the Extended Identification Act on 1 January 2005 (Wet op de Uitgebreide Identificatieplicht) made it obligatory for every person over the age of 14 years to carry identification, whereas before this would hold only in specific situations.

Discussion: much research ground to be covered

The assumption that recent social, political and legal developments have increased the possibility for ethnic profiling in the Netherlands is strongly supported in the literature, policies and legislative changes reviewed above. A complex mix of background factors neatly fitting within the wider cultural-security complex is causing this changing opportunity structure for ethnic profiling. Yet, it should be realised that changing data infrastructures and emphasis on the need to use them (through, for instance, intelligence-led policing) have also contributed to these developments. In the existing Anglo-American literature, which is strongly focused on police culture and institutional racism, this aspect has received little attention.

With respect to research, we must conclude that sound and actual empirical research of the practice and effects of ethnic profiling is lacking, which is in stark contrast to the amount of research on the over-representation of migrants in registered crime and disorder. For a long time the selectivity discussion in the Netherlands was seen as old-fashioned. Researchers adopted a pragmatic stance, assuming that ethnic profiling or biased policing was not taking place. Still today, registered data are not readily available. Unlike in the UK there are no stop and search forms, and the police is not held accountable for their decisions as long as no complaints are filed.

Future research must find a way around the major problem that it is not clear what the baseline – normal treatment should be (Reitzel and Piquero 2006). With quantitative research, researchers may be able to show a disparity along ethnic lines, concluding that this is necessarily ethnic profiling is less clear-cut. Qualitative research, on the other hand, may unravel rationales behind police decisions. Therefore, a mixed approach appears to be most promising.

With respects to citizens' perceptions of police and police stops, we also have very little reliable studies, despite it being an important area of inquiry. If minority groups believe that they are treated differently, this may hugely impact on trust in the police and even backfire directly on police work.

A third type of research which is largely lacking are studies on the view of the police with respect to profiling. Rather than assuming that police officers are generally inclined to distrust ethnic minorities, which has been dominant in the existing literature, this would require more research including observations and interviews. In the present article we have put emphasis on the police, but it can be argued that the questions we have dealt with are just as relevant for other controlling agents, for instance, those working at borders or in private companies.

Note

1. Common terms in Dutch policy circles apart from 'non-western allochtonous' are 'ethnic minorities' or 'migrants', terms often referring to policy categories rather than to ethnic groups. The term race is hardly ever used.

References

Adler, F., 1983. *Nations not obsessed with crime.* Littleton, CO: F.B. Rothman.

Bauman, Z., 2000. *Liquid modernity.* Cambridge: Polity Press.

Blom, M., *et al.*, 2005. *Verdacht van criminaliteit. Allochtonen en autochtonen nader bekeken* [Suspected of crime. A closer look at persons of foreign and Dutch heritage]. Den Haag: WODC.

Boekhoorn, P., Speller, T., and Kruijssen, F., 2004. *Evaluatie Vreemdelingenwet 2000, Operationeel vreemdelingentoezicht door de politie* [Operational surveillance of foreign nationals. Evaluation of the powers of the police for the surveillance of foreign nationals in the Aliens Act 2000]. Den Haag: WODC.

Boutellier, H., 2004. *The safety utopia: contemporary discontent and desire as to crime and punishment.* Dordrecht: Kluwer Academic.

Bovenkerk, F., 1991. Het vraagstuk van de criminaliteit der Marokkaanse jongens. *De Gids*, 150 (12), 8–28.

Bowling, B., 1990. Conceptual and methodological problems in measuring 'race' differences in delinquency, a response to Marianne Junger. *British Journal of Criminology*, 30 (4), 483–492.

Bowling, B. and Philips, C., 2007. Disproportionate and discriminatory: reviewing the evidence on police stop and search. *Modern Law Review*, 70 (6), 936–961.

Bridges, L., 1999. The Lawrence inquiry – Incompetence, corruption, and institutional racism. *Journal of Law and Society*, 26 (3), 298–322.

Cavadino, M. and Dignan, J., 2006. *Penal systems: a comparative approach.* London: Sage Publications.

COT, 2007. *Preventief Fouilleren in Rotterdam. Maatschappelijk draagvlak, opbrengsten en effecten* [Preventative searches in Rotterdam. Societal support and effectivity]. Den Haag – Rotterdam: COT Instituut voor Veiligheid en Crisismanagement.

COT, 2009. *Preventief Fouilleren in Amsterdam. De balans van 2008* [Preventative searches in Amsterdam. Results of 2008]. Den Haag – Amsterdam: COT Instituut voor Veiligheid en Crisismanagement.

De Boer, M., 2007. Wake-up call for the Lowlands: Dutch counterterrorism from a comparative perspective. *Cambridge Review of International Affairs*, 20 (2), 285–302.

De Roos, T.A., 2007. Doelbewust strafrecht en maakbare veiligheid. *In*: M. de Keizer and S.C. Roels, eds. *Staat van Veiligheid.* Zutphen: Walburg Press, 129–149.

Downes, D. and van Swaaningen, R., 2007. The Road to Dystopia: changes in the penal climate in the Netherlands. *In*: M. Tonry and C. Bijleveld, eds. *Crime and justice in the Netherlands.* Chicago: Chicago University Press, 31–72.

Eijkman, Q., 2010. Has the genie been let out of the bottle? Ethnic profiling in the Netherlands. *The Journal of Law and Social Justice*, 5 (2), 1–21.

Engbersen, G., *et al.*, 2011. *Destination Netherlands the evolution of migration from six origin countries to the Netherlands.* Rotterdam: Erasmus University.

Engbersen, G., Van der Leun, J., and De Boom, J., 2007. The fragmentation of migration and crime in the Netherlands. *In*: M. Tonry and C. Bijleveld, eds. *Crime and justice in the Netherlands.* Chicago: University of Chicago Press, 389–452.

European Union Agency for Fundamental Rights (EU-FRA), 2009. *European Union Minorities and Discrimination Survey. Data in Focus Report: Muslims*. Brussels: EUAFR.

European Union Agency for Fundamental Rights (EU-FRA), 2010. *EU-MIDIS 5 Data in Focus report: Multiple discrimination*. Brussels: EUAFR.

Europese Commissie tegen Racisme en Intolerantie, 2008. *Derde Rapport over Nederland*. Straatsburg: Raad van Europa.

Feeley, M. and Simon, J., 1992. The new penology: notes on the emerging strategy of corrections and its implications. *Criminology*, 30 (4), 449–474.

Feeley, M. and Simon, J., 1994. Actuarial justice: the emerging new criminal law. *In*: D. Nelken, ed. *The futures of criminology*. London: Sage, 173–201.

Garland, D., 2001. *The culture of control: crime and social order in contemporary society*. Chicago: University of Chicago Press.

Geddes, A., 2003. *The politics of migration and integration in Europe*. London: Sage.

Haen Marshall, I., 1997. *Minorities, migrants, and crime diversity and similarity across Europe and the United States*. New York: Sage.

IND, 2004. *Status of the policy for highly skilled migrants* [online]. Available from: http://www.ind.nl/en/inbedrijf/wonenenwerken/standvanzakenkennismigranten.asp [Accessed 28 April 2011].

Junger, M., 1989. Discrepancies between police and self-report data for Dutch racial minorities. *British Journal of Criminology*, 20 (3), 273–284.

Junger, M., 1990. *Delinquency and ethnicity an investigation on social factors relating to delinquency among Moroccan, Turkish, Surinamese and Dutch boys*. Deventer/Boston: Kluwer.

Junger-Tas, J., 1997. Ethnic minorities and criminal justice in the Netherlands. *In*: M. Tonry, ed. *Ethnicity, crime and immigration. Comparative and cross-national perspectives*. Chicago and London: University of Chicago Press, 257–310.

Kamerstukken II, 2001/2002. http://www.rijksoverheid.nl/documenten-en-publicaties/kamerstukken [Accessed 28 April 2011].

KLPD, 2010. *Gerichte Alcohol Controles* [Targeted alcohol checks] [online]. Available from: http://www.politie.nl/klpd/nieuws/100820gerichtealcoholcontroles.asp [Accessed 20 August 2010].

Kommer, M., 1994. Het Nederlands Strafklimaat in Internationaal Perspectief. *In*: M. Moerings, ed. *Hoe punitief is Nederland?* Arnhem: Gouda Quint, 313–330.

Maasstad Pers, 2010. Lapt Leefbaar Rotterdam de rechtsstaat aan de laars? *Maasstad Pers*, 1 Sep.

Miller, J., 2010. Stop and search in England. A reformed tactic or business as usual? *British Journal of Criminology*, 50, 954–974.

Ministerie van Justitie, 1985. *Samenleving en Criminaliteit. Een beleidsplan voor de komende jaren*. Den Haag: Staatsuitgeverij.

Moerings, M., 2003. *Straffen met het oog op veiligheid, een onderneming vol risico's*. Leiden: Leiden Law School (inaugural lecture).

Muller, E.R., Kummeling, H.R.B.M., and Bron, R.P., 2007. *Veiligheid en Privacy*. The Hague: Boom Legal.

Nationale Ombudsman, 2009. *Onderzoek inval vreemdelingenpolitie in Amsterdams café*. The Hague: Nationale Ombudsman, Report 2009–170.

Open Society Justice Initiative, 2009. *Ethnic profiling in the European Union: pervasive, ineffective and disciriminatory*. New York: Open Society Institute.

Pakes, F., 2004. The politics of discontent: The emergence of a new criminal justice discourse in the Netherlands. *Howard Journal of Criminal Justice*, 43 (3), 284–298.

Philips, C. and Bowling, B., 2003. Racism, ethnicity and criminology. Developing minority perspectives. *British Journal of Criminology*, 43 (2), 269–290.

Reitzel, J. and Piquero, A.R., 2006. Does it exist? Studying citizens' attitudes of racial profiling. *Police Quarterly*, 9 (2), 161–183.

Roethof Commission, 1984. *Interim-rapport Commissie Kleine Criminaliteit*. Den Haag: Staatsuitgeverij.

Rovers, B., 1999. *Klassenjustitie. Overzicht van onderzoek naar selectiviteit in de Nederlandse strafrechtsketen*. Rotterdam: Erasmus University.

Rutherford, A., 1996. *Transforming ciminal policy*. Winchester: Waterside Press.

Salet, R., 2009. Preventief fouilleren als praktijk. *Nederlands Juristenblad*, 84 (27), 1724–1728.

Sampson, R.J. and Lauritsen, J.L., 1997. Racial and ethnic disparities in crime and criminal justice in the United States. *In*: M. Tonry, ed. *Ethnicity, crime, and immigration: comparative and cross-national perspectives*. Chicago: University of Chicago Press, 311–374.

Steffensmeier, D.J., Ulmer, J.T., and Kramer, J.H., 1998. The interaction of race, gender, and age in criminal sentencing: the punishment cost of being young, Black, and male. *Criminology*, 36 (4), 763–797.

Stumpf, J., 2006. The crimmigration crisis: immigrants, crime, and sovereign power. *American University Law Review*, 56 (2), 368–419.

Tillyer, R. and Hartley, R.D., 2010. Driving racial profiling research forward: learning lessons from sentencing research. *Journal of Criminal Justice*, 38 (4), 657–665.

Van der Leun, J.P., 2003. *Looking for Loopholes. Processes of incorporation of illegal immigrants*. Amsterdam: Amsterdam University Press.

Van der Leun, J.P., 2010. *Crimmigratie*. Apeldoorn/Antwerpen: Maklu (inaugural lecture).

Van der Leun, J.P. and Ilies, M., 2010. The Netherlands: assessing the irregular population in a restrictive setting. *In*: A. Triandafyllidou, ed. *Irregular migration in Europe. Myths and realities*. Farnham, Burlington: Ashgate, 187–206.

Van der Leun, J.P., *et al.*, eds. 2010. Criminaliteit, migratie en etniciteit. Nieuwe richtingen binnen een complex en beladen onderzoeksterrein. *Tijdschrift voor Criminologie*, 52 (2) 107–121.

van der Woude, M.A.H., 2009. Brede benadering terrorismebestrijding. *Openbaar Bestuur*, 11, 2–5.

van der Woude, M.A.H., 2010. *Wetgeving in een Veiligheidscultuur*. Den Haag: Boom Juridische Uitgevers.

van der Woude, M.A.H., 2011. Is het Nederlandse antiterrorismebeleid écht zo degelijk vormgegeven? Een bespreking van recent uitgevoerd evaluatieonderzoek. *PROCES*, 90 (3), 125–141.

Van Swaaningen, R., 2005. Public safety and the management of fear. *Theoretical Criminology*, 9 (3), 289–305.

Weenink, D., 2009. An analysis of the outcomes of Dutch prosecutorial decision making. *British Journal of Criminology*, 49 (2), 220–242.

Wetenschappelijke Raad voor Regeringsbeleid, 1979. *Etnische minderheden*. The Hague: Sdu Uitgevers.

Wetenschappelijke Raad voor Regeringsbeleid, 2007. *In debat over Nederland*. Amsterdam: Amsterdam University Press.

Wilson, J.Q., 1989. *Bureaucracy. What government agencies do and why they do it*. New York: Basic.

Wittebrood, K., 2004. Van delictmelding tot officïële aangifte – sprake van sociale ongelijkheid? *Tijdschrift voor Criminologie*, 46 (56), 56–71.

Zedner, L., 2005. Securing liberty in the face of terror: reflections from criminal justice. *Journal of Law and Society*, 32 (4), 507–533.

'It sounds like they shouldn't be here': immigration checks on the streets of Sydney

Leanne Weber

School of Political and Social Inquiry, Monash University, Melbourne, Australia

Australian state police have historically held wide-ranging powers which reflect their origins as all-encompassing administrators and agents of control over unruly colonial subjects. Contemporary police powers to stop and question individuals to establish whether they are lawfully present stem from at least 1958 when they were incorporated into section 188 of the *Migration Act*. There is no official monitoring of the use of stop and search powers in this or any other context, and the capacity for police to make on-the-spot checks has been enhanced by the establishment of the Immigration Status System which provides immediate feedback about immigration status, 24 hours a day. This paper will draw on statistical data, survey responses and interviews with senior New South Wales police to build up a picture of their immigration status checking practices, concentrating on opportunistic street encounters. The reported starting point – of directing attention to those who are perceived to be 'out of place' – embeds street-level border control into everyday practices of order maintenance policing. Questions of immigration status are found to be closely intertwined with determinations of identity, highlighting the importance in a globalising world of marking non-citizens as 'surveillable subjects', and raising deeper questions about entitlement and belonging.

Australian police wield immigration enforcement powers which are remarkable in terms of their scope, and because of their apparent acceptance by the population at large. While heated public debate surfaces periodically around the unauthorised arrival of asylum seekers by boat, the everyday role of police in the production of the *internal* border maintains a low public profile. Even the accidental death in September 2006 of Wah Aun Chan, an unlawfully present Malaysian national who fled from police following a vehicle stop (Johns 2008), failed to ignite public interest about the police role in immigration enforcement. In this paper, I will paint a picture of the everyday involvement of state police in the production of the internal border, drawing on data collected for a study on immigration enforcement in the Australian state of New South Wales (NSW) funded by the Australian Research Council.[1]

Migration policing in Australia

Australian police have historically held wide-ranging powers which reflect their origins as all-encompassing administrators and agents of control over unruly colonial subjects.

> The police in Australia were founded in a specific colonial context which gave them an important *political and administrative* role: guaranteeing the success of settler dispossession of Aboriginal land, sustaining the boundaries of urban order, acting as agents of the state in the collection of taxes, conducting elections, and counting the population. (Finnane 1994, p. 34; emphasis in original)

This is nowhere more apparent than in NSW, in which the first Australian penal colony was established at Sydney Cove in 1788. One legacy of this foundational role for state police has been a capacity to garner significant resources and powers (Brown *et al.* 2006, Finnane 2009), coupled with a relative lack of democratic accountability. As Goldsmith (2005, p. 452) notes: 'in colonial societies, there historically was less effort given to justifying police policies and actions in terms of broad public support'. From the time of federation in 1901, and in the absence of national law enforcement agencies, state police remained the only resource available to enforce the new federal mandate to control immigration (Finnane 2009). Despite the subsequent establishment of both a national police authority and a specialist immigration authority, state police maintained an ongoing involvement in the control of 'aliens' – a term which has now given way to the legal category of 'unlawful non citizens'.

Section 14 of the *Migration Act 1958* categorises all non-citizens who enter or remain in Australia without a valid visa as 'unlawful non-citizens'. State and federal police, along with customs and immigration officials are 'designated officers' under the Act. Section 188 requires any person who is 'reasonably suspected of being a non-citizen' to present evidence of their lawful status (such as a valid visa) to a designated officer, or at least to establish their identity. No equivalent power exists for police to demand proof of identity from apparently law-abiding citizens. The precise wording of the section indicates that the power applies not merely to those who are 'reasonably suspected' of being *unlawfully* present, but extends to anyone suspected of *not being a citizen*. The legislation therefore licences the questioning of anyone whose 'Australianness' is considered suspect, and creates a clear demarcation in law between the liberties enjoyed by citizens and non-citizens.

There is no requirement on police to produce monitoring data, or account for the exercise of their *Migration Act* powers. According to the most recent annual report from the Department of Immigration and Citizenship (DIAC), 80% of the 14,169 'locations' of unlawful non-citizens across Australia during the 2009–2010 financial year were due to 'voluntary' reporting, with the remainder detected either through DIAC field operations or by referrals from police (DIAC 2010). If police are assumed to contribute around the same number of 'locations' as DIAC (consistent with previously reported figures) this amounts to around 1400 unlawful non-citizens identified in a year by police across Australia, many of these from street stops. The capacity for police to make on-the-spot checks was enhanced in 2006 by the establishment of a 24-hour system operated by DIAC which provides immediate feedback about immigration status. The Immigration Status System (ISS) was introduced in the wake of scandals concerning the wrongful deportations and prolonged detentions of hundreds of overseas-born Australian citizens and lawful residents (Palmer 2005). Although characterised by authorities as 'mistakes' these outcomes were the product of an 'automated' deportation system which operated with few checks and balances (Nicholls 2007). The subsequent emphasis on using technology to establish identity and immigration status stands in stark contrast to these earlier practices, described here by a senior immigration official: 'So the police would say to us, we have this person and you know they're unlawful. We would take their word for it and without doing anything more than perfunctory checks we would accept that' (Interview 47, Canberra DIAC). According to statistics provided by DIAC, NSW Police have been the most frequent users of the ISS system, generating more than 50% of the 11,672 queries recorded in the first 20 months of its operation.

Immigration checks by NSW police

The Migration Policing project

The aim of the Migration Policing project is to examine multi-agency networks directed towards the detection of unlawful non-citizens. The role of police was given a central place in the study but the data reported here was collected with a view to identifying the range of immigration-related activities engaged in by police, and understanding their interactions with other agencies, and was not specifically directed towards debates within the stop and search literature. The police data was collected through a series of mixed method case studies based around three metropolitan police stations in Sydney and two police stations in rural NSW at which significant use of the ISS was recorded. The sampling rationale for the study sites was purposive, that is, intended to identify as wide a range of migration policing practices as possible, rather than to be representative of the NSW Police as a whole.

A survey of operational officers was conducted at each location between January and October 2008. The survey provided a glimpse into everyday practices, albeit through self-reports rather than direct observation. A total non-probability sample of 371 responses was achieved. Due to the strictures of the operational policing environment, sampling methods differed across stations according to agreements made with each Local Area Commander. A mix of general duties officers, detectives and other operational personnel was obtained but it is not possible to determine whether the profile in Table 1 is statistically representative since requested breakdowns of the workforce at each site were not provided. Each police case study ended with a formal interview with the Local Area Commander at which the results of the survey were discussed. This discussion will draw on interviews with these Sydney-based commanders, two interviews with officers in specialist urban units, and

Table 1. Profile of survey sample by rank, role and years of service (percentages shown exclude missing values).

Rank	Probationary constable	Constable	Senior constable	Sergeant	Senior sergeant	Inspector	Missing	Total
	41 (11%)	115 (32%)	135 (38%)	57 (16%)	4 (1%)	8 (2%)	11	371
Role		General duties	Highway patrol	Intelligence /pro-active	Detectives	Other	Missing	Total
		203 (62%)	25 (8%)	16 (5%)	44 (13%)	39 (12%)	44	371
Years at station		< 1 year	1 < 2 years	2 < 5 years	5 < 10 years	10+ years	Missing	Total
		31 (9%)	80 (23%)	135 (39%)	79 (23%)	24 (7%)	22	371
Years in police		< 1 year	1 < 2 years	2 < 5 years	5 < 10 years	10+ years	Missing	Total
		16 (5%)	36 (10%)	79 (23%)	111 (32%)	108 (31%)	21	371

extracts from interviews with senior immigration officials at DIAC headquarters in Canberra.

Self-reported migration policing practices

There was considerable variation between officers in the number of immigration checks they reported, with a modal frequency of once or twice a year (see Figure 1). Higher frequencies might be due to an individual propensity to initiate checks, or may simply reflect differing opportunities for immigration checking according to operational roles. While local area commanders believed that immigration checking would occur mainly in police stations, the most commonly reported method for requesting immigration checks was via the radio despatch system (185 reports), suggesting that on-the-spot checks during police patrols were a significant feature of street policing.

Police officers reported conducting immigration checks during routine patrols, traffic stops and street stops; in the course of criminal investigations; in response to reports or when called to a house; and even when individuals presented as victims. Amongst respondents who identified as general duties officers, 78% reported conducting an immigration check at least once in the previous 12 months. Amongst highway patrol officers and detectives the percentages were 87% and 84%, respectively. One local area commander depicted immigration checking as just part of routine information-gathering about a wide range of individuals encountered by police: 'Yeah, we like to know who we are dealing with, so anyone – whether they are a victim, a witness, a complainant, a suspect – everyone gets run through the mincer – the machine – so that we know who we are dealing with' (Interview 23).

Statistics supplied by DIAC indicate that around 13% of the 8986 ISS checks conducted nationally between 20 February 2006 and 31 October 2007 resulted in the identification by police of an unlawful non-citizen, a total of 1185 'locations'. From a community policing point of view, it is the cases in which immigration checks confirm lawful status (70%) or citizenship (17%) that may be the most significant. Studies on procedural fairness in policing frequently conclude that unwarranted questioning by police erodes perceptions of legitimacy, not just amongst individuals

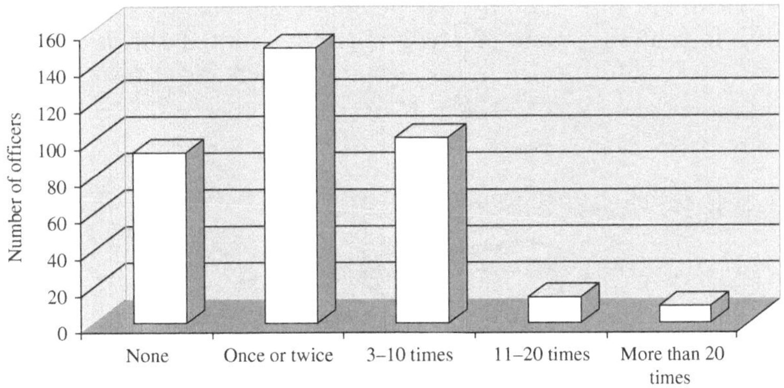

Figure 1. Reported frequency of immigration checks by operational police ($n = 371$) in previous 12 months.

exposed to it, but also more widely amongst family and community members, particularly if stops are conducted in an abusive or disrespectful manner (Skogan 2005, 2006, Brunson and Miller 2006, Sharp and Atherton 2007, Bradford *et al.* 2008). On the other hand, the survey results indicate that many of the immigration checks instigated by police in NSW take place without the individual being present, often in the course of criminal investigations, and may therefore have less impact on community perceptions. Similarly, immigration checks carried out in the individual's presence as part of a range of checks (e.g. following a lawful traffic stop) may not come to the attention of the individual concerned unless they confirm unlawful status. In these cases, whatever impact is experienced is more likely to be associated with the conduct of the stop itself, rather that the immigration check per se. The impact on community relations of the vast majority of immigration checks conducted nationally that *do not* confirm police suspicions about unlawful status remains an important, but as-yet unanswered question.

The reported basis for immigration checks

Police respondents were asked to indicate their reasons for conducting immigration checks by choosing as many options as applied to them from a pre-determined list. The responses are shown in Figure 2. By far the most frequently reported reason for conducting an immigration check was uncertainty over identity. This seems circular since the ISS requires a name in order to check immigration status. Senior police explained in interviews that descriptive information provided by the system could help officers judge whether the person before them matches the profile recorded against the name the individual has provided. Using the ISS as a way of verifying identity opens up possibilities beyond the identification of unlawful non-citizens, such as issuing on-the-spot fines, making warrant checks and pursuing other policing outcomes. Police and immigration authorities could therefore have differing perspectives on the use of the system, as alluded to by this DIAC official: 'Well they'll have a case and a client who they think may be of immigration interest. How they determine that sometimes, considering that 90% of the cases are lawful, or could be Australian citizens, leaves some questions unanswered' (Interview 42, Canberra DIAC).

Other stated reasons for making immigration checks concerned various indicators of 'foreignness', none of which aligns substantially with the category of 'non-citizen'. It is difficult from this data to disentangle instances in which

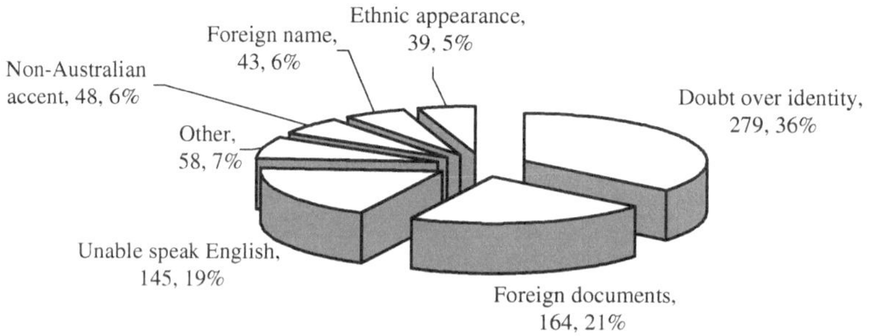

Figure 2. Reported reasons for checking immigration status (776 responses).

individuals are stopped solely on suspicion of being a non-citizen, from circumstances in which an immigration check follows a stop for some other purpose. Notably, ethnic appearance is the only characteristic reported in Figure 2 that would be available to police *prior* to questioning an individual. This suggests either that ethnic appearance may be used as the sole basis for a stop more frequently than was reported in the survey, or that immigration checks arise most often from encounters instigated on other grounds. Notwithstanding that legal authority *does* exist in the *Migration Act* to stop suspected non-citizens in the absence of any crime-related suspicion, police officers invariably supported the latter view.

> Police need to detect something else before they check a passport. If there are minor offences we need to validate who they are. Without any real reason we may use an immigration check to verify what they are saying ... you can't look at people and suspect he or she is illegal in our society. Normally something else comes first. (Interview 11, Police Commuter Crime)

Although immigration status was always described as a secondary concern, it is apparent that a very fine line divides questions of 'identity' from judgements about belonging and entitlement, and suspicions could be aroused by indications of being socially 'out of place': 'It is not about the name or the circumstance, it is about their observations of the individual that they doubt that they are a resident. So by the discussion that they are having with them it sounds like they are not here – *that they shouldn't be here*' (Interview 40, Police Headquarters). Moreover, these assessments could be mediated by ethnicity, as described in this hypothetical account:

> Yeah, and again to people who shouldn't be here ... The biggest giveaway, a Black-African gentleman, someone from Sudan or Uganda or something like that and they have got a credit card on them in the name of John Smith. I am sorry, but you don't look like John Smith. (Interview 26, Local Area Commander)

The legal, social and institutional context for immigration checks

The picture emerging so far embeds immigration checks arising from street stops within everyday policing tactics directed towards order maintenance and crime control. This interpretation is reinforced by the observation that 177 of the survey respondents claimed never to have exercised their *Migration Act* powers, despite all but 97 of them reporting having made an immigration status check in the past 12 months. Only 111 said they had exercised *Migration Act* powers, and 72 said they did not know. Further confirmation came from the interviews: 'The cops would be far less knowledgeable in the *Migration Act* than what they would for the nuts and bolts proactive policing legislation' (Interview 18, Local Area Commander). In order to understand the context for immigration checks it is therefore necessary to discuss them in relation to broader legal powers, political directives and general stop and search practices.

Proactive policing in New South Wales

Historically, the policing of public places in NSW has impacted overwhelmingly on Aboriginal populations. These cycles of over-policing and resistance are widely understood as perpetuating the dynamics of colonisation (Cunneen 2001, 2007). In recent years enthusiasm for intelligence-led policing methods amongst politicians and senior police has led to the targeting of known offenders and geographical hot spots, supported by technologies such as CCTV: 'So it is very likely that every time a police officer goes out onto <location> they are going to say – I know that person, their picture is up in the police station – So that gives them the cause to at least go up and speak to them' (Interview 23, Local Area Commander). While ostensibly directed towards the identification of particular suspects, these tactics clearly operationalise broader categories of risk based on suspect typifications and localities, as apparent in the following statement.

> For example, the Pizza Hut at <location> has been robbed three times by a South East Asian identified male, or suspected male who looks five foot nine and South East Asian appearance. So we have got a police patrol in <location> and they see three during the day – people who fit that description. They have got reasonable cause to actually go and speak to those people. So it is all about the information that is given to them. (Interview 18, Local Area Commander)

When patrolling 'risky places' officers were expected to use their own judgement to direct their attention to local policing priorities. One Local Area Commander said he expected his patrol officers to 'interfere' with 'people who are making a nuisance of themselves on the street-swearing, yelling out, obviously intoxicated, assaulting other people, acting in an anti-social manner' adding that 'they are the types of things that they are directed to come down on hard, and not so much because a person's heritage is other than white Caucasian' (Interview 23). Another commander explained how he tried to encourage his young officers to 'identify crooks' by 'teaching them about how to look at who is actually acting in a suspicious manner' (Interview 18). Along with all the other commanders interviewed, he expressed unqualified confidence in proactive street policing as a successful crime prevention measure, attributing drops in local crime largely to 'targeting specific criminals and being suspicious about the activity of people within our environment'. Local area commanders also described how they believed immigration checks might arise within these street-level encounters.

> This is exactly what happens. You'd stop and prop[2] a group of kids that were waiting at the train station at nine thirty at night, and say 'What are you doing here? Who has got identification?' ... So you would start to ask those questions of somebody who doesn't have reliable valid-type identification stuff. And then you'd probably start to do the check, well how long have you been living there for? Who is living there with you? Then you would probably do a check. (Interview 6, Local Area Commander)

The legal basis for 'stop and prop'

Current police powers in NSW derive mainly from the *Law Enforcement (Powers and Responsibilities) Act 2002* (LEPRA), supplemented by special legislation often hastily enacted in response to political pressures (Dixon and Schimmel 2002, Brown *et al.* 2006). The only restriction on officers deploying LEPRA powers is that they must identify themselves, give verbal reasons for deploying their powers, and explain that failure to comply is an offence. The full range of street policing powers cannot be outline here, but this comment from a local area commander gives an indicative overview:

> So, we have that basis, our move-on powers, someone obstructing a pedestrian, a vehicle or traffic, they are causing a nuisance and generally causing a bit of a pest of themselves, we could move them on from the area. We also have at the extreme end the powers of arrest, and there is nothing to stop us just going up and talking to someone to go and gather intelligence. So the whole basis of our proactive intervention, if you like is that four pronged attack of intelligence, move on, search, and at the extreme arrest. (Interview 23, Local Area Commander)

Police survey responses tie immigration checks most closely to questions of identity which, it is claimed, arise most often in relation to stops made for other purposes. Section 11 of LEPRA – which reads as an invitation to intelligence-gathering – empowers police to require disclosure of identity 'if the officer suspects on reasonable grounds that the person may be able to assist in the investigation of an alleged indictable offence'. Subsequent sections create offences for failing to disclose one's true identity. Vehicle stops are authorised without reason for the purposes of random alcohol and drug testing, and where a car or a person inside is wanted in connection with an offence – after which a general power to request a driver's licence from anyone in control of a vehicle can be used to authorise an identity check (*Road Transport (General) Act 2005* s173). An officer from the Commuter Crime Unit (Interview 11) explained that other legislation not related to the regulation of motor vehicles required only that name and address be provided. Still, he contended, the onus was generally on a person approached by police to satisfy the officer of their identity, even in the absence of any clearly defined power. In interviews, it became apparent that there was often a 'catch' to these initially 'consensual' interactions:

> At the end of the day if the police don't have that reasonable suspicion, then I don't have to tell you who I am–go away. I don't have to tell you anything. And that is your right. But then if the police believe that they have reasonable suspicion, well then they need to be able to explain their powers to the people, and in accordance with LEPRA they need to identify themselves, tell the person the powers that they are exercising, what the consequences are if the person fails to abide by police directions. They may render themselves liable to arrest, etcetera etcetera ... you know if they start to burr up or walk away or whatever, it may increase your suspicion of them as to why they are trying to avoid talking to the cops. (Interview 23, Local Area Commander)

As Dixon (1997, p. 95) concluded from his research on the exercise of police powers in both England and NSW, 'the very process of trying to obtain consent allows officers to test their suspicion about a person'. Advocates for young people who are targeted by these policing tactics therefore temper their legal advice with a heavy close of pragmatism: 'Police have a right to ask you to identify yourself, but in most cases you do not have to do so. It is usually a good idea to tell the police your name and address, or show them some ID, otherwise they might make trouble for you or even arrest you' (The Shopfront Youth Legal Centre 2008).

Conclusion: policing the internal border

In this closing section, I consider some key questions about immigration checking by NSW Police. Why is there an absence of research and public debate about the sweeping *Migration Act* powers to question non-citizens about their immigration status? What can be said about the effectiveness, fairness, legitimacy and accountability of these practices? And what broader significance should be placed on the introduction of the ISS and the growing emphasis placed on establishing identity?

As to the first question, the normalisation of police powers to stop and question suspected non-citizens in NSW stands in stark contrast to the vocal opposition to similar proposals in Arizona (see Provine and Sanchez, this issue). Many socio-legal and historical differences are at play here, the most important of which, I argue, is Australia's colonial legacy. Patrolling the boundaries of belonging has been an accepted role for colonial police in Australia, with indigenous Australians the primary targets. Cunneen (2001) has charted the historical use of public order policing as a tool of governance to exclude Aboriginal people from public space through arrest and moving-on. The normalisation of immigration checks may have some continuities with these established patterns of street policing aimed at producing order through exclusion – in this case through deportation – of those who 'shouldn't be here'.

Australia has consistently maintained a high rate of deportation by world standards (Nicholls 2007). However, unlike the United Kingdom and Japan (see Namba, this issue) where governments have openly pledged to meet specified removal targets, successive Australian governments have invested their material and symbolic capital in the defence of the *external* border. In place of harsh rhetoric about 'criminal immigrants', as in the Netherlands for example (see van der Leun and van der Woude, this issue), Australian politicians direct their demonising rhetoric towards the small numbers of asylum seekers arriving without authorisation by boat, and the people smugglers who assist them (Weber and Grewcock 2011). Public debate, research and activism have largely followed this policy focus offshore. Even revelations reported earlier about the wrongful detention and deportation of Australian citizens have not translated into sustained questioning of the routine detection processes that feed into these outcomes; and while a popular television series depicts immigration officers conducting workplace raids and checking visas at airports, the role of police in patrolling the internal border remains largely invisible.

What can be said about the effectiveness, fairness, legitimacy and accountability of immigration checking practices by police? In the absence of government targets rewarding the detection of unlawful non-citizens, there is no evidence at present that street policing in NSW is actively directed towards this purpose. Nevertheless, proactive policing tactics ensure that police play a significant role in performing the internal border through opportunistic checks of immigration status that arise in the context of other policing activities. While a 13% 'success' rate would be a low return on resources deployed *solely* for the identification of unlawful non-citizens, the embedding of immigration checking within everyday order-maintenance policing decreases the net cost of these activities for police. None of the senior police interviewed for the Migration Policing study considered that immigration enforcement created an undue financial burden. While immigration authorities sometimes queried the low return rate from ISS checks, police forces nevertheless contribute as many 'locations' of unlawful non-citizens nationally as the more targeted activities of much smaller teams of specialist DIAC compliance officers.

There is no statistical data with which to assess the fairness of checking practices by NSW Police in terms of nationality or ethnic origin. The broad drafting of the *Migration Act* powers and the accessibility to police of the ISS suggest that immigration status checks will be conducted at will, and are likely to be prompted by judgements of non-belonging mediated by ethnicity, and other indications that individuals are 'out of place'. Irrespective of overall measures of equity or disproportionality, it has been argued that the 'subjective experience of *feeling* profiled' may be just as damaging to confidence in police as 'the objective one of *being* profiled' (Tyler and Wakslak 2004, p. 254). Immigration checks which fail to uncover breaches of immigration law, where they are conducted with the knowledge of individuals concerned, send a powerful message of non-belonging which could impact negatively on perceptions of police legitimacy and on social cohesion more broadly. The prospect of being identified as an unlawful non-citizen is likely to render those without lawful status unwilling to access police services when needed (see Weber forthcoming). Australia's colonial history has arguably reduced the emphasis on public accountability normally associated with police governance in democratic societies and there is little evidence that NSW Police are giving any thought to the community implications of their migration policing role. ISS records *could* become the basis for public accountability with respect to powers exercised by police under section 188 of the *Migration Act* since patterns of immigration checking by nationality could be discerned from this data. But in the absence of obvious public concern there is no indication that this application of the data is being considered.

This brings us to the final question about the implications of the ISS as an adjunct to emerging forms of surveillance-based governance. The ISS was developed primarily to ensure that individuals transferred from police into DIAC custody were, in fact, unlawfully present, and to establish their identities beyond doubt. A document detailing a 'Strategic Plan for Identity Management in DIAC', authored by a specialist Identity Branch of DIAC, reveals the growing importance of identity verification technologies across a range of border control strategies, including the use of biometrics to 'anchor' identity. The purpose of these technologies is said to be to 'establish a consistent foundation identity for non-citizens to use in the community' (DIAC 2007, p. 4). The extent of DIAC's surveillant capacities is explained here by this senior official:

> If the name that we're given is correct we've been able to verify that in our systems. And you know Australia's virtually unique. Australia, New Zealand and Japan are the only three countries in the world who can actually do that because we're the only countries in the world that have virtually universal visa systems or entry and exit systems from the country. (Interview 45, Canberra DIAC)

While identity verification may open up access to positive entitlements and prevent 'mistakes' such as wrongful detention and deportation, it also represents a major advance in the construction of non-citizens as surveillable subjects who are vulnerable to any future ramping-up of exclusionary policies. The content of the 'Strategic Plan for Identity Management' also indicates a merging of identity verification capacities with broader concerns about identity fraud in relation to immigration programmes, crime and terrorism. These developments parallel the proliferation of transnational databases in Europe, aimed at separating *bona fide* EU citizens from what Aas (2011) describes as 'crimmigrant others'. In her view, these technologies signal the emergence of new forms of global governance in which verification of identity becomes a key to producing mobile juridical subjects who can be sorted for inclusion and exclusion in a 'globally divided polity'.

To return to questions of stop and search, Delsol and Shiner (2006) have recommended that 'race' should remain an important focus for stop and search monitoring and research, but that other bases for disproportionality should also be considered. I have argued elsewhere, with Bowling, that expanded categories of 'otherness' are merging in response to insecurities arising from rapid social change, institutional failure, and increasing global interconnectedness associated with globalisation (Weber and Bowling 2008). This suggests that immigration status – a non-observable characteristic, likely to be operationalised in street policing through visible ciphers based on 'race', class and ethnicity, and other indicators of non-belonging – should be investigated as a powerful category of 'otherness' in future research on stop and search practices.

Acknowledgements

Amanda Wilson, Jenny Wise and Alyce McGovern all provided skilled and enthusiastic research assistance to the Migration Policing Project which is gratefully acknowledged.

Notes

1. 'Policing Migration in Australia: an analysis of onshore migration policing networks' Australian Research Council Discovery Grant DP0774554; Chief Investigator Leanne Weber; Research Team Amanda Wilson, Jenny Wise, Alyce McGovern.
2. Although not appearing in legislation, this was the term of preference for NSW police and was used repeatedly in interviews. The author takes 'prop' to be an abbreviation for 'proposition' or questioning, indicating the emphasis on intelligence-gathering. The keywords 'stop and search' appear very rarely in Australian criminological literature, and these practices are more commonly referred to as 'proactive policing' or – particularly in relation to Aboriginal populations – as examples of 'over-policing'.

References

Aas, K., 2011. 'Crimmigrant' bodies and bona fide travelers: surveillance, citizenship and global governance, *Theoretical Criminology*, 15 (3), 331–346.

Bradford, B., Jackson, J., and Stanko, E., 2008. Contact and confidence: revisiting the impact of public encounters with the police. *Policing and Society*, 19 (1), 20–46.

Brown, D., Farrier, D., Neal, D., and Weisbrot, D., 2006. *Criminal laws: materials and commentary on criminal law and process in New South Wales*. 4th ed. Sydney: Federation Press.

Brunson, R. and Miller, J., 2006. Young black men and urban policing in the United States. *British Journal of Criminology*, 46, 613–640.

Cunneen, C., 2001. *Conflict, politics and crime: aboriginal communities and the police*. Sydney: Allen and Unwin.

Cunneen, C., 2007. Reflections on criminal justice police since the Royal Commission into Aboriginal deaths in custody. *In*: N. Gillespie, ed. *Reflections: 40 years on from the 1967 referendum*. Adelaide: Aboriginal Legal Rights Movement.

Delsol, R. and Shiner, M., 2006. Regulating stop and search: a challenge for police and community relations in England and Wales. *Critical Criminology*, 14, 241–263.
DIAC, 2007. *Identity matters: strategic plan for identity management in DIAC 2007–2010*. Canberra: Department of Immigration and Citizenship.
DIAC, 2010. *Annual report 2009–10*. Canberra: Department of Immigration and Citizenship.
Dixon, D., 1997. *Law in policing: legal regulation and police practices*. Oxford: Oxford University Press.
Dixon, D. and Schimmel, J., 2002. What's wrong with the Law Enforcement Bill? *Law Society Journal*, 40 (1), 58–61.
Finnane, M., 1994. *Police and government: histories of policing in Australia*. Melbourne: Oxford University Press.
Finnane, M., 2009. Controlling the 'alien' in mid twentieth-century Australia: the origins and fate of a policing role. *Policing and Society*, 19 (4), 442–467.
Goldsmith, A., 2005. Police reform and the problem of trust. *Theoretical Criminology*, 9 (4), 443–470.
Johns, F., 2008. *Findings in the matter of Wah Aun Chan*. Adelaide: South Australian Coroner's Court.
Nicholls, G., 2007. *Deported: A history of forced departures from Australia*. Sydney: UNSW Press.
Palmer, M.J., 2005. *Inquiry into the circumstances of the immigration detention of Cornelia Rau*. Canberra: Commonwealth of Australia.
Sharp, D. and Atherton, S., 2007. To serve and protect? The experience of policing in the community of young people from black and other ethnic minority groups. *British Journal of Criminology*, 47, 746–763.
Skogan, W., 2005. Citizen satisfaction with police encounters. *Police Quarterly*, 8 (3), 298–321.
Skogan, W., 2006. Asymmetry in the impact of encounters with police. *Policing and Society*, 16, 99–126.
The Shopfront Youth Legal Centre, 2008. *Police powers and your rights*. Sydney: The Shopfront Youth Legal Centre.
Tyler, T.R. and Wakslak, C.J., 2004. Profiling and police legitimacy: procedural justice, attributions of motive, and acceptance of police authority. *Criminology*, 42, 253–282.
Weber, L., forthcoming. Policing a world in motion. *In*: S. Pickering and J. McCulloch, eds. *Borders and transnational crime: pre-crime, mobility and serious harm in an age of globalization*. London: Palgrave.
Weber, L. and Bowling, B., 2008. Valiant beggars and global vagabonds: select, eject, immobilise. *Theoretical Criminology*, 12 (3), 355–375.
Weber, L. and Grewcock, M., 2011. Criminalising people smuggling: preventing or globalizing harm? *In*: F. Allum and S. Gilmour, eds. *The Routledge handbook of transnational organized crime*. London: Routledge, 379–390.

Suspecting immigrants: exploring links between racialised anxieties and expanded police powers in Arizona

Doris Marie Provine and Gabriella Sanchez

Justice and Social Inquiry, Arizona State University, Tempe, AZ, USA

Immigration enforcement has become an important site of expanded police powers to stop and search as the USA attempts to remove more unauthorised immigrants from its interior. Arizona has enthusiastically embraced this approach, treating Latino immigrants as a quasi-criminal element. State legislation requiring municipal police to engage in immigration enforcement, along with past local police practice directed at immigrant removal, strident political rhetoric, and the federal government's own deportation initiatives, have legitimised an enforcement regimen that: (1) blends techniques of control used on the border with those used in interior enforcement; (2) mixes criminal and administrative approaches to apprehension, detention and deportation; (3) invokes national security as a rationale for strict, uncompromising enforcement and (4) hypes the violence aspect of human smuggling and border crossing to support more aggressive interior enforcement. This policy mix, current practices suggest, encourages entho-racial profiling, hyper-surveillance, abusive stops, problematic searches and unwarranted detention of suspected unauthorised immigrants.

Introduction

The state of Arizona has passed many laws to discourage unauthorised immigrants from entering or staying within its borders, but it was the 2010 adoption of SB 1070, *The Support Our Law Enforcement and Safe Neighborhoods Act*, that cemented the state's reputation as a trend-setter in immigration enforcement. Among its provisions, the most notable is the requirement that a police officer ascertain the legal status of anyone stopped if the officer suspects that person might be undocumented. If suspicions persist, the officer must detain the individual and contact federal immigration authorities. Failure to comply can lead to a suit for damages by any Arizona citizen. This law expands the powers to stop and search in Arizona and offers a blueprint for other states to express their determination to fight unauthorised immigration by deploying municipal police in the effort.

While cooperation between federal and local police agencies to enforce immigration law in the United States is nothing new, SB 1070 breaks legal ground. It rejects the traditional role of states as subordinate partners in this process. Arizona has, in effect, taken the lead away from the federal government by mandating its own comprehensive and on-going plan for immigration policing at the local level, while at the same time legitimising the racialised stops and searches that were already growing more common in the state. Although the federal government has sued to block enforcement of this law, its own emphasis on increasing deportations fosters similarly racialised stop and search practices at the federal level and tolerance for abuses of traditional police powers at the state level.

This essay describes the socio-political context in which SB 1070 became law, including the racialised stop and search powers already exercised by some law-enforcement officers against suspected undocumented immigrants from Mexico. We turn then to the federal level, which is also expanding its stop and search powers. The federal government, despite its lawsuit to block SB 1070, has done little to discourage Arizona's aggressive approach. Policies directed towards the removal of settled immigrants from a nation's interior, we argue, invariably reproduce and exacerbate already-existing ethno-racial inequality, much as security-focused initiatives do (Bowling and Phillips 2007). Both rely on the expansion of police powers to stop and search beyond traditional boundaries in pursuit of vaguely defined objectives. And in both cases, a primary goal is to calm public anxieties. In Arizona the fear is of 'Mexicanization' with associated cultural, language and economic changes that are unwelcome to the Anglo majority. Policing takes on elements of political theatre as enforcement efforts concentrate on people socially constructed to be, not just undesirable, but also dangerous.

Latino immigrants in Arizona

According to data from the 2010 US census, Arizona is the second-fastest growing state in the nation. Latinos now make up nearly 30% of the state's residents, up from just over 25% in 2000. Much of this growth has occurred in small towns outside of metropolitan Phoenix area, which remains the largest urban concentration of Latinos in the state. Unauthorised residents, primarily of Mexican origin, make up about 9% of the population and 10% of the state's labour force (Passel and Cohn 2010).

A significant Latino presence in Arizona is not new. The United States acquired part of the Arizona territory in 1853 as part of the Gadsden Purchase. Mexicans residing in the new territory were entitled to American citizenship. The formal status of citizenship, however, did little to eliminate systematic discrimination against them by Anglos, who immediately assumed control of the state government and commerce (Gomez 2007). This has not changed, despite continued immigration from Mexico into the state. During the Mexican Revolution of 1910, large numbers of Mexican citizens moved to Arizona to escape the violence in their country and to seek employment in the booming mining industry. Their labour, by virtue of their origin, entitled them to less than half the Anglo wage (Gordon 2001). During harsh economic times immigration raids against Latinos were common. Local law enforcement removed over 1000 foreign workers from Bisbee, Arizona in 1917, sending them in boxcars to the New Mexico desert (University of Arizona 2011). During the Depression of the 1930s many Mexican and Mexican-American workers and their families were deported from Arizona by the federal immigration service.

These events have their parallel in more recent efforts to control the state's Latino population. In 1997 the Chandler Roundup – a weeklong series of immigration raids – generated national attention. Local police, in collaboration with federal authorities, stopped and questioned dozens of Latino immigrants on the basis of their physical appearance, leading to unjustified arrests and a successful lawsuit based on civil-rights violations (Romero and Serag 2004, Romero 2006).

Maricopa County sheriff Joseph Arpaio has continued this tradition with workplace raids and 'crime suppression sweeps' in predominantly Latino neighbourhoods in the Phoenix metropolitan area. His jurisdiction includes most of the city and its surrounding suburbs, some of which have large concentrations of Latino residents. The raids, marketed to the public as efforts to remove criminals, are in reality aimed at detecting and deporting unauthorised residents and reminding Latino residents, regardless of their immigration status, of the power that law enforcement holds over their lives. The continued popularity of the sheriff and a continual stream of anti-immigrant rhetoric and legislation from the state legislature re-enforce an overall sense of second-class status among Latinos in the state. A study of the sense of safety Latina immigrant women feel in Phoenix and Tucson revealed widespread fear of leaving home, even among women with secure legal status. Sheriff Arpaio and his deputies were cited more often than anyone as the source of this pervasive sense of fear (McDowell and Wonders 2010).

The heritage of discrimination and lack of educational and economic opportunities, in tandem with surveillance and intimidation of Latino residents throughout the state's history, have created obstacles to the growth of strong Latino leadership in the state and have impacted the development of an energised electorate. Latinos are therefore vulnerable to hostile legal initiatives sponsored by politicians anxious to cash in on the fears and antipathies of voters unprepared for demographic change (see e.g. Zúñiga and Hernández León 2005, Singer *et al.* 2008).

SB 1070

SB 1070 represents the culmination of more than a decade of anti-immigrant legislation. Statutes requiring the use of English in government transactions and restricting welfare or public benefits to those who can prove legal status already shape public services. The state has also experimented with criminal sanctions: in 2007 the legislature approved the denial of bail to unauthorised immigrants accused of serious crimes, and in 2008 it adopted an Employer Sanctions Law to punish employers who knowingly hired unauthorised workers by suspending or revoking their business licenses.

The objective has always been the same: to express displeasure with the presence of unauthorised immigrants, popularly equated with poor Latinos, and to encourage them to leave. It is important to note the specificity of these laws. Arizona welcomes legal immigrants from all over the world, including large numbers of impoverished refugees. Unauthorised immigration from Mexico, however, has made the state uneasy since territorial days. This attitude remains politically significant. In 2011 the legislature considered bills to require local teachers to report the immigration status of students and their parents and to require landlords to check immigration status before leasing, along with proposed restrictions on birth certificates for the babies of unauthorised residents. These latest initiatives were defeated only after forceful complaints by state business leaders.

SB 1070 is distinctive among the steady stream of laws directed at unauthorised immigrants in Arizona in focusing on police agencies. Its mandate that all police units participate actively in immigration enforcement forces city governments and urban police departments to adopt an approach that some of them have rejected. This mandated uniformity and the enhanced stop and search powers directed towards suspected unauthorised immigrants are SB 1070's primary innovations, though there are other provisions beyond the scope of this article that enhance police powers to arrest unauthorised immigrants.

The requirement that police investigate the immigration status of those whom they suspect are undocumented has been put on hold by a federal judge. At a political level, however, Arizona has successfully signalled to the world how a state legislature can override local opposition to immigration enforcement and at the same time force the hand of the federal government, which is widely perceived as insufficiently committed to preventing unauthorised entry from Mexico. The political message is that the nation faces a crisis of such massive dimensions that other priorities must give way, including efforts to foster community trust, efficient allocation of policing resources and sensitivity to individual rights.

The legislature and governor have cultivated this sense of crisis for years, but the 2010 Arizona election escalated the rhetoric to include (false) stories about headless bodies in the desert and other atrocities allegedly produced by Mexican drug cartels and human smugglers. The rhetoric helped propel the entire Republican slate into office in statewide elections and has enhanced the name recognition of the political officials who supported SB 1070's passage. Most significantly in the long term, SB 1070 helps to condition the public to accept police stops based on ethno-racial profiling, legitimising practices that already existed in some police agencies when the law was adopted.

Stop and search in Arizona before SB 1070's adoption

Even before the adoption of SB 1070, Arizona laws and policing practices threatened the most basic civil, human and constitutional rights of Latinos, including those with legal status. Unwarranted searches, stops based on ethnic appearance, and checkpoints in predominantly Latino working class neighbourhoods have been common for at least a decade. Undocumented immigrants who have experienced violence along their journeys have been unable to count on local law enforcement for help. Resident Latinos who live in mixed-status families and mixed-status neighbourhoods have been reluctant to seek assistance. Scholars have studied the fears of Arizona victims of domestic violence who are afraid to contact local police for fear of deportation of a loved one or other immigration-related consequences (see e.g. Menjivar and Salcido 2001). Job hunting, particularly in a time of recession and high unemployment has become hazardous and problematic for Latinos, whose right to work is questioned and challenged by employers weary of being accused of hiring undocumented workers. Day labourers, many of whom are of Latino origin, are under suspicion and some municipalities have prohibited them from congregating in public areas to offer labour services. Law-enforcement agencies in Arizona have occasionally enforced these ordinances, arresting Latino men who, despite being

American citizens, are subjected to stops on the basis of their use of language, their attire or choice of location (Varsanyi 2008). Checkpoints have become another form of intimidation against Latino workers and their families, as these operations tend to be launched only in immigrant communities or work areas during regular commuting hours. None of these policing practices are enforced as part of an overall crime-fighting strategy.

As we describe below, evidence of aggressive, racially based stops and searches comes from accounts of Latino and Latina workers arrested during employment raids, smuggling interdiction patrols and crime suppression sweeps. Statements from participating law-enforcement officers show how ethno-racial profiling – using physical appearance and socially constructed notions of race and ethnicity – subjects working-class Latinos to special scrutiny, stops and searches. These residents experience racialised law-enforcement practices as law-enforcement policy. The policy appears to those who feel its effects as a racially motivated attempt to inscribe illegality and citizenship on the basis of physical characteristics, that is, on the basis of bodies rather than law. Racially-based stop and search to enforce immigration law thus helps to establish, maintain and reinforce Latinos second-class citizenship.

Policing 'employer' sanctions through stops and searches of immigrants

Arizona's *Legal Arizona Workers Act*, commonly referred to as the state's employer sanctions law, prohibits businesses from knowingly or intentionally hiring an 'unauthorized alien'. The law also requires employers in Arizona to use the E-Verify system, a free Web-based service offered by the Department of Homeland Security to verify the employment authorisation of all new employees.

While business owners initially opposed the measure in court, enforcement practices soon revealed that the real target was unauthorised workers. Only two companies have been penalised since the sanctions law entered into effect in 2008. One was Waterworld, an amusement park that had closed and filed for bankruptcy before any determination of wrongdoing. The other was a sandwich shop that was ordered to close its doors for only one day: Thanksgiving.

Yet at the same time, the law has been used instead to justify employment-site raids against businesses that are believed to hire undocumented immigrants. Most cases arise from tips provided by disgruntled employees and managers within the companies themselves, or from citizens who report seeing 'illegals' on the business' premises, their suspicions aroused by hearing 'Mexican' music or Spanish being spoken between staff members. The Maricopa County Sheriff Office and the county attorney have responded to these reports as credible enough to open official investigations.

Details of arrests in the Waterworld case, gleaned from case files, indicate problematic police behaviour. In one instance, although there was no public stop and search, there was highly intrusive surveillance. Undercover officers followed five Latina employees suspected of being undocumented to and from work for several days, even before their employment eligibility was verified. The women were shadowed as they drove to their children's schools, visited relatives, shopped for groceries and attended church. The officers justified their intrusive surveillance as necessary to ensure their own safety.

In another instance, the police stop seems clearly to have been unnecessarily violent. Celia Alvarez, a janitor and mother of four US-born children, was arrested when sheriff officers burst into the landscaping firm she had worked at for five years, acting on a tip from a 'concerned' supervisor who allegedly reported that the company hired undocumented workers. Alvarez described in court testimony how deputies wearing ski masks entered the building, warning the occupants they were looking for 'illegal aliens'. The officers found Alvarez hiding under a table, 'lifted her off her feet, and slammed her face into a wall', causing injuries on her face, jaw and teeth. Another officer allegedly hit her with a clipboard for trying to speak to another detainee.

A third lawsuit involves a stop and interrogation based on ethno-racial profiling, followed by a gratuitously humiliating detention. The case involved Julian Mora, one of Alvarez's co-workers, who was detained during the same operation where she was arrested. A legal permanent resident, Mora was on his way to work when two Maricopa County sheriff's vehicles blocked his progress. The deputies arrested Mora and his son, a US citizen, who was accompanying him. The officers handcuffed them and held them without explanation for three hours. Mora, a diabetic, was not allowed to use the restroom, but was eventually granted permission to urinate by the side of a truck as deputies watched. He and his son were eventually released. The lawsuit that the American Civil Liberties Union filed on the Moras' behalf alleges that father and son were stopped because officers interpreted Julian Mora's skin colour and the denims he was wearing as indicators of illegality.

Policing human smuggling through stops and prosecution of smuggled immigrants

A similar pattern of ethno-racial profiling can be seen in the enforcement of Arizona's unique human-smuggling statute. In 2005, in response to public concern over increased smuggling of drugs, weapons and humans through the state, the Arizona legislature approved an anti-human trafficking law. The statute established prison terms for the men and women involved in the transportation of people known or presumed to lack legal status to be in the state. It also expanded the definition of human smuggling, allowing for the detection and arrest of those suspected to be engaged in smuggling activities. This vague definition created a legal mechanism by which undocumented immigrants entering the country with the assistance of a human smuggler or coyote could be accused of conspiring to commit an act of human smuggling – their own.

Over one thousand undocumented Latino immigrants, many of whom had been victims of border violence, had been successfully prosecuted under the statute by mid-2011. The prosecutions have continued despite legal challenges. The volume of cases is great enough to create backlogs in court processing. An immigrant charged with conspiracy to be smuggled into Arizona can expect to wait an average of three months in custody before the case will be heard; state law prevents pre-trial release. If convicted, these people face deportation as well as possible federal criminal charges if their presence in the country is determined to be the result of an illegal re-entry.

The importance attached to the issue of human smuggling has justified aggressive anti-smuggling interventions in predominantly low-income, Latino sections in the

Phoenix metropolitan area. In March 2009, for example, a human-smuggling investigation led to the stop and detention of Refugio Serna, who was handcuffed and driven around the cities by state police officers for 11 hours. Serna, a US citizen and an employee of the Department of Homeland Security, was picking up his brother-in-law at a parking lot in a predominantly immigrant neighbourhood in Phoenix. The police report cited Serna's 'bold and very confident demeanor while driving a truck [and] playing Mexican music very loud' as sufficient probable cause for stopping and questioning him. A detective handcuffed Serna and put him in the back of a police vehicle, alleging concerns for his own safety. Serna spent the rest of the day handcuffed in the police vehicle. The officers told him that he was not under arrest, suggesting that he could get out and go home if he so desired as they drove through a desolate area. Serna's frustration was evident in his statements to court investigators. They reveal the embarrassment and pain he felt while the officers paraded and questioned him in public, especially when he was later ridiculed in front of his very concerned family and neighbours. He was forced to resign from his job as a result of the criminal investigation launched against him, though no charges were filed.

The human smuggling law has also led to police roadblocks and patrols that engage in questionable stops in areas designated as 'human smuggling corridors'. Maricopa County Sheriff deputies frequently conduct 'smuggling interdiction patrols' along heavily transited areas near the border with Mexico in an attempt to detect groups of undocumented immigrants in transit. A survey of probable-cause statements used in the prosecution of cases arising out of these patrols reveals a disturbing pattern of justifications for stops.

Deputies often cite minor traffic violations to justify their stops, but their descriptions of these situations include characterisations of these drivers and their passengers as foreign, undesirable and potentially criminal (Sanchez 2011). Some probable-cause statements refer to Latino suspects as 'smelling like illegal aliens', or cite as reasons for suspicion as 'speaking only Spanish' or 'looking dirty and soiled'. One statement cited 'fail[ing] to make eye contact with [the officer] while on the freeway' as a justification for further investigation. These references appear alongside pre-fabricated, boilerplate narratives designed to increase the odds that the probable-cause statement will hold in court.

These practices are troubling on a variety of grounds. They ignore the 'reasonable suspicion' standard that is supposed to protect the freedom of residents to move about without interference from police. (Even SB 1070 purports to adhere to this standard.) The justifications described here smack of ethno-racial profiling and stereotyping that uses physical appearance to make assumptions about legal status and behaviour. These stops and the reasons used to justify them also tend to conflate the role of the Border Patrol with that of local police. The US Border Patrol is not limited by the reasonable-suspicion requirement. Nor is it prohibited from taking ethnic or racial characteristics into account as part of an overall justification for proceeding. The blending described here effectively removes the 100-mile limit on the more intrusive stops that has been established by law for the Border Patrol, and replaces it with a more generous standard to be carried out by agents of the State of Arizona, rather than the federal agency authorised by law.

The federal government's complicity in racialised stops and searches

The federal government has never effectively challenged Arizona's harsh approach to unauthorised immigrants. Nor is it likely to bring strong pressure for changes because its own policies have hardened considerably over the past two decades. Like Arizona, the federal government is primarily concerned with unauthorised immigration from Mexico. This focus is not surprising in light of the fact that Mexicans make up slightly over half of the unauthorised population within US territory. It does, however, mean that the federal government, through the weight of its authority, is helping to frame unauthorised immigration in racialised terms, highlighting the faces of Latino immigrants, particularly those from Mexico, rather than reminding law enforcement and the public that persons without legal status can be found in all colours and among all classes and every nationality (Provine and Doty 2011).

Federal immigration stops and searches: the ethno-racial dimension

The hardening of the federal position on immigration from Mexico began with Operation Gatekeeper and Operation Hold-the-Line in the mid-1990s. These programmes fortified the border in populated areas, while relying on the inhospitable desert and the reality of dehydration and death to discourage immigration from other areas (Nevins 2002, Doty 2010). Over 85% of US Border Patrol agents are currently deployed along the southern border and they have been supplemented by deployments of the National Guard, federal investigators and federal drug-control agents (Haddal 2010). Federal enforcement priorities at the border pay little heed to basic rights or dignity. Federal judges in border districts have seen their courtrooms inundated with people charged with federal crimes under Operation Streamline, a programme to prosecute those caught crossing the border. The process begins with apprehensions of people caught crossing illegally by the Border Patrol or another police authority. Those caught are held in detention until time can be found for a court hearing. Some will not be charged because the court cannot handle the caseload. So detainees wait, not knowing whether they will be among those criminally charged or not. Those who are charged are arraigned and processed in groups of up to 10 at a time. They face a lengthy prison term unless they plead guilty to the crime of unauthorised entry, which gives them a criminal record. The criminal record makes them felons, which in turn helps to justify stronger enforcement measures against 'dangerous' criminals.

Federal activities in the interior of the country have also been ramped up in recent years. For a time federal agents staged highly publicised workplace raids, mostly directed against Latino immigrants. The usual charge was using false identity documents. This policy included some legally indefensible actions against immigrants, such as the federal raid in Postville Iowa, where the US Supreme Court, in a unanimous opinion, rebuked prosecutors for over-charging the largely Guatemalan workforce to get guilty pleas. Recently the strategy has changed to federal audits of company records, which leads to the firing of unauthorised workers, rather than their arrest.

The National Fugitive Operations Program has also expanded dramatically. Created in 2003, the programme's mandate was to locate, arrest and remove immigrants with old orders of deportation, focusing particularly on fugitives who threaten national security or endanger communities. That requirement was soon dropped, however, as the size, scope and cost of the programme steadily increased. Now 100 enforcement teams operate across the country, often conducting house raids that involve questioning the legal status of the entire household and arresting anyone who cannot prove their legal status.

Researchers have found a decided tendency of these teams to ignore constitutional requirements against breaking into homes without legal authority, searching without authority, and seizing innocent people. The data also suggest racial profiling of Latinos. In two locations studied by researchers from the Benjamin Cardozo School of Law, collateral arrests of Latinos outstripped, by over 20%, targeted arrests, suggesting that non-targeted arrestees were stopped and questioned on the basis of appearance alone (Chiu *et al.* 2009). An analysis by the Migration Policy Institute found that over 70% of those apprehended had no prior criminal convictions (Mendelson *et al.* 2009).

Enhanced federal enforcement efforts have also targeted legal permanent residents. Congress has lengthened the list of crimes that result in deportation, and Immigration and Customs Enforcement (ICE) has responded with increased levels of enforcement. Mexican-origin residents, according to a study by Human Rights Watch, were vastly over-represented, at 78.2% of the total, over the 10-year period the group studied (Human Rights Watch 2009).

Local police in some places are doing their part to help this programme net as many deportations as possible. A recent study of one county's arrest records for a 23-month period found that as the federal programme grew more technologically sophisticated, arrests of Latinos increased dramatically. The trend was most notable for traffic offenses. Although the Criminal Alien Program has been advertised as a means of removing dangerous felons from American neighbourhoods, only 2% of those detained were charged with felony offenses; 98% of the cases involved only misdemeanors (Gardner and Kohli 2009).

Federal partnerships with local police

As it has increased its own interior-enforcement efforts, the federal government has, for the first time, created formal, on-going immigration-enforcement partnerships with local police, a policy that envisions local police as a 'force multiplier' to enhance federal enforcement. Congress created a legal structure for such partnerships in 1996 within the Illegal Immigration Reform and Immigrant Responsibility Act. Under an arrangement stipulated in the statute, cooperating agencies sign a formal memorandum of understanding to train local officers to either assist in the identification of immigrants while they are booked in jail, or to question and detain immigrants on patrol after the commission of an offense. The programme, which became known as '287g' after its legislative moorings, at first drew little interest, but some law-enforcement organisations began to sign on after the 2001 terrorist attacks on the World Trade Center and Pentagon. The agency in charge of enforcement, ICE lists 71 active agreements on its webpage.

The 287g Program was only the beginning of the federal government's effort to involve local police in immigration enforcement. In 2003 the Justice Department authorised the addition of civil immigration data – such as outstanding deportation orders – to databases that local police use in pursuing criminal suspects across state lines (Gladstein *et al.* 2005). The number of federal immigration agents embedded in local departments has also been increasing. A series of three nationwide surveys of local police executives in cities and county sheriffs reveals that consultation between local police and federal officials is routine in connection with specific cases, while formal agreements remain exceptional (Decker *et al.* 2011).

Local/federal partnerships have been touted as a way to gain more control over serious crime, but the evidence is strong that the real priority has been to increase the numbers of immigrants detained and deported, which have been growing rapidly and are now at historic highs. The communities that have signed agreements tend not to have out-of-the-ordinary crime rates, though they do have high rates of recent immigration (Shahani and Greene 2009, p. 16). The General Accounting Office found that some police departments were routinely using their 287g authority on people arrested for minor traffic violations (GAO 2009). A 2011 report by the Migration Policy Institute found that half of the cases resulting in deportation involved low-level misdemeanour or traffic cases. Federal officials have ignored such evidence of widespread racial profiling and pretextual stops. Failure to safeguard against these abuses has led to recommendations that the programme be cancelled from various observers, including the Inter-American Commission on Human Rights, an arm of the Organization of American States (Semple 2011).

The 287g Program, however, will soon be overshadowed by a much more comprehensive and far-reaching initiative: Secure Communities. The concept behind Secure Communities is shared data availability – local jails make all their booking data available to the federal government, and in return they receive information on immigration violators and criminal matters. This programme, which appears to be mandatory, is being implemented without any safeguards against arrests conducted purely for the sake of immigration control. Full implementation across the United States is anticipated for 2013.

There are already indications that Secure Communities, like previous federal programmes designed to focus only on dangerous offenders, is not achieving its ostensible goals. A study by the *Arizona Republic* found that nationwide, 60% of those deported were either low-level criminals or had no criminal record at all. In Arizona, the rate was 66%, mostly thanks to the efforts of Maricopa County sheriff's office, which leads the nation in both the number of immigrants arrested (30,052 in a two-year period) and the number deported (12,089) (Gonzales 2011). These statistics strongly suggest that local policing based on immigration status is already a reality in Arizona, even without implementation of SB 1070.

Conclusion

Returning now to the four worrisome trends described at the outset, it is clear that both the Maricopa Sheriff's Department and the federal government have contributed to the blending of border enforcement with interior enforcement. Sheriff deputies are conducting stops on highways near the border, stops that strongly suggest racial profiling, which they are not authorised to do. At the same time, the federal government is devolving authority to the local level through its 287g Program and Secure Communities, both of which make immigrants vulnerable to appearance-based stops and arrests. Secure Communities also exhibits the second tendency: mixing criminal and administrative approaches to apprehension, detention and deportation. Civil immigration warrants are now part of the National Crime Information Center Database. The federal government has justified these programmes as well as its Fugitive Alien Program and Criminal Alien Program in terms of national security concerns, the third tendency we noted at the outset. The fourth tendency we noted – hyping of violence as a reason for more aggressive interior enforcement – has fallen mostly to states like Arizona, which have made immigration-related violence part of their platform for elective office.

The policies Arizona and the federal government are following have an impact on all immigrants who 'look Mexican', regardless of their legal status. This is because immigration enforcement in the interior of the United States requires appearance-based criteria to be effective. Race, in other words, is an essential part of this kind of law. And such laws build on long-standing antipathy towards Latinos in the United States, which helps make them politically palatable (Massey 2007, Chavez 2008). Arizona's Latinos feel this hostility, particularly in the wake of SB 1070. Polls reveal their view that they are under special scrutiny and that SB 1070 has exposed 'a deeper sense of racism' in the community (Gonzales 2010).

References

Bowling, B. and Phillips, C., 2007. Disproportionate and discriminatory: reviewing the evidence on police stop and search. *Modern Law Review*, 70 (6), 936–961.

Chavez, L.R., 2008. *The Latino threat: constructing immigrants, citizens, and the nation*. Palo Alto, CA: Stanford University.

Chiu, B., *et al*., 2009. *Constitution on ICE: a report on immigration home raid operations*. New york: Cardozo Immigration Justice Clinic.

Decker, S., *et al.*, 2011. *Immigration and local policing in smaller municipalities: results from a national survey of law enforcement executives* [online]. Available from: http://ccj.asu.edu/research/immigration-research-section/current-project/immigration-and-local-policing-in-smaller-municipalities-results-from-a-national-survey-of-law-enforcement-executives/view [Accessed 18 Feb 2011].

Doty, R.L., 2010. SB 1070 and the banality of evil. *Z Magazine* [online], 9 Oct. Available from: http://www.zcommunications.org/sb1070-and-the-banality-of-evil-by-roxanne-doty [Accessed 31 July 2011].

Gardner, T. and Kohli, A., 2009. *Racial profiling in the ICE criminal alien program*. Policy Brief, The Chief Justice Earl Warren Institute on Race, Ethnicity, & Diversity. Berkeley: University of California Law School.

General Accounting Office (GAO), 2009. *Immigration enforcement: better controls needed over program authorizing state and local enforcement of federal immigration laws*. Washington, DC: U.S. Government Accountability Office.

Gladstein, H., *et al.*, 2005. *Blurring the lines: a Profile of state and local police enforcement of immigration law using the National Crime Information Center Database, 2002–2004*. Washington, DC: Migration Policy Institute.

Gomez, L., 2007. *Manifest destinies: the making of the Mexican-American race*. New york: New York University Press.

Gonzales, D., 2010. Poll: many say migrant debate stirs racism. *Arizona Republic*, 2 Aug, pp. A1, A4.

Gonzales, D., 2011. Senate Bill 1070: 1 year later. *Arizona Republic*, 23 Apr, pp. A1, A10.

Gordon, L., 2001. *The great Arizona orphan abduction*. Cambridge, MA: Harvard University Press.

Haddal, C.C., 2010. *Border security: the role of the U.S. Border Patrol*. Washington, DC: Congressional Research Service.

Human Rights Watch, 2009. *Forced apart (by the numbers)*. New York: Human Rights Watch.

Massey, D.S., 2007. *Categorically unequal – the American stratification system*. New York: Russell Sage.
McDowell, M. and Wonders, N., 2010. Keeping migrants in their place: technologies of control and racialized public space in Arizona. *Social Justice*, 7 (2), 54–72.
Mendelson, M., Strom, S., and Wishnie, M., 2009. *Collateral damage: an examination of ICE's fugitive operations program*. Washington, DC: Migration Policy Institute.
Menjivar, C. and Salcido, O., 2001. Immigrant women and domestic violence: common experiences in different countries. *Gender & Society*, 16 (6), 898–920.
Nevins, J., 2002. *Operation Gatekeeper and beyond: the war on 'illegals' and the remaking of the U.S. – Mexico boundary*. New York: Routledge.
Passel, J.S. and Cohn, D., 2010. *U.S. unauthorized immigration flows are down sharply since mid-decade*. Washington, DC: Pew Research Center.
Provine, D.M. and Doty, R.D., 2011. The criminalization of immigrants as a racial project. *Journal of Contemporary Criminal Justice*, 27 (3), 261–277.
Romero, M., 2006. Racial profiling and immigration law enforcement: rounding up of usual suspects in the Latino community. *Critical Sociology*, 32 (2–3), 447–473.
Romero, M. and Serag, M., 2004. Violation of Latino civil rights resulting from INS and local police's use of race, culture and class profiling: the case of the Chandler Roundup in Arizona. *Cleveland State Law Review*, 52, 75–96.
Sanchez, G., 2011. Border crossings: smuggling operations in the southwest. Unpublished Ph.D. dissertation. Arizona State University.
Semple, K., 2011. Immigrant detentions draw international fire. *The New York Times*, 18 Mar. [online]. Available from: http://www.nytimes.com/2011/03/18/us/18detain-1.html [Accessed 31 July 2011].
Shahani, A. and Greene, J., 2009. *Local democracy on ice: why state and local governments have no business in federal immigration law enforcement*. New york: Justice Strategies.
Singer, A., Hardwick, W.S., and Brettell, C., eds., 2008. *Twenty-first century gateways: immigrant incorporation in suburban America*. Washington, DC: Brookings.
University of Arizona, 2011. *The Bisbee deportation of 1917* [online]. Available from: http://www.library.arizona.edu/exhibits/bisbee/ [Accessed 31 July 2011].
Varsanyi, M.W., 2008. Immigration policing through the backdoor: city ordinances, the 'right to the city' and the exclusion of undocumented day laborers. *Urban Geography*, 29 (1), 29–52.
Zúñiga, V. and Hernández León, R., eds., 2005. *New destinations: Mexican immigration in the United States*. New York: Russell Sage.

Stop and search in global context: an overview

Ben Bowling[a] and Leanne Weber[b]

[a]*School of Law, King's College, London, UK;* [b]*School of Political and Social Inquiry, Monash University, Melbourne, Australia*

Reflecting on the evidence presented in this collection, this overview explores the purposes for which stop and search powers are deployed, whether their use can be described as effective and whether the infringements of liberty and privacy that stop and search entails can be justified. We conclude by considering the impact of stop and search on citizenship and mobility and examining questions of fairness, legitimacy and justice.

The police power to stop and search

The words 'stop, police' in any language assert authority, power and control. They announce and initiate a coercive practice that resists being countermanded. Stop and search can be based on legal powers relating to specific offences, including drunk driving and un-roadworthy vehicles (Marks), terrorism (Parmar, Belur) and illegal entry (Namba, Weber, Provine and Sanchez). It can be focused on specific locations and restricted to a designated time, or used routinely as a generalised power (Tóth and Kádár, van der Leun and van der Woude, Wortley and Owusu-Bempah, Quinton). What unites these diverse practices is the state-sanctioned use of intrusion and coercion.

When a police officer stops someone walking along a street or driving their car, they are detaining them. This might be brief – long enough to check their driving licence or other documents or to question them about the reasons for their presence in a place. It could initiate a longer period of on-street questioning or end in an arrest. There is of course a distinction between arresting someone and detaining them for the purpose of such a search. But in any case, a stop amounts to a deprivation of liberty. As Bowling and Phillips (2007, p. 940) argue, 'there can scarcely be any meaning to the word "stop" if it does not indicate an attempt to detain someone from continuing his or her free passage on foot or in a vehicle'. The European Court of Human Rights supported this view in the case of Gillan, concluding that being deprived of freedom of movement during the course of a stop and search was indicative of a deprivation of liberty within the meaning of Article 5 of the European Convention on Human Rights. However the Court was not required to determine this question because Article 8 was unquestionably violated in the case.

When a police officer asks a person to account for himself or herself they are intruding into that person's private life. In some places, identity checks are legally empowered and routine, either in general or in relation to particular groups. In other places the police have no such power. In all cases, a stop is a *non-negotiable coercive power*. The police monopolise coercive force and have express powers to compel compliance and to use 'reasonable force' such as physically detaining a person attempting to resist. Individuals stopped must comply with the police officer's order and may face criminal prosecution if they refuse. In Hungary, for example, people unwilling or unable to prove their identity may be taken into custody and fined (Tóth and Kádár). In India, refusal to comply with a police officer's demand to stop can result in a fine or up to six months imprisonment (Belur).

A search is clearly more intrusive than the stop which usually precedes it.[1] The manner in which searches are conducted is a primary source of dissatisfaction and feelings of having been treated with disrespect. It might only involve a brief pat down or 'frisk' of a person's outer clothing, but sometimes consists of an extensive search of clothing, bags or in the passenger area or boot of a motor vehicle. If a police officer's suspicion is confirmed as a result of the search – for example, if they cannot verify a person's identity, if their immigration status is found to be unlawful, if contraband is discovered, or if there is a warrant for their arrest – this can result in criminal charges, deportation or arrest.

The effects of stop and search

In a democratic society, it is axiomatic that the police powers of bodily coercion or intrusion into privacy cannot simply be taken for granted; they must be justified in general and in each individual case. As Kleinig (1996, p. 13) puts it, there is 'a moral onus on those who limit the freedom of others to provide a justification of that limitation'. This principle, derived from Lockean contract theory, underpins discussions of policing and human rights. Applying this axiom to stop and search, we can say simply that a police officer must always have a good reason for stopping someone, and this should be accounted for in ways that are explanatory, cooperative, obedient and subordinate to the will of the people (Marshall 1978). This is enshrined in civil or human rights law that restricts police intervention to those instances where it is legal, necessary, proportionate, parsimonious and accountable (Bowling *et al.* 2004). As becomes clear when looking at practical examples, the reality of contemporary policing is often inconsistent with these principles.

What is the purpose of stop and search and how well does it achieve its goals? The question of evaluation is extremely difficult, but it seems plausible that it must have some value if only because it is so ubiquitous. Advocates cited in this collection of articles argue that the power is useful for, inter alia, the purposes of public protection, public order, public safety, crime control and the early detection and prevention of crime. These nebulous claims can be divided into an investigative justification and a deterrent justification, and each will be examined in turn.

The investigative justification

The most common justification for stop and search powers is crime investigation – to detect people engaged in, or planning, crime. In this sense, the power enables police to allay or confirm suspicions about individuals without exercising their power of arrest. Without this intermediate power, police officers investigating criminal allegations must choose between doing nothing and arresting anyone accused by witnesses. A power to search a person reasonably suspected of wrongdoing without needing to arrest them seems to be rational in principle (Bowling and Phillips 2007, p. 961).

In practice, however, there are problems with this justification, the first of which is calibrating the appropriate threshold at which intrusion is justified. The threshold is often set quite high – no one should be stopped and searched unless a police officer has 'reasonable suspicion' that they are involved in wrongdoing. But what does this mean in practice? On what objective criteria should suspicion be based? How accurate and reliable should suspicion be before it can be described as 'reasonable'? In practice – as Quinton shows – police can find almost anything suspicious, including personal characteristics such as style of clothing, age or physical appearance. The targeting by police of 'young men on a two wheeler, of a certain build and age, generally carrying a backpack' at Mumbai roadblocks (Belur) is a case in point. Tóth and Kádár note that, in Hungary, police require only 'simple suspicion' which presumably need not be reasonable. The literature is replete with police officers' comments about intuition, hunches and general signals of disreputableness which would not satisfy a neutral observer. Moreover, objections by those targeted for stops may provide a post-hoc justification in the minds of police, where the original basis for the stop is open to question. Often suspicion is linked to more general views about marginal communities and stereotypical beliefs about their criminal behaviour.

The use of power to stop in order to identify 'illegal immigrants' raises particular problems. In such instances, suspicion stems from the view that a person 'looks foreign', speaks a foreign language, reads a foreign language newspaper (Namba), 'looks like they shouldn't be here' (Weber), listens to 'ethnic music', 'looks dirty' or 'smells like an illegal alien' (Provine and Sanchez). It is well established in a number of contexts that 'categorical suspicion' – based on the social category to which the individual belongs – is often used as the grounds for a stop. The use of cues of this sort has the effect of making suspects out of entire communities. Of course, those who cannot provide evidence of their legal status are liable to detention and deportation. In Japan's 'war on illegal immigrants', stop and search contributed to the detection and deportation of more than 90,000 people (Namba). Similar policies have been deployed in many other places around the world.

In systems where stop and search powers are justified on the basis of investigating allegations of crime, police officers frequently use the power for other purposes. These include 'gaining intelligence' on people who are 'known' to the police (Weber), and to break up and move groups of people simply for the purposes of 'social discipline' (Choongh 1997). Moreover, powers initially designed for investigative purposes may be readily adapted towards the politically attractive goal of pre-emption (van der Leun and van der Woude). Although these practices often have no basis in law, they are widespread. Taking the elasticity of the notion of reasonable suspicion together with the 'mission creep' of the investigative justification, it is not surprising that only a very small proportion of all stop and searches yield any investigative value.

In the UK, about one in every 10 stops and searches based on reasonable suspicion results in the discovery of unlawful items or the arrest of an offender (Bowling and Phillips 2007). 'Hit rates' reported in this collection range from a 3% arrest rate and the instigation of petty offence procedures in 18% of cases following ID checks in Hungary (Tóth and Kádár); the identification of unlawful non-citizens in 13% of the immigration checks conducted by Australian police (Weber); to the seizure of just seven weapons, two arrests of wanted persons and the discovery of one stolen vehicle from over 42,000 *nakabandi* conducted by police in Mumbai (Belur). Significantly, of the 100,000 searches under the *Terrorism Act* 2000, none resulted in the identification of a terror suspect; the most frequent result was a street warning for cannabis possession (Parmar). By comparison, South African 'super roadblocks' resulted in the issuing of an enormous 2.3 million fines over a four-month period, the arrest of 10,000 drunk drivers and the removal of more than 24,000 un-roadworthy vehicles (Marks). Despite these apparent indicators of success, several senior officers still doubted their effectiveness when compared with more targeted approaches, indicating the elusiveness of judgements about the effectiveness of these policing strategies. The key point is that the burden of proof lies with the state to show that intrusion and coercion are justified, and therefore that stop and search has a value in effectively and efficiently investigating crime. This collection of essays provides little support for this contention.

The deterrent justification

A related, but distinct, justification is that stop and search powers deter wrongdoing. This could be achieved in a number of ways. Firstly, crime detection can bring offenders to the courts to face justice which may deter them from committing further crimes. Of course, this justification rests on the effectiveness and rectitude of stop and search as an investigative tactic which, as explained earlier, is questionable. Secondly, the memory or anticipation of being stopped might lead people to 'think twice' before committing crime or carrying weapons. If stop and search is carried out extensively, either at random or targeted at the presumed proximate causes of crime and disorder, criminals may be less likely to engage in crime. The core belief among many police officers that the primary function of street patrol is the 'rigid and unrelenting enforcement of the law ... to prevent and control crime' (Brown 1981, p. 198) was evident amongst some police, but not all, in Durban (Marks) and England (Quinton and Parmar), and uniformly amongst senior officers interviewed by Weber in New South Wales who were committed to this form of 'proactive' policing.

A principled objection to what might be called the 'deterrence thesis' of stop and search is the Kantian dictum that no human being should be treated merely as a 'means to an end'. Unlike the investigative justification, which limits stop and search to suspicious people and thus treats people as 'ends in themselves', the deterrent justification permits people to be stopped and searched without suspicion. Whether this is random or targeted, the implication is that many people will be subject to interference by the state irrespective of their involvement in crime. This seems unacceptable, especially when highly discretionary powers are used disproportionately against specific populations identified by 'race', ethnicity and social class.

An empirical objection to the deterrence thesis is the lack of any compelling evidence in this collection of essays that stop and search does in fact deter. This is consistent with the conclusions of earlier reviews of the international research evidence that stop and search makes 'only a limited disruptive impact on crime by intercepting those going out to commit offences' but does not play a significant role in controlling crime or in maintaining public order (Miller *et al.* 2000). While many senior police officers cling to the belief that stop and search deters terrorism, there is no evidence to support this contention (Parmar, Belur). Other authors argue that poorly targeted stop and search is counter-productive, undermining confidence and trust in public authorities (Parmar, Weber). How extensively stop and search powers are used varies widely within and between countries. This seems to be unrelated to crime patterns but depends to a large extent on tradition within local forces, the ethos of the high command and the political value placed on visible street policing. There is little evidence that the widespread use of stop and search is an operational necessity (Bowling 2007, EHRC 2010).

Inequity, unfairness and legitimacy

In many jurisdictions, stop and search powers are used extensively and aggressively against particular groups. This applies in general to urban, male, working-class or poor communities and to ethnic minorities. Early examples of targeting the socially marginal are laws attempting to control the movement of gypsies and travellers in seventeenth-century Europe, North American 'slave codes' prohibiting travel without a ticket, 'protectionist' policies governing the lives of indigenous people in Australia and South African pass laws (Weber and Bowling, 2004, 2008). Japan's 'closed country policy' resulted in an ethnically homogenous society with tight migration and residential control and deeply entrenched xenophobia. In the twentieth century, 'the other' was socially constructed in racial terms, and debates about crime, migration and the primacy of police enforcement were often, but not always, expressed in terms of racial, ethnic or national territory (Hall *et al.* 1978). The term 'racial profiling' emerged in the USA in the 1990s to refer to a practice that had occurred for many years, especially in relation to inter-state travel in which African-Americans were more frequently stopped on the basis of an explicit suspect profile. More recently, the term has been used to describe situations where particular groups are targeted for suspicion on the basis of 'ethnicity' or 'race' irrespective of whether this is a *deliberate* policy of targeted stop and search, or a more deeply embedded routine practice more aptly described as 'institutional racism' (Bowling and Phillips 2007).

In this context, it is no surprise that minority communities emerge as police targets in many of the papers in this collection. In Hungary, Roma are targeted for ID checks (Tóth and Kádár), and in Toronto and England it is the black community (Wortley and Owusu-Bempah, Quinton). Culture or religion act as markers to construct 'Muslim youth' as the archetypal 'others' in London (Parmar) with the apparent endorsement of the British Home Secretary who stated that Muslim communities must simply face the 'reality' that they would be the principal targets of counter-terrorism law enforcement. In South Africa (Marks) and India (Belur), the boundaries of suspicion seem to be drawn in more subtle ways, less clearly aligned with the categories of 'race' and ethnicity.

Explicit targeting policies were most evident amongst the contributions in this issue in relation to non-citizens, whose otherness (recalling Hall *et al.* 1978) is defined by their lack of legal right to remain on national territory (Namba, van der Leun and van der Woude, Provine and Sanchez). And while there is clear evidence of racial profiling against black Torontonians in Canada, which suggests that the issue does not rely on behavioural but categorical cues (Wortley and Owusu-Bempah), generalisations about particular ethnic groups are used in the Netherlands as part of a risk management strategy (van der Leun and van der Woude). In this context, migration itself is seen as a threat and therefore indications of migratory status – particularly those pointing to irregularity and marginality – provide the trigger for police intervention.

A number of consequences flow from the unfair use of stop and search powers. Firstly, targeting means that wrongdoing among particular communities comes more frequently to the attention of the authorities, which in turn reinforces police and public stereotypes about minority involvement in crime. Secondly, when stop and search is used so widely against ethnic minority communities, a significant proportion of these communities have the experience of being treated as suspects and enduring the embarrassing inconvenience of having their person, bag or vehicle searched. This 'collateral' impact on the law-abiding creates a particularly widespread perception of unfairness (see Wortley and Owusu-Bempah in Toronto, and Parmar in London). Even when stop searches are justified (bearing in mind that the majority are fruitless), the markedly disproportionate impact on minority communities still creates the experience of being unjustly targeted. Tyler and Wakslak (2004, p. 254) argue that the 'subjective experience of *feeling* profiled' may be just as damaging to confidence in police as 'the objective one of *being* profiled'.

Thirdly, stop and search has a corrosive impact on social solidarity. It engenders feelings of exclusion, resentment, distrust of the police, alienation, social and political disenfranchisement. The 87% of immigration checks conducted by Australian police which confirm the subject of the check to be a citizen or lawful resident (Weber) must surely convey a powerful message of non-belonging. Fourthly, the unfair use of stop and search can be criminogenic. The experience of being unfairly targeted for stop and search undermines the legitimacy of policing which has material effects on voluntary compliance with the law as well as disengagement on the part of victims and witnesses (Tyler 1990). Fifthly, it explicitly reinforces social boundaries. The papers in this collection demonstrate that targeted groups have differing capacities to resist and draw attention to their disproportionate treatment. The outrage amongst established expatriate Mexican communities and their supporters in Arizona at being targeted for immigration checks by local police (Provine and Sanchez), stands in stark contrast to both the normalisation and invisibility of immigration checking in Australia (Weber) and the open policies of removal of illegal immigrants in Japan (Namba). Roma unfairly targeted for police attention in Hungary (Tóth and Kádár) seem to have fewer resources at their disposal to draw attention to this injustice, than either black Torontonians (Wortley and Owusu-Bempah) or British Muslims (Parmar), which is not to say that the impact of unfair treatment would be any less acute.

The experience of being asked by a police officer to stop is often one of the first encounters that a person will have with the coercive arm of the state. In some cases, no doubt, stop and search encounters will pass off without friction, but in many instances the experience is deeply resented. Some encounters may be seen as routine and untargeted, such as generalised roadblocks and random stops of motorists for alcohol and drugs testing. Other stops may be perceived to be individually targeted and more intrusive, particularly when they result in being searched in a public place. In the most extreme cases, the inappropriate use of stop and search carries the risk of creating confrontations between police and the public and has the potential to trigger disorder. One cause of the 2011 summer riots in London and across the UK was a catastrophic breakdown in trust in the police among young people.

No democratic policing practice can survive without the constant renegotiation of legitimacy and consent. As Carole Willis has explained, the use of stop and search powers 'needs constantly to be reassessed not merely in relation to arrests or clear up rates, but also in the light of the effect on the community as a whole' (Willis 1983, p. 23). The danger is that aggressive enforcement can contribute to increased criminal victimisation and citizen dissatisfaction, while leaving fear of crime and perceptions of disorder unaffected (Skogan and Frydl 2004). It may also disrupt existing mechanisms of social control. Unnecessary contact with the police reduces public support for the police and undermines voluntary compliance (Tyler 1990, Skogan and Frydl 2004). In other words, the unwise use of stop and search can have precisely the opposite of its intended effects.

Conclusion

The police power to stop and search people is universal but varies in form, function and frequency. It is used very extensively in some places and only rarely in others. It is used routinely for street policing and forms of special intervention such as roadblocks and immigration sweeps. It is used against antisocial behaviour, terrorism, drugs and drunk driving. The incredible variety of circumstances in which the police can stop someone, interrogate or search them, reflects the breadth of the police function as 'a *solution* to an *unknown problem* arrived at by *unknown* means' (Bittner 1974, p. 249). At its heart, the police function is legitimated on the basis that it can provide some important but broadly defined social goods. Few examples illustrate better than stop and search the dilemma at the heart of policing: coercion and intrusion, backed up with the threat of physical violence, is the mechanism that is supposed to deliver the goods of peace, safety and order. The fact that stop and search in practice requires that policing must be *against* some people, that it must deliver the *bads* (or *burdens*) of interference with the fundamental human rights of freedom of movement and privacy against people who are either selected randomly, or targeted on the basis of 'racial profiling' or other categorical signals, makes it imperative that the power can be justified in principle and by its demonstrated capacity to deliver the promised goods. In practice, stop and search powers fall short of these principled justifications.

The pattern of criminalisation of ethnic minorities in the domestic sphere echoes the use of stop and search powers to police borders. This collection has provided situated examples of each of these applications of stop and search in specific contexts. Suspect communities are more extensively stopped and searched at airports, land and sea borders, are detained for more detailed questioning and also face a greater likelihood of being denied entry. Police forces around the globe are working towards intelligence databases shared in real time with police officers in other countries. Ron Noble, secretary general of Interpol, has a 'visionary model' for a global policing doctrine. In this vision, Interpol will provide operational support to domestic police officers so that, 'when they stop someone, they will be consulting global databases to determine who they are stopping' (Bowling and Sheptycki 2011). Advance passenger information systems, posting overseas liaison officers, biometric data requirements for foreign nationals, immigration status databases for beat officers all point in the direction of globally integrated security policing that meshes migration policing and counter-terrorism into domestic street policing and thus into the practice of stop and search.

The time seems ripe for developing transnational and comparative research on stop and search. A *comparative* approach would enable us systematically to compare and contrast experiences in different places around the world so as to develop richer theories with stronger external validity and wider applicability. Comparative survey methods, case studies or ethnography, could shed light on patterns of policing in countries with very different enforcement regimes. Beyond comparison, a *transnational* approach could explore practices that do not belong exclusively in one place or another and are explicable only by analysing linkages between places. This would explore how stop and search practices are *linked* across time and place, how transnational legal regimes and enforcement strategies emerge and how decisions taken in once place impact on people elsewhere.

This special issue makes a start on this transnational and comparative project. It has begun to develop a common language to discuss the use of coercive and intrusive powers in street policing and an agenda for future research. It has explored some conceptual and evaluative principles based on the police role in protecting fundamental human rights and freedoms. It has identified the paucity of data in some locations, the lack of community awareness and concern about inequitable policing in others, and the possibilities for developing a 'globally aware' criminology that addresses some important questions. There is clearly potential for a collaborative global learning process. We hope that this special issue has made a contribution to that goal.

Note

1. Some searches – for example covert searches of belongings and electronic searches using ion scanning or ultrasound 'electronic strip searches' – can be carried out without stopping someone. Bowling and Phillips (2007, p. 940).

References

Bittner, E., 1974. Florence Nightingale in pursuit of Willie Sutton: a theory of the police. *In*: H. Jacob, ed. *The potential for reform of criminal justice*. Beverley Hills: Sage, 30–40.

Bowling, B., 2007. Fair and effective police methods: towards "good enough" policing. *Scandinavian Studies in Criminology and Crime Prevention*, 8 (1), 17–23.

Bowling, B. and Phillips, C., 2007. Disproportionate and discriminatory: reviewing the evidence on stop and search. *Modern Law Review*, 70 (6), 936–961.

Bowling, B., *et al*., 2004. *Human rights and policing: eliminating racism, discrimination and xenophobia from policework*. Geneva: United Nations Institute for Social Research and Development.

Bowling, B. and Sheptycki, J., 2011. *Global policing*. London: Sage.

Brown, M.K., 1981. *Policing the street: discretion and the dilemmas of reform*. New York: The Russell Sage Foundation.

Choongh, S., 1997. *Policing as social discipline*. Oxford: Oxford University Press.

EHRC, 2010. *Stop and think: review of stop and search powers.* London: Equality and Human Rights Commission.
Hall, S., *et al.*, 1978. *Policing the crisis; mugging, the state and law and order.* London: Palgrave Macmillan.
Kleinig, J., 1996. *The ethics of policing.* Cambridge: Cambridge University Press.
Marshall, G., 1978. Police accountability revisited. *In*: D. Butler and A.H. Halsey, eds. *Policy and politics.* London: Macmillan.
Miller, J., Bland, N., and Quinton, P., 2000. *The impact of stops and searches on crime and the community.* Police Research Series Paper 127. London: Home Office.
Skogan, W. and Frydl, K., 2004. *Fairness and effectiveness in policing: the evidence.* Committee to Review Research on Police Policy and Practices, National Research Council. Washington, DC: National Academy of Sciences.
Tyler, T., 1990. *Why people obey the law.* New Haven, CT: Yale University Press.
Tyler, T. and Wakslak, C., 2004. Profiling and police legitimacy: procedural justice, attributions of motive, and acceptance of police authority. *Criminology*, 42, 253–281.
Weber, L. and Bowling, B., 2004. Policing migration: a framework for investigating the regulation of global mobility. *Policing & Society*, 14 (3), 195–212.
Weber, L. and Bowling, B., 2008. Valiant beggars and global vagabonds: select, eject, immobilize. *Theoretical Criminology*, 12 (3), 355–375.
Willis, C.F., 1983. *The use, effectiveness and impact of police stop and search powers.* Research and Planning Unit Paper 15. London: Home Office.

Index

Page numbers in **BOLD** represent Figures.
Page numbers in *Italics* represent Tables